# VOICES FROM THE PAST

THE KHOISAN HERITAGE SERIES

Series Editor: David Lewis-Williams

14/5/98

Khisann

First prize in the 1998 Study Abroad Programme: South African Literature. Hope you have a very stimulating career, studywise + careerwise. Let me know how you're doing...

Hélène van Vuuren

*Dorothea Bleek*

*Wilhelm Bleek*

# VOICES FROM THE PAST

## /Xam Bushmen and the Bleek and Lloyd Collection

Edited by
Janette Deacon and Thomas A. Dowson

WUP WITWATERSRAND UNIVERSITY PRESS

# THE KHOISAN HERITAGE SERIES

Series Editor: David Lewis-Williams

**Other titles in the Khoisan Heritage Series**

*Contested Images*
*Diversity in Southern African Rock Art Research*
Edited by Thomas A Dowson & David Lewis-Williams

*Women Like Meat*
*The Folklore and Foraging Ideology of the Kalahari Ju/'Hoan*
Megan Biesele

*Rock Engravings of Southern Africa*
Thomas A Dowson

Witwatersrand University Press
1 Jan Smuts Avenue
Johannesburg
2000 South Africa

First published 1996

ISBN 1-86814-247-7



Cover design by Franscois McHardy

The portrait on the cover is of //Kabbo or Jantje Tooren (c.1871), one of Wilhelm Bleek and Lucy Lloyd's informants. It was painted by the Cape Town artist WK Schroeder and was used as the frontispiece of Bleek and Lloyd's *Specimens of Bushman Folklore* (London: George Allen, 1911).

Frontispiece pictures by kind permission of Dr KMF Scott and Patricia Scott

Typeset by Photoprint, Cape Town

Printed and bound by : Federal Business Communications , Woodstock

# Contents

# Preface

The papers published in this volume are a selection of those presented at a conference in 1991 entitled 'Bleek and Lloyd: 1870-1991'. The purpose of the meeting was to celebrate the qualities of what have become known as the Bleek and Lloyd records, and to bring together the scholars actively working on them to identify research needs and to share common concerns.

The manuscript and published records that have generated so much interest were the work of Wilhelm HI Bleek and Lucy C Lloyd who interviewed a small group of /Xam and !Kung San-speakers in Cape Town between 1870 and 1884. The result of the combined efforts of the San (Bushmen) and the Bleek and Lloyd families have produced a testimony in more than 11 000 pages that provides a glimpse into the life-styles, language and beliefs of some of the survivors of a population that at one time inhabited the whole of southern Africa. Bleek and Lloyd's work was taken further in the first half of the twentieth century by Bleek's daughter, Dorothea, who died in 1948. It was not until the 1970s, however, that interest was revived by the research of Roger Hewitt, David Lewis-Williams, Patricia Vinnicombe and others. They, in turn, inspired a new set of researchers whose interests have ranged from linguistics to rock art, and modern San narratives to archaeology, and it is their work that is at the heart of this volume.

The Bleek and Lloyd Conference was held in Cape Town from 9 to 11 September 1991, eighty years after the publication of *Specimens of Bushman Folklore* in 1911. This remarkable book was compiled by Lucy Lloyd who had carried on the work of recording and translating after Wilhelm Bleek died in 1875 and presented not only English translations of a selection of the narratives, but also the verbatim /Xam and !Kung texts as recorded between 1870 and 1884.

One afternoon during the conference the delegates visited the site of the Bleek home in Mowbray, the cemetery in Wynberg where Wilhelm Bleek, Dorothea Bleek and Lucy Lloyd are buried, the South African Museum where the Bleek collection of San artefacts is housed, the Jagger Library at the University of Cape Town where the Bleek and Lloyd manuscripts, letters and papers are kept, and the last remaining portion of the original Breakwater

Prison where most of the /Xam had spent some time before going to live at the Bleek's home. After the conference, a few of the delegates were able to join a four-day field trip to the Northern Cape to see some of the places where Dia!kwain, //Kabbo and /Han≠kass'o had lived. Their voices reached into our subconscious minds as we slept under the same stars of which they had spoken and gazed on the panoramic view of the Flat Bushman country from the top of the Strandberg.

With financial assistance from the Wenner Gren Foundation for Anthropological Research in New York, the organising committee of Janette Deacon and John Parkington in Cape Town and Thomas Dowson and David Lewis-Williams in Johannesburg were able to invite thirty scholars from South Africa, Namibia, Germany, the United States, Canada and Britain to attend. It was the first opportunity that many of us had had to meet people with whom we had corresponded on details of content and interpretation of the Bleek and Lloyd Collection. Inevitably, a few of the key researchers could not be there and we were unable to make contact with several others, but the range of interests discussed made the effort worth while.

The librarians from the Manuscripts Department of the Jagger library, Leonie Twentyman-Jones and Etaine Eberhard, were invaluable for the biography they compiled on Bleek and for the information they had on what the Bleek and Lloyd Collection comprises. Nigel Penn described interactions between the /Xam and the Cape colonial regime from 1740 to the early nineteenth century. Rainer Vossen and Mathias Guenther spoke about the ideological and historical context in which Bleek and Lloyd had worked and how this affected the authenticity and representivity of their collection. Four women from across the Northern Hemisphere, Sigrid Schmidt (Germany), Nadine Howard (USA), Elena Kotlyar (Russia) and Melissa Heckler (USA), presented papers analysing the meaning of the folktales both to the /Xam and to us in the twentieth century. Linguistic aspects of the /Xam and !Kung records were highlighted too: John Argyle analysed the place of Southern San in the Khoisan language family, Franz Potyka spoke about the phonology of clicks in /Xam and about /Xam sentence construction and text architecture, and Patrick Dickens compared Lucy Lloyd's !Kung texts with the language and vocabulary of modern Ju dialects. Megan Biesele's experience of Ju/wa narratives from Namibia and Botswana enabled her to find an equally significant link between the /Xam and the Ju/wasi. This presentation was followed by a video taken by Thomas Dowson during an interview with Ju/'hoansi in Namibia in 1991. The enormous contribution that the Bleek and Lloyd records have made to the interpretation of San rock art was demonstrated again by David Lewis-Williams, while John Parkington and his co-authors Tony Manhire and Royden Yates showed another way in which rock art can be 'read'. A third viewpoint, this time from an art history perspective, was introduced by Pippa Skotnes who was critical of the methods used by archaeologists to study rock art. Finally, ways in which archaeological methods can be used to elaborate the information on /Xam lifestyles and beliefs in the Bleek and Lloyd collection were explored by Anne Solomon, Lyn Wadley and Janette Deacon.

Regrettably, it has taken five years for the papers to be published. Some authors did not submit papers and financial constraints further limited the number that could be included. Those that are included, though, give more than adequate coverage of the ideas and concerns that were raised during the meeting and are still as pertinent as they were in 1991.

The papers in Part One provide background information on the lives of the people whose voices were heard and of the people who heard them. During the last few decades there have been many discussions about the value of linguistic and ethnographic records such as those collected by Bleek and Lloyd. Some have questioned their accuracy, implying that an ethnographer is inevitably too immersed in his or her own society to make unbiased observations about other societies. Other critics believe that ethnographies serve only to reinforce the Western domination of indigenous people, while another group sees ethnographies as vehicles for experimenting with cultural critique through cross-cultural comparisons. The emphasis in the records on the intellectual achievements of the Bleek family, for example, contrasts with the emphasis on the physical attributes of the /Xam. By describing how tall each of the informants was it is as if Bleek and Lloyd were trying to make their observations scientific; yet we have no record of how tall Bleek himself was, nor what distinguishing physical features characterised Lucy Lloyd. Whatever shortcomings one may identify, however, the contributions in this volume show that the Bleek and Lloyd collection is still accessible after more than a century and provides much fuel for challenging the racial stereotypes and perceptions held about the San of southern Africa.

Part Two presents original research that has used the Bleek and Lloyd collection in a variety of ways in the fields of folklore,linguistics and archaeology. While some of the papers display a cautious acceptance of the concept of a general similarity in the cognitive system of San in many parts of southern Africa, others are more critical of the dangers of reductionism and the failure to recognise diversity. There is clearly awareness of the interactions between different groups of people in the region and of the implications that these interactions have for our understanding of social processes in the past. The authors are also deeply conscious of changes that have occurred through time in the language beliefs and life-styles of the San.

We had planned to have a third section in the volume but the cost would have made the book available only to the very wealthy. This section would have included a detailed index, compiled by Janette Deacon and Anne Holliday, to the Bleek and Lloyd notebooks in which the /Xam and !Kung interviews were recorded and translated, and a catalogue of all the material in the Bleek and Lloyd collection at the Jagger library, compiled by Etaine Eberhard and Leonie Twentyman-Jones.*

The 'voices' referred to in the title are those of both speakers and writers. They may be separated by time over a period of 126 years and scattered across the world from North America and Europe to South Africa and Namibia, but they have created an understanding of both the history of the San of southern Africa, and of the changing ideologies of the people who have studied this history. The fact that we can still 'hear' these voices is a wonderful tribute not only to the scholarship of Wilhelm Bleek, Lucy Lloyd and Dorothea Bleek, but also to the patience and integrity of //Kabbo, /Han≠kass'o, Dia!kwain, !Kweiten ta //ken, ≠Kasin, /A!kunta, Tamme, !Nanni, /Uma and Da.

Of considerable concern to us, though, is that while the voices echo and reverberate continuously in the academic world, they have yet to be claimed by /Xam and !Kung San descendants. //Kabbo told Dr Bleek in 1873 that, 'The Bushmen's letters are in their bodies,' where presentiments could be felt as a gentle 'tapping'. We hope that the voices in this collection of papers will tap their way into the collective consciousness of all the people of southern Africa. The results of their efforts must be made accessible to the descendants of the /Xam and the !Kung. In the future, people interested in the 'Bushmen's letters' will no doubt continue experimenting, as others have done, with methods of presentation and so end the cycle of academic domination by Europeans and their descendants.

We are deeply grateful to the many people who have helped to publish this book and thank them most sincerely. Jo Sandrock and the Director and staff of

* We could make this information available on disk or CD for a small charge. Enquiries should be directed to the Librarian, Manuscripts Department, Jagger library, University of Cape Town, 7700 Rondebosch, South Africa.

the Witwatersrand University Press have borne the brunt of the copy-editing and production. The authors of the papers have shown great patience and understanding during the period of gestation, as have those whose papers could not, in the end, be included. The Wenner-Gren Foundation and the University of Cape Town generously provided funding for travel and conference costs. The Jagger Library and the South African Museum set up exhibitions during the conference. Farmers in the Northern Cape lavished hospitality on those who braved the field trip. And when Dr Marjorie Scott, granddaughter of Wilhelm Bleek, generously gave us copies of family photographs for reproduction here, several conference participants reciprocated by contributing to the costs of repairing and cleaning the Bleek family grave. Finally, we thank all our contributors for forgoing royalties so that the price of this book could be kept within the reach of those who wish to continue the initiatives of Wilhelm Bleek and Lucy Lloyd and work towards the recognition of the /Xam as key players in the history of South Africa.

*Janette Deacon*
*Thomas A Dowson*

*All the papers in this volume were submitted for publication within twelve months of the Bleek and Lloyd Conference held in 1991*

# Biographical Introduction

## *WILHELM BLEEK*

Wilhelm Heinrich Immanuel Bleek, PhD, was born in Berlin on 8 March 1827 and died in Mowbray, Cape, on 17 August 1875. He was the eldest son of Professor Friedrich Bleek, Professor of Theology at Berlin University, and later at the University of Bonn, and his wife Augusta Charlotte Marianne Sethe.

Bleek graduated from the University of Bonn in 1851 and achieved his ambition of going to Africa when he was appointed official linguist to Dr W D Baikie's Niger Tshadda Expedition in 1854. Unfortunately ill health forced Bleek to leave the expedition when they reached Fernando Po. He returned to England where he met J W Colenso, Bishop of Natal, who invited Bleek to accompany him to Natal in 1855 in order to help him compile a Zulu grammar.

When this project had been completed, in 1856 Bleek accepted an invitation from the Governor of the Cape, Sir George Grey, to become his official interpreter in Cape Town. When Sir George was appointed Governor of New Zealand, he presented his very valuable library to the South African Public Library. A condition of this gift was that Bleek should be appointed curator of the Grey Collection, a post he held from 1862 until his death.

Bleek continued with his philological research and published his findings from time to time. He also wrote leading articles for the English edition of *Het Volksblad* for a number of years. From 1870 Bleek had access to Bushman prisoners at the Breakwater Prison and some of them were released into his custody. They lived at his home in Mowbray where their language and folklore was recorded with the assistance of Bleek's sister-in-law Lucy Lloyd.

Bleek published a number of articles, reports and books during his lifetime, mainly concerning his philological studies and Bushman folklore. Many years after his death his sister-in-law published *Specimens of Bushman Folklore* in London (1911), based on their joint research.

He married Jemima Lloyd in 1862 and they had seven children, one son and six daughters. Their son and one daughter died in infancy. Bleek is buried in the Wynberg cemetery.

## *LUCY LLOYD*

Lucy Catherine Lloyd was born in Norberry, Staffordshire, England, on 7 November 1834 and died in Mowbray, Cape, on 31 August 1914. She was the second eldest daughter of the Reverend William Henry Cynric Lloyd and his first wife Lucy Anne Jeffreys. After her mother's death she and her three sisters went to live with her maternal aunt, Caroline Dundas, and was privately educated. When her father was appointed Colonial Chaplin for Natal in 1849 she accompanied him and his second wife and family to Durban.

After her sister Jemima married Wilhelm Bleek in 1862 Lucy Lloyd lived with them in Cape Town and was trained by her brother-in-law to help him with his work, particularly with his Bushman studies, and she proved to be a very able pupil. When Bleek died she was asked to take over some of his duties in the Grey Collection, and at the same time she continued her work with the Bushmen for a number of years.

Lucy Lloyd played a leading part in founding the South African Folklore Society and also in the establishment of the *Folk-lore Journal* in 1879. During the 1880s she went to England and lived there and on the continent for about twenty years but returned to Cape Town some years after the Anglo-Boer War. Her major publication was *Specimens of Bushman Folklore*. In 1912 she was awarded an honorary Doctorate of Literature by the University of the Cape of Good Hope, the first woman in South Africa to be honoured in this way. She is buried in the Wynberg cemetery.

## *DOROTHEA BLEEK*

Dorothea Frances Bleek was born in Mowbray, Cape, on 26 March 1873 and died in Plumstead, Cape, on 27 June 1948. She was the sixth child of Wilhelm Heinrich Immanuel Bleek and his wife Jemima Lloyd. During the 1880s Mrs Bleek took her children to live in Europe where Dorothea attended schools in Germany and Switzerland. She studied at Berlin University, where she trained as a teacher and took a course in African languages.

She returned to South Africa in 1904 and taught at the Rocklands Girls High School in Cradock until 1907. She accompanied one of her colleagues, Helen Tongue, on expeditions to copy rock paintings, and went to London when the paintings were exhibited there in 1908. Some of these paintings were published the following year with notes on the Bushmen by Dorothea and her sister Edith. When she returned from London she devoted all her time to studying Bushman life and languages. She assisted her aunt, Lucy Lloyd, in the preparation of *Specimens of Bushman Folklore* for publication, and edited and published much of the research left by her father and her aunt.

She went on many expeditions to study Bushman dialects and rock art, her travels taking her to the Kalahari, Botswana, Angola and Tanzania. Not only did she record vocabularies, genealogies and rock art in those areas but also took many photographs which illustrated shelters, weapons and types of dress.

From 1923 to 1948 Dorothea Bleek was Honorary Reader in Bushman Languages at the University of Cape Town. Her major achievement was the publication of the *Bushman Dictionary*, published in 1956, eight years after her death. It incorporated the lexicon started by her father almost a century earlier and added to by Lucy Lloyd. In 1936 the University of the Witwatersrand wished to confer an honorary doctorate on her, but she is reputed to have declined on the grounds that there could only be one Dr Bleek.

She died in Plumstead in 1948.

# PART I

# THE PEOPLE AND THEIR WORK

*/Xam-speaking men photographed at the Breakwater Prison in Cape Town in about 1870 or 1871. Back row, l. to r. Khauru (Soopie) from the Strandberg; !Xaitatin (Lellerbay) from the Strandberg; Kusi (Koos Pleitje) from 'among the Boers'; !Xwariitten (Jacob Nel) from Witteklip; !Gubbu (Klaas) from north-west of the Strandberg. Front row, l. to r. /Hankum (Marcus) from Rietfontein; !Herri-i (Oud Toontjie) from north-west of the Strandberg; Tshorru (Cornelis) from the Strandberg; Gautarru (Klaas) from north-west of the Strandberg; //Oe (Adam Fix) from Haasfontein.*

# The /Xam Informants

Janette Deacon

The people who worked most diligently to record the /Xam San folkore and language described in this book came from only four extended families. Although some information on Bushman languages had been collected earlier than the 1870s, the majority of the interviews referred to by researchers came from six /Xam-speaking people who represented three families. They taught their language to Wilhelm Bleek and Lucy Lloyd and shared their folklore and personal experiences unstintingly. /A!kunta, //Kabbo, /Han≠kass'o, Dia!kwain, ≠Kasin and !Kweiten ta //ken were a very small sample of the descendants of the tens of thousands of Southern Bushmen who lived throughout southern Africa at the time of European contact. By the same token, in the 1870s out of the tens of thousands of Europeans in southern Africa, Bleek and Lloyd were two out of only five who took the trouble to try to learn a Bushman language and then to write down what the Bushmen had to say. The other recorders were the traveller Dr H Lichtenstein and two missionaries, C F Wuras and G Krönlein, all of whom wrote down only short vocabularies and a few sentences (Bleek 1873:2; Bleek & Lloyd 1911:441-42).

The relationship between an ethnographer or linguist and his or her subjects is a complex one. There is the inevitability of becoming involved with each other's lives and the danger of losing objectivity. Just how much 'the truth' is altered by such a process is difficult to quantify, but it is always affected in one way or another. Despite such problems, it is evident that the Bleek and Lloyd records were the result of remarkable mutual respect and co-operation between interviewers and interviewees. On the one side were individuals whose lives had been turned upside down by events beyond their control: 'progress', colonialism and interracial conflict; on the other side was a family of scholars, committed to a cause that must have seemed esoteric in the extreme to many of their contemporaries. The thousands of hours they spent together probably led to tension and frustration as well as to a sense of achievement.

The responsibility the work placed on Lucy Lloyd and, later, on Dorothea Bleek, both of whom spent a major part of their working lives on the texts, must have been considerable. This is hinted at by Lloyd in her preface to her final report (Lloyd 1889) when she apologises for the delay in submitting it, 'caused by some years of overwork and many of ill-health'. The remarkable dedication of Lucy Lloyd and her sisters and nieces, no doubt finely honed by their Victorian sense of duty and Bleek's wish, written into a codicil in his will (Spohr 1962:41), that they carry on with the work after his death, has meant that we are still able to use the records of /Xam folklore more than a hundred years later and to learn something new every time we read them.

A contemporary of Lloyd's who visited Cape Town and saw the Lloyd/ Bleek household in action four years after the death of Wilhelm Bleek, was Elizabeth Lees Price, a daughter of Robert Moffatt and sister-in-law of David Livingstone. She, too, was the wife of a missionary and wrote to her children about her meeting with Jemima Bleek, her daughters and her sister Lucy Lloyd in February 1879:

> Mrs Bleek immediately invited us all out together to her country house at Mowbray ... These ladies are great students of Bushman & other African languages & habits ... All the sisters (four) dressed in the same neat way, and the house was very very plain and simply furnished, with very little indeed in the way of ornament, a little too plain & bare I thought, but it was such a relief to feel in the company of people, refined, intellectual & cultivated, yet simple & homely as the humblest cottagers ... Mrs Bleek has a Bushman family – father, mother & two children – living on their premises, expressly for the purpose of learning & studying their language. The man had lived at Kuruman once, & knew Uncle Robert [Robert Moffatt Jnr, who died in 1862]. (Long 1956:304-305)

In another account, Edith and Dorothea Bleek (1909) described how the convicts were accommodated at their home. When /A!kunta and //Kabbo first came to Mowbray, their father hired an ex-warder who was armed with a gun to watch over them. To make doubly certain of their safety, the men were locked up at night in a room with bars over the window. These precautions were soon dispensed with, however, as /A!kunta was too happy and //Kabbo was too feeble to escape. Dia!kwain 'was sometimes an escort to our lady friends, going home alone at night. One of them recently asked after "my father's pet murderer", whom he had offered to protect her on her somewhat lonely way home' (Bleek & Bleek 1909:40).

In addition to the written records, there is a collection of drawings made by several of the adults and children who had stayed at the Bleek's home, some of which have been published (Bleek & Lloyd 1911; Rudner 1970). They also made clay models, mostly of animals, and some crude arrows and other artefacts (Goodwin 1945; Deacon 1992). These are curated at the South African Museum together with a fine collection of leather garments, artefacts and musical instruments obtained from /Xam visited by Dorothea Bleek in the northern Cape in 1910 and 1911.

This paper is a companion to the biographies of Bleek and Lloyd and follows the lives of the /Xam informants. It is divided into two main sections. The first is a chronological account of the work undertaken by Bleek and Lloyd from 1857 to 1884, set against the broader backdrop of events which led to the /Xam coming to Cape Town where the interviews took place. The second section follows the life histories and genealogies of the six /Xam informants whose testimony forms the bulk of the Bleek and Lloyd collection.

## *THE LEARNING PROCESS*

The first Bushman-speaking people interviewed by Bleek were a few men and women from the Colesberg and Burghersdorp districts of the eastern Cape who had been sent to prison on Robben Island and at the Cape Town Gaol and House of Correction in 1857. At that time, Bleek tested Lichtenstein's short vocabulary of Bushman words and sentences on them. He concluded that 'the different Bushman dialects spoken within this Colony vary very little from each other, and that one language, quite different from Hottentot, is spoken by all these Bushmen' (Bleek 1873:2; Bleek & Lloyd 1911:442-43). He concluded, too, that 'the Bushman language is certainly not nearer akin to the Hottentot than e.g. the English language is to the Latin; but it may be that the distance between Bushman and Hottentot is indeed far greater than between the two above-mentioned languages' (Bleek 1873:8).

The first /Xam-speakers to be introduced to Bleek were brought to Cape Town in 1863 by Mr Louis Anthing, Resident Magistrate and former Civil Commissioner of Namaqualand and a champion of the cause of the Bushmen of the northern Cape. It is worth while outlining here the reason for their visit to Cape Town as it draws attention to the precarious political situation in which the /Xam had been placed in the late nineteenth century by the expansion of the British Empire.

The northern Cape portion of the Cape Colony between the Sak and

Orange Rivers was known as Bushmanland. It had been claimed by the British crown as recently as 1847 by Sir Harry Smith and until then had belonged to the /Xam and their neighbours the Korana. Prior to 1847, the British had believed the land was not worth owning because it had few opportunities for agriculture. After the introduction of merino sheep to the Karoo, however, the situation changed and the colonists put pressure on Britain to annexe the land and stop cross-border conflict.

Not surprisingly, the /Xam and Korana resisted the European colonists and entered into a battle of attrition to retain control of the rare water sources in this dry land. Requested by the Governor, Wodehouse, to investigate reports of marauding Bushmen in the territory in 1862, Anthing established a base near present-day Kenhardt. He travelled extensively, interviewing anyone willing to talk, including *smouse* (itinerant traders), Basters, trekboers and Bushmen. A trader, Nicholson, told him that the wholesale extermination of the Bushmen had occurred in the area mostly since 1859 (Cape Archives CO 4414). Anthing met a Bushman named Herklaas (Hercules), a survivor of a massacre of about two hundred /Xam murdered near Bosduif in 1853, who said it was bitterness and revenge for the murder that had made him become a bandit. Another group of about two hundred /Xam had been killed in the Kareeberg at about the same time (Cape Archives CO 4414).

In his report dated 1 April 1862, Anthing recommended that the Bushmen be given land of their own as well as sheep and goats to enable them to start farming. He wrote to the Colonial Secretary, 'The true solution is to be found in the principle which recognizes the necessity and the justice of compensation for the occupation of the veld [by the Europeans]' (Cape Archives, CO 4414), but his pleas fell on deaf ears. After several more incidents, there was a revenge attack on Basters who were murdered by two Bushmen. Anthing persuaded Herklaas to turn in the guilty parties, one of whom was Herklaas's own son, as he was afraid that if a commando was mounted to look for them, the Bushmen would surely be murdered. Herklaas brought in the two men and, lacking a formal prison building, Anthing kept them in a large brush enclosure around a thorn tree in Kenhardt (Findlay 1977).

The Colonial Secretary approved his actions and Anthing began plans to build a magistrate's office and prison at Kenhardt. After another attack by Bushmen on a farm in the vicinity, Anthing took the entire band, about eighty strong, into custody, keeping the twenty who had been involved in the robbery and murder in the brush enclosure as the doors for the prison had not yet arrived. Unfortunately, ten of the awaiting-trial prisoners escaped, including seven who were being held for the murder of the Lourens family at Kalbasput near Vanwyksvlei. To make matters worse, Anthing then received a letter from the Colonial Secretary saying that he had exceeded his powers and had incurred unreasonable expenses. He was to stop all plans to prepare for a magistracy in Kenhardt and return to Springbokfontein. Anthing was deeply disappointed as he genuinely believed that his negotiations with the Bushmen around Kenhardt could lead to a situation of mutual trust. When Herklaas and his men returned the ten escaped prisoners, Anthing set the group of eighty free, sent the seven involved in the Kalbasput murder to the Circuit Court in Beaufort West and left two in custody with a constable in Kenhardt.

However, instead of returning to Springbokfontein as instructed, he arrived in Cape Town on 9 February 1863, bringing with him Herklaas, Herklaas's son and his accomplice, and a /Xam man who had been wounded in another incident in which /Xam had attacked a trader and killed a farmer (Findlay 1977). Anthing hoped that they would be tried in the Supreme Court, but the Attorney-General waived the prosecution (Cape Archives, A39-'63:12). Anthing himself set about completing his report to the Colonial Office but was to find that the government was more concerned with paying off the debts he had incurred than implementing his suggestions to alleviate the plight of the Bushmen in the northern Cape (Findlay 1977:45).

In May 1863 Anthing went back to Kenhardt to close down his office there. On the way there he was moved by the condition of /Xam who stopped his cart and begged him to employ them. During his stay he gave them sheep and goats until the annual springbok migration began and they could hunt their own meat. Over the following year, Anthing's actions were severely criticised in documents laid before the House of Assembly and he was accused of illicit trading. Amongst other charges, it was alleged that he had supplied buckets of brandy to 'Hottentots' and that he had given guns and gunpowder to Bushmen to shoot ostriches in order to obtain skins for trade (Findlay 1977:48-49). Although he repudiated the charges, Anthing was transferred to a post in Cradock but, as scandal continued to follow him, he resigned in November 1865 (ibid.).

Anthing's presence in Cape Town may well have influenced Bleek to persist in his endeavour to record a Bushman language and probably played a part in his later success in interviewing /Xam at the Breakwater Prison. Although public opinion as expressed in the newspapers criticised Anthing for favouring the interests of the Bushmen over those of the colonists, he also had his supporters (Findlay 1977) and Lloyd remembered him warmly in her acknowledgements at the end of her final report on the project (Lloyd 1889:28). Herklaas, too, appears to have been an articulate man and certainly formed a bond with Anthing. Who it was that made the effort to contact the other is not known, but Bleek's notebook entry (Jagger Library MS BC 151 B-IX:908 rev.) gives a list of names of /Xam men, including Herklaas, who were in Cape Town with Anthing in 1863. He notes that they were members of the Flat, Berg and Hardast River groups from the vicinity of Kenhardt and Vanwyksvlei so he must have had the opportunity to meet them personally. Nearly a decade later, these same /Xam were mentioned as acquaintances by the Flat Bushmen interviewed by Bleek and Lloyd in the 1870s. For example, /A!kunta told Bleek in 1870 that 'Hartklaas' son is Boor, grown-up name of Hardklaas. He dreams of his wife' (BI:305).

In June, July and August 1866 two more Bushman prisoners, this time from the Achterveld east of Calvinia, were transferred from the Breakwater to the Cape Town prison to make it possible for Bleek to interview them. The words and sentences he recorded at that time, together with the English index and alphabetical vocabulary, covered nearly 140 manuscript pages (Bleek 1873:2). One of the men was Adam Kleinhardt. A loose page in Bleek's B-I notebook says Adam's father was a Korana and his mother was a 'real Bushman'. He had no beard, but his brother did. He mentioned also the Brinkkop and the Hartbeest (or Hardast) River, both places well known to the /Xam interviewed later by Bleek and Lloyd (Deacon 1986, 1988).

In 1870 Bleek heard of the presence of 28 Bushmen at the Breakwater Prison and the Reverend G Fisk, the prison chaplain, selected for him 'the best-behaved Bushman boy', known as Stoffel or /A!kunta. In August 1870 Her Majesty's Colonial Government gave permission for /A!kunta to live at the Bleek's home in Mowbray to enable Bleek to receive instruction in the Bushman language (Bleek 1873:2). However, as he did not know much about folklore, an older man, //Kabbo or Old Jantje, was also allowed to live at Mowbray. Over the next few years, Dia!kwain and his sister and brother-in-law ≠Kasin spent varying periods there and, after Bleek died in 1875, //Kabbo's son-in-law, /Han≠kass'o, lived with the household too, to be interviewed by Lucy Lloyd until 1879.

The circumstances surrounding the imprisonment of the 28 Bushmen reflect again the tense situation that had developed in the northern Cape in the latter half of the nineteenth century, and mirror similar events that took place both earlier and later in southern Africa as the European colonists inexorably claimed the land of the indigenous people by genocide and subjugation.

The arrest, conviction and imprisonment of the /Xam who were at the Breakwater in 1870 came in the wake of the Korana War of 1868-69. After Anthing's unsuccessful efforts to persuade the colonial government to set land aside for the Bushmen, the European farmers became increasingly entrenched in the northern Cape and continued to acquire loan and quitrent farms. While it had been relatively easy to murder itinerant Bushman groups, however, the colonists found it more difficult to overcome the pastoralist Korana who had been well established along the Orange River for many centuries. Particularly during times of drought when there was considerable pressure on scarce water and grazing resources, the Korana began to perfect the art of raiding European farms and settlements. Marais (1939) has remarked that by the end of the 1860s the 'Korana had taken the place of the Bushmen as "the enemy" on the northern frontier'.

By the middle of 1868, a year in which the theft of 2 000 cattle, 10 000 sheep and 240 horses was reported by colonists and Basters in the area between Kenhardt, Brandvlei and Vanwyksvlei alone, raids were so frequent that the Korana, often aided by /Xam, were said to be in possession of most of the country between the Kareeberg and the Orange River, and the leased land on either side of the Hartbees River was almost completely deserted (Cape Archives A.54-'68, Steyn to Calder, 3 August 1868). Several other farmers had also deserted their leased lands for fear of depredations by Korana who had the advantage of a more intimate knowledge of the terrain and were unencumbered with wagons, goods and families (Cape Archives HA 80, Erasmus to Resident Magistrate, Victoria West, 19 Oct. 1968). The Korana would not only attack farms, but also targeted traders and farmers returning from provisioning trips to Cape Town, thereby replenishing their own supplies of food, horses and ammunition. As Strauss (1979:118) has pointed out, cattle raiding was an integral feature of Korana society; the Korana exploited the availability of the colonists' cattle to the full.

After several petitions to the Cape Parliament, the Northern Border Protection Act was passed in August 1868 (Strauss 1979:39). It made possible the appointment of a Special Magistrate, Maximilian James Jackson, who was ordered to set up a magistracy in Kenhardt. He went there in October 1868 with a mounted police force of 50 men (ibid.). These raw recruits, untrained even in basic police work, were singularly unsuccessful in countering the Korana, and by January 1869 half the horses were either dead or out of action and Jackson and his men were discouraged. On one hand there were too few men, too few horses and too little water and fodder, and on the other hand the area they had to cover was too large, the men were unfamiliar with the terrain, and it took a long time for news of raids to reach the magistracy in Kenhardt. Jackson was frustrated, too, at the attitude of the Colonial Secretary who seemed not to understand the seriousness of the situation (Cape Archives G.61-'79. Report from Jackson to Colonial Secretary, 11 Jan. 1869).

After several disastrous encounters in which policemen were killed and guns and ammunition lost to the Korana (Strauss 1979:46ff), in May 1869 Sir Walter Currie arrived in Kenhardt with reinforcements. A few weeks later, 258 men were assembled and marched to De Neus drift on the Orange River to attack the Korana at their strongholds on islands in the river. They were assisted by a Korana leader, Cupido Pofadder, and his men who had already aided the British by returning stolen cattle for a reward. Although the British managed to drive Korana from three of the islands, they simply reassembled on other islands and no real victory was achieved. Currie recommended that the Korana be starved out of the islands by establishing a strong force all along the south bank of the river. He hoped this would prevent their making use of the grazing, but this, too, was unsuccessful.

In October Jackson changed his tactics and sent for the Korana leader Klaas Lukas. He threatened to attack Lukas's settlement unless he invited the other three Korana leaders, Piet Rooy, Jan Kivido and Carel Ruiters, to visit him. When they did so on 26 October, Lukas took them all prisoner. Although Ruiters escaped, the other two were handed over to Jackson in Kenhardt on 1 November. Their capture and subsequent imprisonment on Robben Island led to the disintegration of the groups they had led, and by February 1870 the remaining Korana moved northwards across the Orange River (Strauss 1979:52ff). Lukas and Pofadder signed a treaty with the British and were rewarded with cattle. The treaty recognised them as the sole leaders of all the Korana who were granted the territory on the northern bank of the Orange River from the Aughrabies Falls to Griqualand West.

In December 1869 Jackson sent 104 Korana prisoners to Victoria West for trial; these included Kivido and Rooy, as well as 215 destitute Korana and San who had either been arrested over the previous year for offences such as loitering or stock theft, or who were simply starving as a result of the drought and were 'without doubt the chief cause of the numerous thefts' (Cape Archives CO 3163, Jackson to Colonial Secretary, 6 April 1869). Those who were found guilty of a punishable offence were sentenced to imprisonment. After a spell of hard labour at Victoria West, the majority of the Bushmen and Korana were sent to the Breakwater Prison in Cape Town, the Korana leaders going to Robben Island. Destitute people who had not committed any crime were distributed as servants among farmers throughout the Cape Colony (Strauss 1979:53). Carel Ruiters and 25 of his followers were captured later and sent to Victoria West on 18 April 1870 (CO 3179, Jackson to Colonial Secretary, 30 April 1870) and from there Ruiters, too, went to Robben Island (Strauss 1979).

Amongst those convicted for stock theft and sentenced to two years' imprisonment from October 1869 were /A!kunta, //Kabbo and /Han≠kass'o (Cape Archives, Convict Service Number Registers 1/78, PBW Vol. 81 1864-76).

In relating the events surrounding his arrest, //Kabbo said:

> The Kafir took me; he bound my arms ... We were in jail. We put our legs into the stocks. The Korannas came to us, when our legs were in the stocks ... we ate sheep on the way ... to Victoria [West]; our wives ate their sheep on the way, as they came to Victoria. We came to roll stones at Victoria, while we worked at the road ... We again had our arms bound to the wagon chain; we walked along, while we were fastened to the wagon chain, as we came to Beaufort [West] ... We came into Beaufort jail ... We walked upon the road ... We walked, following the wagon, being bound ... until we came to the Breakwater ... A white man took us to meet the train in the night ... the train ran, bringing us to the Cape. We came into the Cape prison house when we were tired, we and the Korannas; we lay down to sleep at noon. (Bleek & Lloyd 1911:291-95)

In a second account, //Kabbo said:

> The Magistrate came to take our legs out of the stocks, because he wished that we might sit comfortably, that we might eat; for it was his sheep that we were eating. Katten ('Piet Rooi') [who was leader of the Katte, a Korana group] came (and) ate with us of the Magistrate's sheep, while we were eating it; also another man, Kkabbi-ddau [possibly Jan Kivido?]; also !Kwarra-ga-/k(e)ow/k(e)ow ... Other Korannas also came, they came into another house, another 'jail's house'. (Bleek & Lloyd 1911:297)

The cost to the Colonial Government of this 'rounding up' operation was considerable. In an account of the sum spent on rations for prisoners and destitute persons sent to Victoria West between 1 August 1869 and 30 April 1870, Jackson claimed £1 280.16.4 for the purchase of 3 169 sheep that provided 4 lb (nearly 2 kg) of meat per person per day (CO 3179, Document 11, Jackson to Colonial Secretary, May 1870).

The circumstances surrounding the arrest and conviction of the two Grass Bushmen, Dia!kwain (David Hoesar) and ≠Kasin (Klaas Katkop), were somewhat different, but also resulted from disputes over land ownership. They were accused of stealing sheep by a farmer, Jacob Casper Kruger, who accosted them alone at their camp one Sunday morning. Dia!kwain shot Kruger in self-defence with a gun. Kruger died a few kilometres away from their settlement. When his friends found the body, Jackson was alerted in Kenhardt on 5 February 1869 and he sent a small police escort to investigate. He reported in a letter to the Colonial Secretary in Cape Town dated 25 February (Cape Archives HA 80) that his men were unfamiliar with the terrain around N'arries (west of present-day Brandvlei) and their horses were unable to obtain fodder, so they engaged the services of three local farmers as guides and Special Constables for the sum of £9.8.0.

In a letter dated 16 March, the Resident Magistrate in Calvinia, P de Smidt, reported that three of the four men they were seeking had been apprehended. They were David Hoesar, Klaas Hoesar and Jantje Japhta. Japhta had been shot in the leg while trying to escape. The fourth, Klaas Katkop, was still at large, but his capture was reported in a later letter dated 30 March (Cape Archives, HA 80). Of David Hoesar and his arrest, De Smidt wrote:

> The principal murderer however is secured, David Hoesaar who boldly confesses that he fired the first and fatal shot at Kruger – Klaas Katkop having fired the second which hit the saddle. He seems to show the greatest indifference as to his crime and its results and says that he did it because Kruger had told him and his comrades, on riding away from their werf, that he would return with his men and exterminate them because they had stolen his sheep.
>
> I deem it right to bring to His Excellency's notice the admirable manner in which the three Constables whom I had sent to capture the murderers effected their hazardous task.
>
> For thirty days they hardly took any rest, but day and night slowly but surely tracked the murderers until they found and caught them.

> The difficulty and danger of their duty may be fully realized from the fact that these culprits have for years been the terror of the Aachterveld being unerring marksmen and the swiftest runners in the Country.

When the case came to trial, the Judge gave Dia!kwain the benefit of the doubt because he pleaded that he had acted in self-defence. The records at the Breakwater Prison (Cape Archives, General Description Register of Convicts, PBW 73) indicate that David Hoesaar (*sic*) and Klaas Katkop were convicted of culpable homicide and sentenced to 5 years' imprisonment on 1 November 1869.

In September/October 1873 both Bleek and Lloyd recorded a few words and names from two Bushmen in what Bleek describes as the Stuurman's Fontein dialect, apparently in the Kareeberge (BXXIV:2261; LII-35:3160-65). Amongst the genealogies in the Bleek and Lloyd collection at the Jagger Library there is one for a 60-year-old man from the Kareeberge named /Aken//kautin au kamman (Oortman) (Jagger Library BCA 151:27).

Several more /Xam informants were interviewed briefly by Lloyd in October 1875 and March 1876, but they gave only a few words and sentences and information on their genealogies. Their names were ≠Giri-sse or Jan Ronebout (also spelled Rondabout) and his elder brother //Xou//ku'a or Hendrik or Daki, Jan Plat and Klaas Paai. They were in prison at the Breakwater for stock theft and Hendrik was interviewed at the Breakwater hospital. Jan Plat, said to be of mixed Griqua, Hottentot and Makatees descent (LVII-1:6046 a-j), was married to Dia!kwain's niece (Deacon 1986:138) and was a servant of a Mr Willmot. Genealogies were recorded for the Ronebout brothers who were said to be Berg Bushmen (Jagger Library BCA 151:32). Their mother, !Kwarra-an or Mietje, was a celebrated medicine woman who was still living in Flat Bushman country in 1874/75 (LV-19:5445). Their father, who had the same name as Jan, was killed by a farmer, Hans Basson (LV-19:5453).

After Bleek's death, Lloyd continued to make use of the connections they had built up. Her efforts to find Dia!kwain were unsuccessful, but /Han≠kass'o was contacted and spent several years at Mowbray. To provide companions for him, Lloyd asked J M Orpen to assist her in finding a Bushman family from the diamond fields around Kimberley. Unfortunately, a Korana family was sent instead in January 1879 and it is they who were mentioned by Elizabeth Lees Price in her letter of February 1879, quoted above. They stayed for a year because of the death of a child and the ill-health of the mother. The father, Piet Lynx, was interviewed both by Lucy Lloyd and by her niece Isabella Lloyd and two Korana folktales were recorded. The notebooks with these interviews were given to L F Maingard by Dorothea Bleek in 1931 and are now housed in the manuscript collection of the Sanlam Library and the University of South Africa in Pretoria (Maingard File 2.1.2.1).

Also in 1879, Mr W Coates Palgrave arranged for two young !Kung boys, !Nanni and Tamme, from Namibia (Damaraland) to spend some time with Lloyd and her sister, Jemima Bleek, and they were joined in 1880 by two younger boys, /Uma and Da. The two older boys returned home in 1882 but /Uma and Da left in 1881 and 1884 respectively. Lloyd was also able to speak to a young boy in 1877 and a young woman in 1878, both from Lake Ngami in Botswana who gave her words and sentences for which the Reverend Krönlein supplied the corresponding terms in Khoikhoi (Lloyd 1889:5).

Lastly, in 1884, a group of Bushman men and women who apparently came from the Kenhardt/Prieska area arrived in Cape Town by sea from Port Nolloth. They were living at Salt River but the circumstances surrounding their move to Cape Town are not clear. One of these people, a woman named /Xaken-an (also spelled /Ogan-an) or Mikki Streep, lived at Mowbray for a short period where she was interviewed by Lloyd. She was posed with a digging stick weighted with a bored stone that had been collected in the early 1870s in Bushmanland by E J Dunn, a geologist. He later recalled that:

> Miss Lloyd often came to Oaklands, on the Claremont Flats, where we lived while in South Africa. I had collections of horns, Bushman stone implements, and other South African objects. When she came, Miss Lloyd brought her Bushman people with her in order to obtain from them the names or any information they could give about these objects.
>
> The excellent photograph of the Bushman woman with the digging stick reproduced on the cover of 'Bushman Folklore', by Bleek and Lloyd, was taken at Oaklands; the digging stick is still in my possession. (Dunn 1931:38)

The digging stick was later taken to Australia by Dunn, and after his death it was bequeathed to the Pitt Rivers Museum in Oxford where it can still be seen. Lloyd also took the opportunity to show the group at Salt River some copies of rock paintings and their comments were recorded (Lloyd 1889). Unfortunately, the notebooks with these comments were separated from the collection now in the Jagger Library and are missing.

The displacement of /Xam and Korana continued through the 1870s and 1880s. After the treaty with Lukas and Pofadder in 1870, the Korana became dissatisfied with the way in which the colonial government neglected to honour its agreement to prevent colonists from disturbing them north of the Orange River. To make matters worse, numerous Korana, who had crossed the Orange to settle in Koranaland, refused to accept the leadership of Lukas and Pofadder. They were joined by a large number of Griquas, and in 1878-79 they began fighting again for land which they believed was being taken from them unfairly (Strauss 1979:70ff). M J Jackson was sent to settle the matter, but was used as a political scapegoat by the Attorney General, Upington. Jackson, charged with mismanagement, was said to have had more men at his disposal than Cortez required to conquer the Mexican Empire (Strauss 1979:98) and he resigned in April 1879. His replacement, Captain McTaggart, dispersed the Korana and Griquas and captured some of their leaders, but others fled into the Kalahari or regrouped. After the war, which ended officially in August 1879, some eight hundred men, women and children were rounded up and sent as servants to the districts of Beaufort West, Calvinia, Clanwilliam and Springbok. Many of the Koranas refused to work for farmers south of the river, however, and returned to squat in the areas whence they had come (Strauss 1979:115).

## *SIX LIVES*

The six main informants whose histories are described below came from two dialectal groups: the Flat Bushmen who lived between Kenhardt and Vanwyksvlei, and the Grass Bushmen who lived to the west between Kenhardt and Brandvlei. Between them were the Har (also called the Hardast or Hartbees) River Bushmen who lived along the Hartbees River in the vicinity of Kenhardt, and to the south were the Berg Bushmen who lived in the Kareeberg (Deacon 1986, 1988).

The boundaries between these groups were elastic. The informants knew individuals from all the neighbouring groupings, they intermarried, they used the services of the same rain-makers and sorcerors and they conducted trade amongst themselves. While acknowledging different customs such as the materials used for making sieves, the animal skins used for clothing and the animals they ate (Deacon 1986:151), they acknowledged a cohesion amongst themselves in contrast to the relative animosity they felt towards the Korana and the whites (Deacon 1986:150).

Although the informants' home language was /Xam, they had all had some contact with European colonists by the time of their arrest and some had even worked for farmers for short periods. They therefore knew a little Dutch and it was through the medium of this language that Bleek and Lloyd were first able to converse with them (Lewis-Williams 1981:25-27). It seems, too, that they quickly learned to act out sentences to make their meaning clear and also learned some English. They were especially fond of music and the Dead March from *Saul* was a favourite (Bleek & Bleek 1909:40-41). Although they were all knowledgeable about hunting and collecting wild plant foods (Lewis-Williams 1981:28; Deacon 1986, 1988; Hewitt 1986a:31 ff), their hunter-gatherer lifestyle had been impeded by the influx of settled farmers. Their artefacts, too, had changed and included items such as guns, knives, spoons and iron pots.

## *The Flat Bushman Country*

It was //Kabbo who explained that the Flat Bushmen were so called because the country they lived in was very flat. It lies to the east of the Groot Vloer and Verneukpan, an internal drainage basin into which the Sak River flows from the south-west and the Hartogskloof River flows from the south. To the east of the pans, the Hartbees River bed leads northwards to the Orange River. For most of the year, and sometimes for years at a time, however, neither the pans nor the rivers have any visible water.

At the northern end of the Flat Bushman territory is the small town of Kenhardt and some hundred and fifty kilometres south-south-east is the even smaller village of Vanwyksvlei. The Kareeberg mountains lie about thirty to fifty kilometres south of this village. The Flat Bushman country is traversed by a series of dry river beds or 'Leegtes' and by dolerite dykes – low hills capped with large brown boulders. The weathered outer crust of the dolerite provides an ideal surface for rock engravings and there are at least ten rock art sites in this vicinity. Semi-desert conditions prevail and as a result the vegetation is low, sparse scrub with a few thorn trees where the water table comes close to the surface. After rain, the grass grows rapidly but does not last longer than a few months.

Not long after he arrived at Mowbray, //Kabbo gave Bleek sufficient information to enable him to draw a sketch map indicating the position of //Kabbo's home, the Bitterpits (or Bitterputs), in relation to the places where other Breakwater prisoners and //Kabbo's friends and relatives lived. These places have been described in detail (Deacon 1986, 1988) and further information is given in another paper in this volume entitled 'Archaeology of the Flat and Grass Bushmen'.

## */A!kunta*

/A!kunta, or Klaas Stoffel, was described as a 'youth' aged about 18 and was the first of the Breakwater prisoners to stay at the Bleek home. He was there from 29 August 1870 to 15 October 1873 (Bleek & Lloyd 1911:x), yet contributed only two folktales and a number of pages of words and sentences, presumably because he was too young to know much about storytelling (Hewitt 1986a:49). His testimony is recorded in several of Bleek's notebooks and in those labelled LI amongst Lloyd's. In a list of /Xam prisoners at the Breakwater, probably compiled in December 1871 to accompany the photographs taken for Professor Huxley and the British government (see Bleek & Lloyd 1911:434ff), he was measured as being 4 feet 11½ inches (about 1,5 metres) tall. His convict number was 4636 which indicates that he was one of the same party of /Xam admitted with //Kabbo and /Han≠kass'o. He was married to Ka (Marie), but they had no children at the time.

In the genealogies recorded by Bleek and Lloyd (Jagger Library BCA 121:10, 15, 21 and 4), the family histories of both /A!kunta and Ka are traced back to their great grandparents. /A!kunta's brother Yarrisho or Jantje was also at the Breakwater (prisoner number 4626). He was 5 feet (about 1,5 metres) tall and his age was estimated at about 25 years. He and his wife //Karri//karri (Katherine) had two children. The parents of /A!kunta and Yarrisho were !Haken/ya and /Toaken-an. The family came from the vicinity of Sondagspan and the Strandberg (Strontbergen) to the south and east of the Bitterpits (Deacon 1986).

Several other men who came from the Flat Bushman area and were arrested with the two brothers were interviewed and photographed at the Breakwater in the early 1870s. Those whose genealogies were recorded included //Kabathin (Swartbooi or Saarbai) and his brother /Xaitatin (Lellerbay), !Gubbu (Koos Toontjie), Khaurru (Soopie), Kushi (Koos Pleitje), Tshorru (Cornelis), /Kan (Jacob Nijn), /Hankum (Marcus) and !Xwarriitten (Jacob Nel).

## *//Kabbo*

//Kabbo or 'Dream', also known as Oud Jantje Tooren, was estimated by Bleek to have been about 55-60 years old in 1871. Prisoner number 4628, he was recorded as being 5 feet (about 1,5 metres) tall. He stayed at the Bleek's home from 16 February 1871 and left with /A!kunta on 15 October 1873. Lloyd tried, through the help of Mr C St L Devenish at Vanwyksvlei, to contact

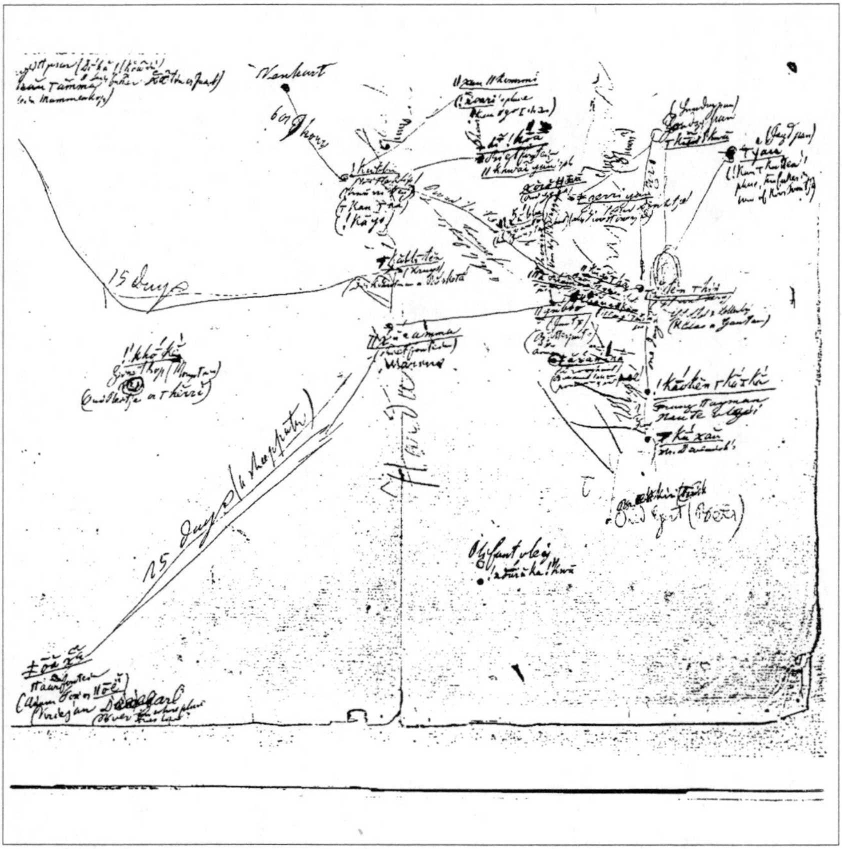


*A map drawn by Bleek on information given by //Kabbo. The distance from north to south is about 150 kilometres. Kenhardt is marked at the top centre, and Haasfontein in the bottom left-hand corner is about 15 kilometres south-east of Brandvlei (see Deacon 1986 for further details).*

//Kabbo and ask him to return, but he died on 25 January 1876 (Lloyd 1889:1). His widow, !Kwabba-an, died in January of the following year before she could travel to Cape Town (ibid.).

//Kabbo's genealogy goes back to his grandparents (BCA 151:1, 9, 5, 11, 12) and also includes mention of his father's brother, //A/khain yan or Oud Bastard, who lived at the Blaauwputs and Oud Bastards Puts south of the Bitterpits (B-II:371) (Deacon 1986:142). //Kabbo's father was Goa/ya (also spelled /Ku/ya) and his mother was !Kwi-an. Her mother, ≠Giri, was said to have been

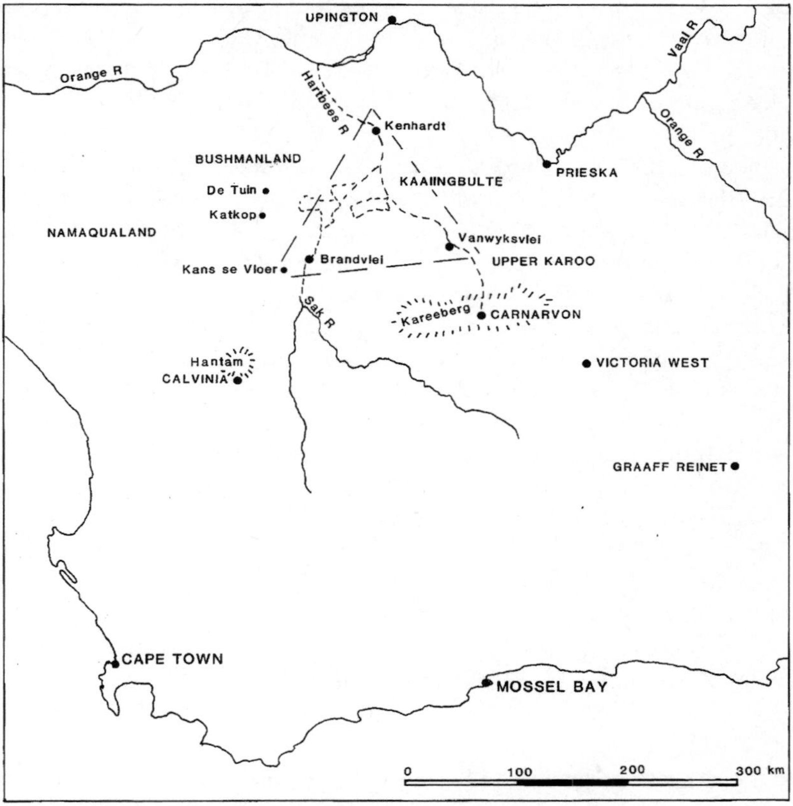


*A map of part of the Cape Colony in the 1870s. //Kabbo's map on the opposite page refers to the area within the triangle. The Grass Bushmen who were interviewed lived between Katkop and Brandvlei and the Flat Bushmen between Kenhardt and Vanwyksvlei. The broken line in the centre of the triangle outlines the Verneukpan.*

killed by a lion, and ≠Giri's first husband and Goa/ya's father, /Torrono, was killed by a rhino. Her second husband, /To/na, died of starvation. ≠Giri was said to have been a *!gixa* or sorceress (LII-37:3337 rev). ≠Giri and /Torrono were not only //Kabbo's maternal grandparents, but were also paternal grandparents to !Kwabba-an, //Kabbo's wife. //Kabbo and !Kwabba-an were therefore first cousins.

//Kabbo and !Kwabba-an (also spelled !Kuobba-an), or Oude Lies, had two children: Suobba-//kein or Sarke (Sarah) who married /Han≠kass'o and died only a year after her mother, and //Goo-ka-!kui, 'Smoke's Man' or Witbooi Tooren. Also amongst his household was Betje, the daughter of his elder brother, whose parents died when she was young. She was older than //Kabbo's children and moved away after she was married (Bleek & Lloyd 1911:307-309).

//Goo-ka-!kui does not appear to have been arrested at the same time as his father. /Han≠kass'o told Lloyd in 1878 that //Goo-ka-!kui has 'seen the wind' at Haarfontein while working at Hartogs Kloof for a Bastard farmer named Jacob Kotze and his wife Silla, a Bushman woman (Bleek & Lloyd 1911:111-13). /Han≠kass'o had also lived there at one time. Hartogs Kloof is about fifty kilometres south-west of the Bitterpits where //Kabbo and /Han≠kass'o were living at the time they were arrested (see Deacon 1986).

//Kabbo's abilities as a storyteller were a great improvement on those of /A!kunta, and his accounts were lively and entertaining. More importantly, many narratives came from his own experience. His name, translated as 'Dream', his references to events in his life and his descriptions of rain-making, presentiments and healing suggest he was a shaman and a rain-maker (Lewis-Williams 1981:27). A highly respected rain-maker, /Kannu or /Kaunu, was said to be '//Kabbo's person' (Bleek 1933b:391) who 'possessed locusts and rain' (Bleek 1933b:388, 391). //Kabbo described how he himself had made it rain in Mowbray while in a dream (LII-6:625-31) and /Han≠kass'o related that //Kabbo 'had Mantises, he was a Mantis's man ... !Gurritan-de was a springbok sorcerer, he had springbok' (Bleek 1936a:143-44; see also Lewis-Williams 1981:27).

//Kabbo spoke poignantly to Bleek and Lloyd about his home and his longing to return and 'He much enjoyed the thought that the Bushman stories would become known by means of books' (Bleek & Lloyd 1911:x). The importance of the part that stories played in his life is related in a piece entitled '//Kabbo's intended return home' (Bleek & Lloyd 1911:299-317), given in July and August 1873, a few months before his departure from Cape Town in mid-October. He explained to Bleek that a story 'is like the wind, it comes from a far-off quarter, and we feel it' and went on:

> The Flat Bushmen go to each other's huts; that they may smoking sit in front of them. Therefore, they obtain stories at them; because they are used to visit; for smoking's people they are (Bleek & Lloyd 1911:301-303).

Further remarks in the same narrative give an inkling of the way in which he and Bleek worked together, of his perceived place in the Bleek household and of his expectations regarding the reward he may receive for the work he had done in Cape Town:

> I ought to talk with my fellow men; for, I work here, together with women; and I do not talk with them; for, they merely send me to work (Bleek & Lloyd 1911:303).
>
> ...
>
> Therefore, I must sit waiting for the Sundays on which I remain here, on which I continue to teach thee. I do not again await another moon ... For I have sat waiting for the boots, that I must put on to walk in. ... I should reach my place, when the trees are dry. For, I shall walk, letting the flowers become dry while I still follow the path. ... for, I must remain at my (own) place, the name of which I have told my Master; ... he knows, (having) put it down. And thus my name is plain (beside it). It is there that I sit waiting for the gun; and then, he will send the gun to me there. ... For, starvation was that on account of which I was bound ... when I starving turned back from following the sheep. Therefore, I lived with him, that I might get a gun from him; that I might possess it; That I might myself shoot, feeding myself, while I do not eat my companions' food. For I eat my (own) game. (ibid:316-17)

//Kabbo's reference above to the fact that he had told Bleek where he lived, and that it had been written down, draws attention, too, to his well-developed sense of place. This is shown not only by the geographical accuracy of the sketch map (Deacon 1986), but also in his frequent references to landmarks in the course of relating narratives.

Hewitt (1986a:240-242) has commented on //Kabbo's capacity for elaborating at length on relatively unimportant details within long narratives, his extraordinary facility for describing the same event from the perspective of several different characters in the story, the outrageous nature of /Kaggen's antics, and the playful banter exchanged between characters. Such are the features of a skilled and practised storyteller.

## */Han≠kass'o*

/Han≠kass'o, or Klein Jantje, was not selected as a possible informant initially and went home in November 1871 after his sentence had been served at the

Breakwater as convict number 4630. His prison record shows no misdemeanours, only a reward of 6 shillings given in November 1870 for good work at school (Cape Archives, PBW Vol 144, Reward and Punishment Book Vol 2: 1869-1873). His age was estimated by the prison authorities at about 21 years in 1869, which would have made him 30 when he returned to Cape Town. His height was given as 5 feet (about 1,5 metres).

/Han≠kass'o was at Mowbray for nearly two years, from 10 January 1878 to December 1879, but his journey there was a traumatic one. At the request of Lucy Lloyd (Lloyd 1889:3), /Han≠kass'o and his wife Suobba-//kein, //Kabbo's daughter, left their small son, !Hu!hun, with friends and travelled from Vanwyksvlei in April 1877 with an infant child. When they reached Beaufort West their baby died and in December Suobba-//kein, in poor health as a result of a brutal attack by a policeman (Bleek & Bleek 1909:41), could not travel further and also died. /Han≠kass'o went on to Cape Town alone but, throughout his time there, was worried about !Hu!hun and was anxious to return home. Edith and Dorothea Bleek recalled that:

> Jantje ..., like the others, was gentle and kindly, but as a rule much graver. Children gave him great pleasure. He would play with the baby and make presents for the little ones' birthdays, a tiny bow and arrows, a doll's chair or a *!goin !goin*. (Bleek & Bleek 1909:41)

/Han≠kass'o's father was Zzorri or Zzorrittu, a Mountain or Berg Bushman from /khu kumm, who did not have a Dutch name as he died before the Boers came to that part of the country (LVIII-1:6052-3). His mother, /Kabbi-an, also spelled /Xabbi-an, or Oud Sarah, was a Flat Bushman woman from //-kuke (Bleek & Bleek 1909:41). Her father, Ts'ats'i, also spelled Tssatssi (Bleek & Lloyd 1911:372) and Tsatsi (op. cit.:359), was related to the rain maker //Kunn or Coos Groot Oog (Bleek 1933b:387) who lived at !khai /ku or Evicass Pits (Bleek & Lloyd 1911:323n). This place is probably the present-day spring at Abiquaputs about thirty kilometres east of Brandvlei. Ts'ats'i was also known to Dia!kwain (Bleek 1933b:385). Ts'ats'i's mother, Ddorruken, was killed by a lion (BCA 151).

/Han≠kass'o's factual accounts of landmarks in the Flat Bushman country, as well as his additional information on people he and //Kabbo knew, have been useful in building up a picture of their life-style and customs (Lewis-Williams 1981; Deacon 1986, 1988; Hewitt 1986a). His descriptions of the making of artefacts such as arrows and dancing rattles, and of the collecting of materials for artefacts reflect his practical nature (Bleek & Lloyd 1911:348-63). On the other hand, his description of the making of clay pots (Bleek & Lloyd 1911:342-47) leaves out the all-important stage of firing. Of particular interest are his interpretations of copies of rock paintings, such as the panel from Ezeljagdspoort (Lewis-Williams *et al.* 1993), which link the rock art unequivocally with rain making. An account of the way in which *//hara* (specularite) and *tto* (red ochre) were collected and the customs surrounding these practices, underscores the ritual significance of paint (Bleek & Lloyd 1911: 374-379).

Guenther (1989:29) votes /Han≠kass'o as the best storyteller amongst the /Xam, and Hewitt (1986a:236, 243) praises the fluent way in which his narratives are constructed. He provided the largest number of songs and 'poems' and gave very lively performances, although he elaborated dialogue within the narratives to a lesser extent than //Kabbo.

Bleek and Lloyd often note at the beginning of a narrative the name of the person who first told the story to the informant. This is most often their mother or their father. /Han≠kass'o was particularly helpful in this regard and sometimes gave an insight into the intimacy between mother and child, the way in which children were taught customs, and the way in which an individual may have built up a repertoire of stories. An example of an occasion that led to his mother telling him a story is in the introduction to The Death of the Lizard (Bleek & Lloyd 1911:214-17, 316-21).

/Han≠kass'o was a young boy at the time and had a young leveret (hare) as a pet that his grandfather, Tsatsi, had caught on the hunting-ground and brought home for him. His mother wanted to kill it and eat it, but 'I was not willing to kill the leveret, because I felt that nothing acted as prettily as it did, when it was gently running, gently running along' (ibid.:319). His mother and grandmother told him to go and fetch water and he tied up the leveret so it would not run away while he was gone. In his absence his mother killed and roasted the leveret. He cried bitterly and asked them to get him another one, but his mother explained

> that I should not play with meat; ... for we lay meat to roast. For the leveret is not a little fat; therefore, we kill it, we lay it to roast, while we do not play with it. (Bleek & Lloyd 1911:321n).

They calmed and soothed him with the story of the lizard 'while they wished that I might quietly listen to them; when I had shut my mouth' (ibid.).

## *The Grass Bushman Country*

There is usually more standing water in the Grass Bushman territory than there is further east which perhaps explains why the grass in the west is such a feature of the landscape. Anthing's 1962 report mentioned the fact that the San relied on grass seeds as a food source. This became scarce when the white settlers moved in with their sheep and cattle as these animals ate the grass and the seeds did not develop. People who called themselves Grass Bushmen were recorded as living in this area from the eighteenth century onwards. Gordon, for example, who travelled through here in 1779, makes reference to the Grassveld Bushmen between Nieuwoudtville and the Orange River (Raper & Boucher 1988:214, 298).

The three representatives of the Grass Bushmen, Dia!kwain, his sister !Kweiten ta //ken and her husband ≠Kasin, came from the Katkop mountains, dolerite hills about a hundred kilometres south-west of Kenhardt and about thirty kilometres north-west of Brandvlei. Other members of their extended family came from a farm now known as Kans about twenty kilometres west of Brandvlei, and from along the Sak River south of Brandvlei. A fourth Grass Bushman, //Oe or Adam Fix, estimated to be 67 years old, was also at the Breakwater and was photographed with the other convicts in 1871 (Deacon 1986:149). His genealogy records the fact that he had five children, but the chart extends back only to his parents (BCA 151:24 & 25). He came from Haasfontein (also spelled Haarfontein) south-east of Brandvlei and was said to be 'a Brinkkop man' (BCA 151:24 & 25).

## *Dia!kwain*

Dia!kwain or David Hoesar (also spelled Hoesaar, Hoezar, Hussar and Husar) was estimated to have been 25 years old when he was admitted to the Breakwater Prison on 1 November 1869 as convict number 4434. His European surname is the same as that of a farm in the vicinity of Katkop, now known as Hoezar Wes. On the sketch map Bleek drew on //Kabbo's instructions, Dia!kwain's place is marked as Klein Mummenkop, a farm known today as Klein Lemoenkop Wes which is about thirty kilometres south of Kenhardt (Deacon 1986:147). At 5 feet $2^3/_4$ inches (about 1,6 metres) he was relatively tall. His other distinguishing feature was a large scar on his right cheekbone.

Dia!kwain's mother, ≠Kamme-an or Doro (Anneke), is said to have come from the same place as /A!kunta (BXXV:2415), i.e. the Strandberg. Furthermore, //Kabbo told Bleek in September 1871 that ≠Kamme-an's brother married //Kabbo's wife's sister (Deacon 1986:151). Dia!kwain told Bleek that his mother had disappeared a few years previously and he thought she had probably been killed by the Boers (BXXV:2414).

Dia!kwain's father, Xatin (also spelled Xattin), came from the Sak River and the Brinkkop (Bleek 1933b:383). Besides their son Dia!kwain, Xatin and ≠Kamme-an had at least three daughters: Whai-ttu (Springbok Skin) or Griet whose daughter Kaitje Lynx married Jan Plat (LV-19:5446); !Kweiten ta //ken who married Klaas Katkop; and /A-kkumm who married Mansse (Bleek & Lloyd 1911:368). A second son, //Xwa:gan-te (Bleek 1933b:383), was married to Du-//hu (ibid.:385). They seem to have been a close family for Dia!kwain was with all three of his sisters when they saw an apparition on the salt pan on their way home after burying his first wife. It was wearing the same cap that his wife used to wear and they all believed it was her at the time the 'sorcerers' were taking her away (Bleek & Lloyd 1911:365-71). By contrast, /Han≠kass'o did not mention his own brothers and sisters.

Dia!kwain's first wife, Mietche, died of an illness in about 1863 near the Sak River at Spreet, south of Brandvlei (Bleek 1932b:249). They were first cousins as Dia!kwain's paternal grandparents, !Xugen di and Twabboken !kanken, were also Mietche's mother's parents. Dia!kwain and Mietche had three children: a son, Booi, and two daughters, Troi and Griet. Griet was 'in service with Boers' at the time the genealogical information was recorded in March 1875 (BCA 151:29 and 1a). His second wife was Johanna, the daughter of Surritte (a Bushman) and Johanna (a Bushman woman) who lived at Katkop.

Mietche's paternal grandmother, /Xarran-/Xarran, also lived at the Sak River and died when Dia!kwain was a youth. She seems to have had special powers as she was said to have had a head like that of an ostrich and to have walked like an ostrich. Even though she was dead, people still called her name if they wanted the wind to blow (Bleek 1932c:334).

Dia!kwain's character is perhaps the most enigmatic of the three main informants. On the one hand he had shot and killed a farmer, and on the other his mild nature had convinced the judge that he had acted in self-defence. Indeed, the Bleek sisters remembered him as 'a soft-hearted mortal, who would not, unprovoked, have hurt a fly' (Bleek & Bleek 1909:40). Yet, in contrast to /Han≠kass'o, he was not a model prisoner. The prison records show that on 19 June 1870 he was given three hours extra labour for disobedience of orders. On a second occasion he was kept two days in the cells on a spare diet from 24 May 1871 for having dagga (hemp or marijuana) in his possession. No stranger to violence, Dia!kwain described how he had been cured of a swollen throat by the sorceress !Kwarra-an after an attack by a 'Kafir' who tried to steal spoons from his mother (LV-4:4200-30).

After his discharge from prison on 29 November 1873, Dia!kwain stayed at the Bleek's home from then until 18 March 1874 and Bleek's last interview with him was dated 16 March. He went home to fetch his sister and brother-in-law and returned for a second spell of nearly two years, from 13 June 1874 to 7 March 1876. It was during this visit that Wilhelm Bleek died in the early hours of the morning of 17 August 1875. No interviews appear to have been done either by Lloyd or Bleek between 13 June 1874 and early January of the following year. They may well have been working to prepare his second Report to Parliament at this time (Bleek 1875), but Jemima Bleek remarked to Sir George Grey in a letter after her husband's death that he had been ill for some considerable time after March 1874 and this probably played a part too (Spohr 1962:40-41). The last date in Bleek's last notebook, BXXVII, is 7 January 1875. Lloyd, on the other hand, worked steadily with Dia!kwain from 7 January until 16 August 1875, after which there was a break of nearly a month when the family were no doubt in mourning. Her last interview with him is dated 5 March 1876.

When Dia!kwain left Cape Town for the second time, he went to work for Dr H Meyer in Calvinia. Lloyd wrote to the doctor some time later asking if Dia!kwain could return to Mowbray. The doctor explained that Dia!kwain had left his home to visit a sister, expecting to return to Calvinia after three weeks and to proceed from there to Cape Town. However, he had not returned and all enquiries to locate him proved unsuccessful (Lloyd 1889:3). According to an account of the incident recorded by W A Burger, a former Principal of the Kenhardt High School, it appears that friends of Jacob Kruger, the farmer who had been shot by Dia!kwain, had heard of his release from prison and of his return to the area. Taking the law into their own hands, they tracked Dia!kwain down and shot and killed him near Kenhardt in retaliation, angry that the court had given him what they considered to be a lenient sentence (Burger n.d.).

Like //Kabbo, Dia!kwain had had direct experience of rain-makers and //Kabbo referred to him as a Brinkkop man (BII:370), probably meaning that he had undergone some training as a shaman (Deacon 1986, 1988). His accounts of rain-making are particularly graphic and detailed. !Nuin-/kuiten, said to be Dia!kwain's paternal greatgrandfather, was called on by Xatin when he wanted it to rain (Bleek 1933b:382), and by Xatin's father to make wind when the mosquitoes were biting him (Bleek 1932c:333). During the course of rain making, they were instructed to climb the Brinkkop and look about for springbok (Bleek 1933b:382-83). However, Dia!kwain said on another occasion that !Nuin-/kuiten was only a friend of Xatin's father and was not his blood relation (Bleek 1936a:131).

Dia!kwain's testimony was the third longest (over 2 400 pages, in contrast to over 2 800 by /Han≠kass'o and over 3 100 by //Kabbo) (Lewis-Williams 1981:27-28). His narratives are often more cryptic than those of //Kabbo and /Han≠kass'o, but they show a great range in subject matter and give valuable detail about beliefs and related social rules and sanctions. Hewitt (1986a:245) rates Dia!kwain's narrative of The Young Man who was Carried off by a Lion when Asleep on a Hill as his most accomplished performance. Dia!kwain's more serious approach to narrating could reflect the fact that the Bleek household was greatly disrupted during his longer second visit as a result of Bleek's continuing illness, his subsequent death and the family's consequent financial problems.

In one particularly tantalising note that Lloyd was not able to follow up, Dia!kwain mentioned in passing that Xatin had done rock engravings depicting animals at a place called /Kann. This is probably the present-day pan called Kans (Deacon 1988) west of Brandvlei. He was therefore the only informant who gave any acknowledgement of a direct link with an artist although most of the others were able to offer comment on copies of rock paintings and engravings that were shown to them (Lewis-Williams 1981:27ff).

### *!Kweiten ta //ken*

!Kweiten ta //ken or Rachel was not in prison so there is no estimate of her age and height on record, but the Bleek sisters recalled that she 'was a pretty little woman, lively and hot-tempered. Her feet were so tiny that the out-grown boots of a small child of eleven were just right for her' (Bleek & Bleek 1909:41). She was at Mowbray for only seven months, from 13 June 1874 to 13 January 1875, initially with her two younger sons aged six and two, and, after 25 October, with her two elder boys as well. The children were very well behaved and a small field was set aside for them to play in. They were never heard to squabble and obeyed their parents implicitly (Bleek & Bleek 1909:41). Although Bleek was clearly worried about the increased expenditure that their stay incurred, !Kweiten ta //ken refused to stay without all the members of her family (Bleek 1875:5).

Bleek must have had little energy at this time as his health was failing (Spohr 1962:40-41) and it was Lloyd who used two notebooks for !Kweiten ta //ken's testimony, amounting to fewer than two hundred pages. The interviews took place over a relatively short period from 6 December 1874 to 12 January 1875, or barely six weeks. The last few pages were not translated until 1911, according to a note on the contents page of the second book (LIV-2). !Kweiten ta //ken's narratives are amongst the shortest in the collection and she seldom elaborated them with dialogue or chants. It is possible that she felt uncomfortable in Mowbray and could not express herself as openly and freely as she might have done under different circumstances. Perhaps her hot temper also played a part and she might have lacked patience in the interview situation. The fact that Lloyd made no attempt to find !Kweiten ta //ken again and invite her to return to Cape Town suggests that she was aware that they had not formed the necessary bond for recording valuable information.

Most useful amongst the comments given by !Kweiten ta //ken are those that relate to what women do, for example, what maidens do with the //ka or red stone and what is done with new maidens. Furthermore, several of her narratives deal with young women (The Maiden who was Changed into a Frog; The Girl's Story; The Frog's Story; About a New Maiden) and Lloyd could have deliberately encouraged her to focus on such subjects, anxious to have a woman's perspective and first-hand accounts of female rituals and beliefs. However, they also cover subjects dealt with by the male informants (The Young Springbok who was Carried off by the Elephants; The Story of the Anteater, Springbok, Lynx and Partridge), and all the other male informants, with the exception of /A!kunta, spoke about new maidens (see Hewitt 1986a:279-86). This would suggest that narratives of all kinds were available equally to both men and women.

## *≠Kasin*

≠Kasin, or Klaas Katkop, was estimated to be 37 years old in 1869 and was 5 feet $^{3}/_{4}$ inches (about 1.5 metres) tall. His father was a Korana captain named Oud Klaas and his mother was a Grass Bushman woman, Oud Griet or Wa≠ko (BXXI:2351ff). The place Katkop is said to have been named after a Korana 'captain' of the same name who must have been related to ≠Kasin, but his genealogy is incomplete so this cannot be verified. He spoke both Korana and /Xam.

At the time of his admission to the Breakwater, as convict number 4435, ≠Kasin was noted as having a double tooth in his front upper jaw and his left wrist was fractured. He was not punished for any misdemeanours while in prison, but was instead recommended for removal from the Probation to the Good Conduct Class on 29 July 1870 (Cape Archives, Record Book of Convict Stations, Table Bay Breakwater 1870, Vol. 6315). Like Dia!kwain, he was supposed to serve five years for culpable homicide. In fact, they were at the Breakwater prison for only four years, although they were in custody for five if the full period from initial arrest in 1869 to departure from Mowbray in March 1874 is taken into account.

The Bleek children thought ≠Kasin was a fierce-looking man (Bleek & Bleek 1909:41). As noted above, he was married to !Kweiten ta //ken and spent two periods at Mowbray. The first began on 1 November 1873, about a month before Dia!kwain joined him, and lasted until 18 March 1874 when both returned home. Bleek remarked that they were so anxious to see their families after their sentence ended that they reached Calvinia, 270 miles away, on 30 March (Bleek 1875:5). They must have walked or been given lifts on wagons as a train journey would have been much quicker. The second visit was with !Kweiten ta //ken and their children from 13 June 1874 to 13 January 1875 (Bleek 1875:5). At one time he lived on the farm Nieuwepoort, said to be about half a day's journey on horseback north-north-east of Calvinia, but he also lived at Katkop and was with Dia!kwain in that vicinity when the farmer, Kruger, was shot.

≠Kasin's testimony was spread over four of Lloyd's notebooks (LIV-1-4) and one of Bleek's (BXXV). Of particular interest to Bleek were the Korana words and sentences that could be compared with the /Xam equivalents. ≠Kasin also identified a number of plant medicines that had been 'found in the hut of a Bushman sorcerer, and were kindly furnished for identification by Mr J. Gibb', and several poisons (Bleek 1875:18-19). His narration skills do not appear to have been as well developed as his age may have led one to expect. Lloyd's first recorded interview with him is dated 4 November 1873 and the last on 23 January 1874. The last translation was done on 20 February 1874, so he does not appear to have been interviewed at all during his second visit. This presumably indicates that, as was the case with his wife, he was not a good subject and Lloyd did not attempt to contact him again after Bleek died.

## POSTSCRIPT

After 1884 Lucy Lloyd's health and Jemima Bleek's decision to take her daughters to Germany to be educated led them both to leave South Africa for nearly twenty years. On their return, both Edith and Dorothea (Doris) Bleek helped Lloyd to prepare the manuscript for *Specimens of Bushman Folklore* and to see it through the press (Bleek & Lloyd 1911). It fell to Dorothea Bleek to take on the responsibility of curating the manuscript collection, continuing where possible with translation, and publishing a series of articles in the journal *Bantu Studies* in the 1930s, a book of /Xam folktales entitled *The Mantis and his Friends*, and a volume of rock painting copies made by G W Stow with a commentary by herself. She was able, too, to almost complete the Bushman dictionary her father and aunt had started, although it was published only after her death (Bleek 1956).

Dorothea Bleek established herself as an ethnographer and was the first member of her family to visit the northern Cape. In 1910 and 1911, a few years before the death of Lucy Lloyd in 1913, she went to Prieska and Kenhardt to try to find descendants or relatives of the people her father and aunt had interviewed. The only such person she met was /Ogan-an who told her that they had disappeared from Salt River in 1884 because they walked back home. They had asked a policeman for directions and he had shown them the way (Bleek 1936c:202).

Although Dorothea Bleek met people there who had lived at the Bitterpits, home of //Kabbo and /Han≠kass'o, and a few who could still speak /Xam, no-one knew any folklore (Bleek 1936c:202), but they still sang and danced. She recalled later:

> Even at Prieska, the very old started the dance of former days after a feast of meat. (Bleek 1924:ix)

She was accompanied on that occasion by staff members of the South African Museum who took a series of photographs and casts of people whom 'the elders themselves guaranteed' were of 'pure Bushman descent' (Bleek 1936c: 203). Some of the casts are still on display in the Museum.

After her aunt's death, Dorothea Bleek went on to study the Nharo Bushmen in present-day Botswana and she undertook several long field trips in that country and as far afield as Angola. She died only a few years short of a century after her father's first interview with Cape Bushmen in 1857.

After their return to the country of the Flat and Grass Bushmen, /Han≠kass'o. !A!kunta, ≠Kasin and !Kweiten ta //ken melted away and we have no record of their further movements. In 1985 I met a farmer, Mr Johannes Hendrikse, on the farm Katkop. He had been born there and remembered a boyhood acquaintance named Klaas Hoezar who once threw a stone at him. Whether Klaas Hoezar was a direct descendant of Dia!kwain or his brother we do not know, but no other Hoezars were known on Katkop or the surrounding farms in the 1980s. The last link I found was an elderly man named Hendrik Gous. He said he knew a few words of /Xam and recited them, giving us the following translation:

> Here come the Boers. We must run away.

## *ACKNOWLEDGEMENTS*

I acknowledge with thanks the financial assistance received for this project from 1985-1988 from the Centre for Science Development, Pretoria, the Wenner-Gren Foundation, New York, and the Swan Fund, Oxford. It was a pleasure working with Helen Barlow, Harriet Deacon and Hannali van der Merwe while compiling information from the Cape Archives and the Jagger Library Mansucripts and I thank them for their help. Elaine Eberhard and Leonie Twentyman-Jones were particularly helpful at the Jagger Library and I would like to thank them especially for their patience and interest.

Parts of this paper have been published in Skotnes, P. (ed.), *Miscast: Negotiating the Presence of the Bushmen*. Cape Town: University of Cape Town Press, 1996.

# A Short Note on Lloyd's !Kung Informants

Janette Deacon

In September 1879, a little more than three months before /Han≠kass'o left the Bleek/Lloyd family for the last time, and some four months before Piet Lynx and his family returned to Kimberley, Lucy Lloyd was given the opportunity of learning something of another Bushman language. Two teenage boys who spoke !Kung (spelled !kun by Lloyd) and came from north-eastern Namibia, were 'placed' in the Bleek/Lloyd household (Lloyd 1889:4), giving Jemima Bleek and Lucy Lloyd the responsibility of feeding, clothing and housing up to seven people in addition to their family for a period of several months. When /Han≠kass'o and the Lynx family had left, the two !Kung boys were joined by two more !Kung children who came to live in the household soon after Lucy Lloyd was given notice by the trustees of the Grey Library.

Mr W Coates Palgrave had known that Wilhelm Bleek was interested in San languages spoken in the northern Kalahari region of present-day Namibia and Botswana and he seems to have brought the boys to Cape Town specifically for Lloyd to interview (Lloyd 1889:4). Palgrave had been sent to Namibia as a British commissioner in 1876 and again in subsequent years to meet Herero leaders and to investigate the possibility of setting up a British protectorate (De Kock 1976:345). Palgrave left Okahandja early in 1879 (Krüger & Beyers 1977:674) and went on a third mission to Damaraland in January 1880 (ibid.) so the two elder !Kung boys were possibly left with Lloyd before his return. The Rehoboth Bastards and the Herero were worried that white farmers from South Africa would invade their territory as the philologist and trader Dr J Theophilus Hahn had encouraged Boers from the Transvaal and the northern Cape to settle there. Hahn, who was the son of a German Rhenish missionary and was born at the Ebenezer mission in Great Namaqualand in 1842, spoke Nama and Herero fluently. He was well known to Wilhelm Bleek who corresponded with him on the subject of Khoisan languages. Aggressive by nature, Hahn crossed swords with Palgrave and with Maherero

*The four !Kung boys interviewed by Lucy Lloyd in Cape Town in the early 1880. They are, from left, !Nanni, Tamme, /Uma and Da. Reproduced from Bleek & Lloyd 1911.*

and as a result he left to settle in Stellenbosch in 1878 where, amongst other publications, he completed the first map of Namibia in 1879 (ibid.).

Two years later, while the !Kung boys were still with the Bleek/Lloyd household, Hahn's career had a devastating effect on Lucy Lloyd when he was appointed as Government philologist at the Cape and replaced her as librarian of the Grey collection. She was given notice in February 1880 (Beyers 1981:315) and he took over the post a year later (De Kock 1976:345). She appealed to the Grey Trustees and the case was taken to the Supreme Court. No final legal decision was reached. Although Hahn resigned in November 1883 after the library committee found his work unsatisfactory (he returned to Namibia in 1889), Lucy Lloyd was not reappointed (Beyers 1981:315; De Kock 1976:345). Probably as a result of the loss of her steady income, she and Jemima Bleek were obliged to leave South Africa for Europe early in 1884.

The two teenagers, !Nanni and Tamme, arrived at the Bleek/Lloyd household in Mowbray on 1 September 1879 and spent two and a half years there before returning to Damaraland on 28 March 1882. The last time that Lloyd interviewed them appears from the unpublished notebooks to have been in October 1881. !Nanni and Tamme were apparently not related and their family units had lived about 80 kilometres apart (Lloyd 1889:4). The Swiss botanist and explorer, Hans Schinz, identified the !Kung as a social and language group in north-eastern Namibia in the 1880s, calling them the I Kun San. A sub-group who lived around the Aha hills he called the I Gu, the present-day Ju/'hoansi (Gordon 1992:46).

!Nanni and Tamme were joined on 25 March 1880 by two younger boys, /Uma and Da, who were also unrelated and also came from different !Kung groups. Da seems to have been no older than about six when he first arrived. He stayed at the Bleek and Lloyd home in Mowbray two years longer than !Nanni and Tamme, until 28 March 1884. Then, at the age of about ten, he was 'replaced' in the care of Mr George Stevens (Lloyd 1889:4), an official of the 'Native Department' (ibid.:28). Employment had been found for /Uma in December 1881, some two months after his last recorded interview. Fewer than a hundred pages of testimony were written down from /Uma and Da, and Da does not seem to have been interviewed at all between October 1881 and March 1884, either because he had little to say or because Lloyd was preoccupied with other matters.

The boys could not converse with /Han≠kass'o or with Piet Lynx as their languages were mutually unintelligible (Lloyd 1889:4), but /Han≠kass'o remarked on 'a partial resemblance between the language of the Grass Bushmen, and that spoken by the !kun' (ibid.). !Nanni and Tamme spoke slightly different dialects, as did Da and /Uma. Despite these initial problems, Lucy Lloyd was able to understand enough !Kung to write down 1 233 pages of text, of which 1 103 had been translated into English by 1889 (Lloyd 1889:5) and the rest later. Lloyd remarked that !Kung appeared to contain only four clicks with the lateral one pronounced slightly differently from the pronunciation used by the /Xam (ibid.).

In addition to linguistic information (see Dickens, this volume), !Nanni and Tamme related a number of narratives, drew and painted pictures and made arrows for Lloyd. Of particular interest to Lloyd was the fact that a large number of narratives included the character /xue who was similar to the Mantis in the /Xam tales in that he could assume many forms (Lloyd 1889:4). Some examples of these narratives have been published (Bleek & Lloyd 1911: 404-13). !Nanni, Tamme and, to a lesser extent, /Uma, apparently enjoyed drawing and painting and some of their pictures were reproduced in *Specimens of Bushman Folklore* (Bleek & Lloyd 1911) and by Rudner (1970). The pictures of plants and animals were accompanied by !Kung words and their translations so may have been used by Lloyd as a device for interpreting what was said. Da, however, did not develop his artistic skills and his sketchbook contains only 'pencil scribbles' (Rudner 1970:153). We do not know which of the arrows in the collection at the South African Museum were made by the boys, but Lloyd noted that they were feathered more elaborately and in a different way from those made by the /Xam (Lloyd 1889:5).

The personal circumstances of the four !Kung boys are not described by Lloyd and it is not clear whether they were orphans or had been taken into some form of voluntary or involuntary service. Tamme described (MS pages 9216-9221) how the Makoba people, who lived in the Okavango (Rudner 1970:148), had taken him and given him to the Ovambo. This, together with the long account by !Nanni of The Treatment of Thieves (Bleek & Lloyd 1911:416-415), attests to a society in which violence and social disruption were not unknown. The boys probably had no choice but to live in Mowbray until it suited others to move them.

One can only speculate on the personal interactions that developed over the years the !Kung boys lived in the Bleek/Lloyd household. It is unlikely that the children saw Jemima and Lucy as surrogate mothers. They probably kept their distance in a benign employer-employee relationship. In any case, a considerable adjustment must have been required of the children but only the teenagers seem to have been able to give Lucy Lloyd any of the information she wanted of them. For her part, the boys arrived just before a traumatic time in her life when she lost her job to Hahn and was caught up in a legal and emotional battle that was never successfully resolved. It is small wonder that interviews ceased in October 1881 and, after /Uma left in December of that year, !Nanni and Tamme went home a few months later. Only Da remained until the family left for Germany in 1884.

# Scientific Reasons for the Study of the Bushman Language

By W.H.I. Bleek, Ph.D.
*F. Memb. of the R. Bav. Academy of Sciences at Munich*

Thirty or forty years ago a philological knowledge of the Bushman language would have been a matter of a good deal of political importance in this Colony; for it would at once have decided the question brought into such loud and violent discussion by the publication of Dr. Philip's Researches, as to whether the Bushmen were originally Hottentots who had been robbed of their cattle by the Boers. A very slight knowledge of the two languages (Hottentot and Bushman) would at once have negatived this proposition. But the present attempt thoroughly to master the Bushman language, although it must be of benefit to those who will have to do with the Bushmen (a race who still hold the keys of that Interior beyond the Orange River which is the unknown region of South Africa, and may, for all we know, be full of the richest treasures), has not been dictated by political, but by purely scientific motives. To understand this, it is necessary to throw a glance at he whole field of South African philological inquiry.

For the general science of comparative grammar, the languages spoken within or on the borders of this Colony are of the highest importance; – Kafir, as giving us the key to the great mass of kindred Negro (Prefix-pronominal) languages which fill almost the whole of South Africa, and extend at least as far to the north-west as Sierra Leone; – and Hottentot, as exhibiting the most primitive form known of that large tribe of languages which is distinguished by its Sex-denoting qualities, which fills North Africa, Europe and part of Asia, which includes the languages of the most highly cultivated nations on earth, and which may be even of far greater extent than we have any idea of at present.

Whilst the languages to which the understanding of these two South African tongues gives us the best key, comprise together about three-fifths of the languages known on earth, the remaining two-fifths are at present thrown together into one great class, mainly distinguished by its negative quality of not possessing the features belonging to either of the two other families. Both these families of languages, represented respectively in their most primitive forms by Kafir in the one case and Hottentot in the other, possess classes of nouns originally dependent upon the concord of other parts of speech with certain portions of the nouns, i.e., with the prefixes of the nouns in Kafir, and with the suffixes of the nouns in Hottentot. These classes of nouns had originally no reference to the distinctions of sex as observed in nature, but are purely grammatical; although natural distinctions, like that of sex, may have been later brought into some relation with them, as has been more or less done in the so-called Sex-denoting languages.

That large class of languages which, as yet, can neither be included among the Prefix-pronominal nor the Sex-denoting, is mainly distinguished by the characteristic of not possessing such grammatical classes (or genders) of nouns. The question now is, with regard to this great bulk of genderless languages, whether they have stripped off the grammatical genders (or grammatical classification of nouns based on their concord), or whether they never possessed any. If the latter be the case, they must belong to a far earlier formation of language than either Kafir or Hottentot. If we want to solve this question, we must study those members of this genderless class of languages which appear to be least advanced in culture, and among these none is *prima facie* scientifically more promising that the Bushman language.

The people speaking this language occupy the lowest known position with regard to civilisation. By their want of all numerals beyond three, they show a low stage of arithmetical development, only equalled, but not exceeded, by some Australian tribes. The Bushman language has the roughest and most difficult sounds met with in any known language on the face of the earth. Now, as it is a well ascertained fact that the tendency in languages is always to throw off the sounds which are difficult in pronunciation, and to render the phonetical mechanism of the language smoother, – those languages which abound in uncouth and almost unpronounceable sounds must be presumed to have best retained the ancient phonetic features.

The clicking sounds are also met with in Hottentot, although there neither as numerous nor of as frequent employment; and this, together with a similarity in certain words in both languages, has led people to believe that these are nearly related to each other. This assumption is dispelled by a closer study, which shows that the grammatical structure of each of these two languages is entirely different. Yet this does not exclude the possibility that – like English and Latin, which are, notwithstanding their now entirely different grammatical arrangement, descended from one mother – Bushman and Hottentot may also have sprung from one source, at a very distant period. The solution of this question will probably not only throw light upon the origin of a good many of those languages now included in the genderless (or, as Professor Max Muller calls it, Turanian) class of languages, but will also elucidate early stages in the formation of language, and lay bare most primitive methods of structural arrangement and modes of thought.

And, if we leave out of question the great difference in the structure of the two languages, there is *prima facie* evidence of the probability of a common origin of the Bushman and Hottentot languages in the outward aspect of the two races, in many of their habits and customs, and, lastly, in their mythologies. Yet how both nations, if derived from a common stock, have become so dissimilar in their language, or how, if not related to each other, they exerted so much influence, can only be discovered by a careful comparison of the two languages, based upon a most intimate knowledge of each. Here a thorough knowledge of the Bushman language is an indispensible necessity for the future student of early South African history, – a history which precedes by many ages the written records, as well as the stone implements, to which the present study of prehistoric times is now mainly directed. 'From the facts brought to light by Comparative Philology and Ethnology, a knowledge can be gained, superior in its certainty to that of the historical record – of the descent and mixture of the different nations inhabiting South Africa, their consanguinity with and influence upon each other, their gradual breaking up into several tribes, or the confluence of different tribes into one powerful nation,' &c (Comp. Gramm., Preface to Part 1.)

All South African philological and historical inquiry would be incomplete without a thorough understanding of Bushman. It is not as if Bushman were more important than either Kafir or Hottentot; but whilst missionary labours have furnished us with plenty of means for a knowledge of both the latter languages, nothing but short and very defective vocabulary has been the fruit of missionary work among the Bushmen. I had long hoped that some Society would take up this work, and whilst benefiting the Bushmen, also fill up this great gap in our philological knowledge of South Africa. But as there appeared to be no real prospect of the work being done in this manner, and as the Bushmen in this Colony seemed to be rapidly dying out, I thought that it was not right to neglect an opportunity which had presented itself for preserving what I could of the language and literature of this curious people. If I had not thought it of the highest importance to do this, I should not have deferred for its sake the work which is the main object of my life, the Comparative Grammar of South African Languages, – a work which I wished to proceed with as quickly as possible, but which has had to be laid aside for a time for the sake of these Bushman studies. I am glad to say that the Government, appreciating the importance of these studies, has given me every necessary facility, and has helped me with the expenses incurred by me in making them. The grants made for this purpose have been asked for, not as a reward for my labours, but merely in repayment of expenses which I am myself unable to afford.

I will now, in a few lines, put together the main points why Bushman studies are of primary importance.

Three kinds of Native language are spoken within the borders of this Colony –

1. Kafir, belonging to the great family of Prefix-pronominal languages, which fill almost the whole of South Africa, and extend to the north-west as far as Sierra Leone;
2. Hottentot, the only known South African member of the very extensive Sex-denoting family which has spread itself over North Africa, Europe and a great part of Asia;
3. Bushman, relationship unknown as yet, presenting outward features of the so-called genderless (or, as Max Muller calls it, Turanian) class, if related to Hottentot, so exceedingly metamorphosed as to be more different from it in its structure than English is from Latin; yet very primitive in its uncouth sounds and in certain structural features, whilst many others are evidently the result of processes of contraction, and of strong grammatical and phonetical changes, the explanation of which leads us back far into the former history of this original language. Mythology and many habits and customs of the Bushmen are akin to those of the Hottentot race, &c.

Whilst in Kafir and the kindred languages of Setshuana and Otyiherero, as well as in Hottentot, a large amount of missionary literature exists, there is next to nothing in Bushman, and if this language, and its very curious literature, is not to vanish almost unknown, the work must be done now. These have been my reasons for undertaking it, difficult as it was. As to the results, one can never predict those of any scientific work; but although they are frequently very different from what one expects when one begins the work, yet in most instances they greatly exceeed in real importance one's most sanguine expectations. This is especially the case in South Africa; and from what I can at present see, I have no reason to doubt but that this will certainly be the case with regard to Bushman studies. The traditionary literature of this nation which has been collected has already proved far richer than our wildest imagination could have anticipated, and will throw an unexpected light upon the primitive stages of the mental life of nations of our own near kindred.

*Cape Monthly Magazine*
Volume VII, September 1873, pp.149-53

# Wilhelm Bleek and the Founding of Bushman Research

Etaine Eberhard

> It appears to me that they (the Bushmen) are the most interesting nation in South Africa – at all events they are the most surprising one.
> *W.H.I. Bleek to Sir George Grey, letter, 9 Oct. 1871*

In this chapter an attempt will be made to show how it is possible to discover something about the people who created the Bleek Collection by an examination of the documents, and to give a brief indication as to what documents, other than the well-known notebooks, exist in the collection.

The Bleek Collection in the University of Cape Town Libraries was donated over a number of years from 1936 to 1947 by Miss Dorothea Bleek, daughter of Dr Wilhelm Heinrich Immanuel Bleek, in whose honour the collection is named. Dorothea was at that time Honorary Reader in Bushman Languages at the University of Cape Town. Important material was also donated by Dr Bleek's granddaughter, Dr K M F Scott, now of Grahamstown, in 1948, during the 1950s, the 1960s and in 1988. A typescript of the *Bushman Dictionary* was donated by Professor J A Engelbrecht in 1961, and Dr O Spohr collected photocopies of letters from various sources, including the Free Public Library, Auckland, New Zealand, the Killie Campbell Africana Library in Durban and the Ernst Haeckel[1] Archive at Jena, Germany.

The largest section of the material donated by Dorothea Bleek consisted of books and pamphlets, dealing mainly with African languages. These were catalogued and put into the appropriate section of the Library's stock. The Bleek Collection described here contains the non-book material which formed part of the above gifts, and can best be described as the residue of the research conducted by three talented, hardworking and dedicated scholars, namely, Wilhelm Bleek, his sister-in-law, Lucy Catherine Lloyd, and his daughter Dorothea Frances Bleek.

The first part of the collection consists of word lists and the notebooks in which the Bushman folklore was recorded, and thousands of slips of paper contained in sixty boxes, which make up the lexicon. The lexicon was started by Bleek himself, added to by Lucy Lloyd, with additions by Dorothea Bleek, who used it as the basis of the *Bushman Dictionary*. The rest of the collection comprises letters written and received, drafts of letters and reports, diaries, genealogical material, manuscript and typescript notes, original drawings, newspaper clippings and photographs. When a collection such as this is sorted and arranged it yields a great deal of information about the people who created the papers, as well as the times in which they lived.

Wilhelm Bleek was the eldest child of Professor Friedrich Bleek and his wife, Augusta Charlotte Marianne Sethe, and was born on 8 March 1827 in Berlin, where his father was professor of theology. Two years later his father was appointed Professor of Theology at Bonn University,[2] and it was there that Bleek attended school and later the University, initially, it seems, to study theology, between 1845 and 1848 (Spohr 1965). Bleek went to Berlin to study Hebrew (*DSAB* 1968,1:82) and it was there that his interest in African languages was first aroused. He spent several terms in Berlin between 1848 and 1851, during which time he also prepared his thesis, *De nominum generibus linguarum Africae Australis*, *Copticae*, *Semiticarum aliarumque sexualium*, for which he received a Ph.D from Bonn University in 1851. There is a bound copy of this thesis in the Rare Books Collection of the University of Cape Town Libraries (Bleek 1851).

Bleek went back to Berlin after graduating and worked with Dr Wilhelm K.H. Peters, a zoologist who had spent about six years, 1842-1848, in East Africa, and who was preparing some vocabularies for publication which Bleek was asked to edit (Spohr 1965:2). Also in Berlin at that time was the Egyptologist, Professor Karl Richard Lepsius, who taught Bleek Egyptian privately (Spohr 1965:1) and encouraged his interest in African languages.

Bleek was keen to go to Africa and was appointed official linguist to the Niger Tshadda expedition in 1854.[3] Soon after reaching Fernando Po, however, he became ill and was obliged to leave the expedition and return to England. In London he met J.W. Colenso, Bishop of Natal, and Sir George Grey, newly appointed Governor at the Cape. Bishop Colenso invited Bleek to accompany him to Natal to help compile a Zulu grammar. The party left England in March 1855 and reached Port Natal in May. Bleek went on his first expedition to a Zulu settlement from 19 June to 17 September 1855, and describes this expedition and others in his diary, which is in the collection (Spohr 1965:15).

In a letter to A. Petermann, publisher of *Petermann's Geographische Mittheilungen*, in April 1856 (Spohr 1965:41), Bleek writes, 'During the first month of this year, the prolonged peace drew the Bushmen from their inaccessible hiding-places in the Kahlamba mountains to steal cattle and directed my attention to them once more.' He does not however, mention having actually seen any Bushmen.

In November 1856, after completing the Zulu grammar for Colenso, Bleek left Natal and came to Cape Town where he was appointed interpreter to the Governor, Sir George Grey, and was also asked to catalogue Sir George Grey's very valuable private library.

Bleek continued his philological research and wrote articles for various publications. His publications can be easily traced, and a list was published in the *South African Mail* in 1875 (28 August, p.3), so these will not be dealt with here.

From 1857 to 1859 Bleek worked on the catalogue of Sir George Grey's library and collected manuscripts and printed texts on a variety of languages, particularly African, from missionaries and travellers from all over the world to add to the Library. In 1859 he went to Europe in a bid to restore his failing health, but continued with his philological research on his return to the Cape. When Sir George Grey was appointed Governor of New Zealand in 1861, Bleek's appointment as interpreter ended. Sir George decided in 1862 to present his library to the South African Public Library, a condition of the gift being that Bleek should be appointed its permanent curator.[4]

Among the letters which have survived in the collection are a few to Bleek's parents and to other members of his family. These are all in German. The letters to Jemima Lloyd, his future wife, are in English and as her replies have also been preserved, one can trace through this correspondence the charm of their growing friendship. Bleek also reveals in these letters many details about himself and his relationship with members of his family, as well as his standpoint on certain moral and religious questions.

In 1861 Bleek went to live at a boarding house run by Mrs Roesch[5] where he first met his future wife. For it was at Mrs Roesch's boarding house that Miss Jemima Lloyd and her sister took rooms early in 1861 while Jemima was waiting for a passage to England. At first their letters are fairly formal but become less so after a few months, and towards the later part of the correspondence in 1862, it is clear that they intended to marry as soon as she returned to Cape Town.

On 4 February 1863, in a letter to Sir George Grey, Bleek wrote that he was married on 22 November 1862

> in St Georges Church, by Mr Glover. We went immediately home into a little house, with a garden in front, in New Street,[6] close to the Bridge leading to 'Grey's Pass'; and we have remained at home all the time since then, except a ten days' stay at Rathfelder's,[7] during the time of greatest heat last month ...

Jemima Bleek wrote to her sister Fanny Lloyd on 30 October 1862, giving the following description of the house:

> we have at last taken a house, near the Library. It is situated in New Street ... it has a garden in front and Table Mountain and Devil's Peak in the background. It has six rooms, besides kitchen and servants rooms. We have also got a good servant, the former first cook aboard the Waldensian[8] an American negro ...

Also in his letter of 4 February 1863 Bleek wrote,

> ... I have, however, been able to translate the whole of the Hottentot Fables [Bleek 1864], and am now expecting an answer from Trubner, to whom I have offered them for publication.' Later, on 29 May 1863, he wrote again to Sir George confirming that '... By last mail I sent Trubner the manuscript of Reynard the Fox in South Africa for publication.

Later that year, on 20 October 1863, he mentions that '... The Bishop of Natal's case is to come here on November 17th ...', and informs Sir George that Colenso had no intention of appearing in person and that Bleek would be delivering, as the Bishop's representative, a letter from him to the Bishop of Cape Town's registrar. Bleek's friendship with the controversial Bishop of Natal dated from 1854 when they first met in London, and Bleek supported him very staunchly throughout his ecclesiastical troubles. As testimony to this friendship there are a hundred and fifty photocopies of Colenso's letters to Bleek, from 1854-1872, in the collection.[9]

Bleek's appointment as curator of the Grey Collection carried a salary of £250 a year,[10] and in order to augment this he wrote leading articles in English for *Het Volksblad* (*DSAB* 1968,1:84) on a fairly regular basis during the 1860s.

Seventy of these, clipped and pasted on to folio sheets, have been preserved in the collection, covering the period 1862 to 1866. Bleek is refreshingly outspoken in his leaders and no one, least of all the Governor, was spared if Bleek felt that the official course of action being taken on any public issue was the wrong one.

On 24 September 1867 he wrote to Sir George expressing his concern about the future of his research, and said that he needed substantial aid to support his work. It seems that the Cape Government was suffering real financial hardship at that time, as Bleek reported that his salary at the Library had been reduced by 16 per cent, and as a result he was very hard pressed financially. He also mentioned that he had received encouraging letters regarding his work from Professor Max Muller, Dr Livingstone and many others, so that he thought it right to persevere. He wanted at all costs to continue with the work he had come to South Africa to do. He felt that he would have to go to Europe to seek the substantial funds he needed.

Bleek did in fact go to London and Germany for some months during 1869. His financial burdens were alleviated to some extent when he was granted a pension of £150 per annum from the Queen's Civil List in 1870 (Spohr 1962: 32).

In Bleek's letter to Sir George of 20 July 1870, he wrote of the opening of the Docks and the success of the diamond fields. The latter was of particular interest as there is a file of newspaper clippings, dating from 25 December 1869 to November 1870, about the discovery of diamonds. He wrote also of the language research he was engaged in at that time, and then remarks, '... But it will be more important to me now to study Bushman, for which I have now an excellent opportunity, as there are 28 Bushmen at the Breakwater ...'

Evidently some Bushmen were released into his custody at this time as there is an interesting schedule of expenditure for 1871-72 in the collection, itemising the costs involved in the feeding and clothing of the Bushmen living on Bleek's property.[11] The Cape Government was funding his research to some extent and Bleek had to submit official reports from time to time concerning his research in progress, copies of which are in the collection. The first of these is dated 1871,[12] and is a photographic report of various native races. On 14 May 1872 he sent to Sir George '... photographs of natives (mostly done according to Prof Huxley's instructions) which I beg you to accept as a birthday present ...'

In the same letter, Bleek remarks,

> This year we were again for a month [February] at Kalkbay ... I employed the time in collecting sea animals and sent a pretty large box with a dozen bottles of them to Jena to my cousin, Professor Ernst Haeckel. Last year I had sent a smaller collection, which he had valued very much, there being many new things and a great number [of] rare ones among the specimens sent. Particularly the Calcispongia of South Africa had been hitherto entirely unknown, and he has done me the honor of [calling?] one of this kind of sponges after me, in a work on Calcispongia in three volumes which he is publishing this year. What we are doing with regard to Bushmen, you will see from my report [Bleek 1873], of which I have enclosed a manuscript copy ... At the Library I am hard at work at an accurate Inventory of the Contents.

Although Bleek's interest in the Bushman language was intense, he had other commitments and needed help in recording the Bushman narrators. His sister-in-law, Lucy Catherine Lloyd, proved to be the perfect collaborator. Bleek taught Lucy Lloyd how to record the Bushman language (Dr K.M.F. Scott, personal communication), and she proved to be a very able pupil.

On 1 April (1871?) Bleek reported to Sir George,

> Our Bushman studies are well advanced, although during the last six weeks I have hardly done anything myself in this respect. We have now two Bushmen with us, an old one and a young one ... and they constantly are chattering in their monkey like speech. One of my wife's sisters, of whom two are staying with us, is already further advanced in the practical knowledge of this language than myself, and as she has a far quicker ear, I shall have to trust to her observation in many ways. She is of course also able to devote more time to this study than I can.

In the same letter Bleek informed Sir George of various papers which he had written on the Australian languages which had been communicated to the British Association,

> ... and one on the 'Concord and Classification of Names and the Origin of Pronouns, etc.' was read before the Ethnological Society ... Professor Huxley expressed also the wish to have my paper on the connection of the Papuan and Polynesian languages with those of Africa.

This letter gives us some idea of the scope and volume of work being done by Bleek at that time.

A few months later, on 9 October 1871, Bleek wrote the following to Sir George:

> Our Bushmen studies are going steadily on. It appears to me that they are the most interesting nation in South Africa – at all events they are the most surprising one. Strictly monoganistic, sidereal worshippers who have prayers to moon, sun and stars – know numerous fables, and curious legends – all of a very original character. Yet the sounds of their language, are the most primitive of any known language, and they have no names for any numerals beyond three. In fact as their third numeral is probably of Hottentot origin, it seems as if originally they had only known two numerals. Yet they count pretty well on their fingers, and can tell me the number of children of a person, even when that number exceeds ten ... You would be exceedingly interested, if you could be with us, and see the gradual progress of our studies, and hear their wonderful stories.

Sir George was informed on 15 November 1872 that they were

> still studying with main and might Bushman; but in fear of losing our Bushmen soon, as they are very homesick ... Another two years would make us complete scholars. We have now, I suppose, nearly four thousand columns [of] texts in this language.

Lack of funds seemed always to be a problem for Bleek where his Bushman researches were concerned, and on 7 May 1874 he wrote To Sir George that he was trying to

> impress upon the Government here their duty of doing something for the preservation of the still existing monuments of the various native minds found in South Africa, before they have quite lost their originality. This is in connection with a new report on our Bushman studies [Bleek 1875] in which I am giving also a short account of the folklore of this nation as far as it has yet been collected. You can fancy that the rare and difficult opportunity of having it within my reach to discover not only a language almost wholly unknown, but still more to pursue

> portions of a rich and highly important folklore belonging to so primitive and in point of civilization so low a race, dared not to be neglected by me; and this particularly as there seemed to be otherwise no hope of it being done at all, before the race had become extinct. This made me set aside for the past few years the Comparative Grammar ... On March 18th my last Bushman left me, and on April 25th my collaborator in the Bushman studies (who had more time to give to Reynard [and] had consequently the better practical knowledge of the language) went on a short visit to England.

In the same letter he gives some information about his family and himself:

> I have now four children, all girls[13] ... the youngest fourteen months old. At this moment we are rather anxious about the youngest, who is ill with a bad cold and cough. This is painful to us, as she is to us the most charming child.[14] For my children and for the completion of many important works begun, I wish much to live on; but I feel every year more that this may not entirely depend upon one's wish; and that the end may be nearer at hand than one has any idea of.

When the Bleeks were first married they lived at 25 New Street, near Grey's Pass in Cape Town, and in the Cape Almanac for 1865 and 1866, their address is given as 28 Grave Street, Cape Town. From 1867 to 1876, their address is listed only as 'Mowbray'. It would appear from the letters, however, that the family moved to Charlton House only in February 1875. Prior to this move they had lived, from 1869, at The Hill in Mowbray, which was situated near Charlton House (Scott, personal communication).

On 16 January 1875, Bleek wrote to Sir George,

> I seem now a settled resident here, especially as I have been obliged to buy a house, very much against my wish. My landlord had given me notice, and I could not get a house to hire for love or money. In our own house (Charlton House) we shall be between Sir Thomas Maclear's 'Grey Villa' and Mr Rutherfoord's.

Jemima Bleek corroborates this move in her letter to Sir George of 6 September 1875, in which she says that they received '... notice from our landlord to leave the house where we had been ever since November 1869 ...'

In his letter of 16 January 1875 Bleek also states:

> In my Bushman researches I have involved myself into greater expenses than our Responsible Government is willing to refund me and I shall have to appeal to those who are interested in this matter in England to assist me in such expenses as I am myself unable to bear ... I shall appeal to them for means to enable me to subvent Missionaries and others for the purposes of collecting the Folklore of the Natives, before they are things of the past, forgotten in the increasing rush of civilisation. I laid a plan for this purpose before our Ministry, but Molteno[15] (who is now Autocrat here) did not see its usefulness, and refused to allow anything for this purpose. With a few months interval I have had Bushmen staying in my house for four years and a half – at one time as many as seven, as I could not get one important member of a family without the others. Now I have only one.

On a sad note, in his letter of 21 April 1875 to Sir George, he reiterates the lack of funds for his projects and continues,

> I am making an earnest struggle as far as my very limited strength allows me, to get as much as is possible saved of the folklore of the Natives ... I cannot get our Government to do more than help me with the expenses of my Bushman researches.

He again mentions his need for funds to reward missionaries and others

> for collecting Native folklore ... before the fearful strides of civilisation due to our diamonds and gold, are doing away with all Native originality ... I am now mainly occupied with working at a continuation of my Comparative Grammar. Yet the Bushman is not neglected, although for the present the task of collecting its folklore is left to my sister-in-law, Miss L.C. Lloyd. At present we have only one Bushman, but expect another, our old Bushman narrator, the best one we have had.

Bleek died on 17 August 1875 at the age of 48. His work was praised in all the obituaries preserved in the collection. In the *South African Mail* of 25 August 1875, the following tribute appeared:

> ... a work and life which were great, noble and self-sacrificing to an extent little known. He had no ostentation and pride in his nature ... As a comparative philologist he stood in the foremost rank, and as an investigator and authority on the South African languages, he was without peer.

This modest man left a very rich scholarly heritage when he died. His unfinished work with the Bushmen was continued by his sister-in-law, Lucy Lloyd, with as much dedication and scholarship as her tutor.

---

Lucy Catherine Lloyd was born in Norbury, Staffordshire, England, on 7 November 1834, the second daughter of William Henry Cynric Lloyd and his first wife, Lucy Anne Jeffreys. When his wife died, leaving four young daughters, her sister Caroline and her husband, Admiral Sir John Dundas, took over the upbringing and education of the four young sisters, Frances, Lucy, Jemima and Julia. They were privately educated while they lived in England (Scott, personal communication). In 1849 they accompanied their father and stepmother to Durban, when he was appointed Colonial Chaplain for Natal. The collection does not reveal anything of her youth or life in Natal, but her presence in Cape Town, staying with the Bleeks, is mentioned quite soon after her sister's marriage. It is not clear, however, whether she stayed with them on a permanent basis, or simply for lengthy visits during the 1860s. It is fair to assume, however, that once work on the Bushman language commenced Lucy Lloyd stayed permanently with the Bleeks.

By far the largest number of notebooks in the collection represent the work of Lucy Lloyd. She had proved to be an able pupil and Bleek respected her work with the Bushmen narrators. After his death she continued this work, but this was not all she did.

In a letter to Sir George Grey on 8 September 1875, Jemima Bleek wrote,

> On 28th [August] ... a joint meeting of Trustees [of the Grey Collection] and the Public Library Committee took place, as a result of which we had a visit in the afternoon of that day from Dr Dale, as chairman of the S.A.P.L. Committee, to ask my sister Lucy on behalf of that body to undertake to complete the Detailed Inventory of the contents of the Grey Library, etc, at half salary; giving meanwhile the acting Custodian-

> ship of the Collection to Mr Maskew. Lucy saw many difficulties in the way of attempting to work at all at the Grey Library under such an arrangement, and spoke of these more or less frankly to Dr Dale; besides of course telling him that she had neither the necessary experience or education to enable her to deal with many of the books and manuscripts in the Grey Collection. It appeared that one great reason which had prompted this request to my sister was the knowledge of how long she had helped Dr Bleek in different ways, & would therefore be better able than another to decipher his handwriting etc, & make a fair copy of some portions that he had only as yet prepared in the rough. The Committee appeared to have already thought of my sister's possible difficulty with regard to some books (Greek, Latin etc) & had proposed to meet it by appointing three of their number, Dr Dale, Mr Cameron & Mr Fairbridge, to act as a subcommittee of reference, to give her help where she required it.

Lucy Lloyd's initial reluctance to accept the position seems then to have been based on the fact that she did not think herself to be sufficiently experienced or educated to undertake it. Another reason for her reluctance was based on the fact that Dr Bleek had had a '… deep distrust … of Dr Dale personally, not only since the latter has been one of the S.A.P.L. Committee, but for years previously …'.[16] A further reason was given as

> the personal character of Mr Maskew, whose great ignorance, i.e., both personal absence of education, & also ignorance as to proper methods etc, for conducting even such an institution as the S A Public Library, render him utterly unfit even for the temporary charge of the Grey Collection. Added to this, there is a kind of easy-going carelessness, a want of strict regard for truth, and a want also of moral courage, which renders him not the kind of man with which any person, more especially a comparatively unprotected lady, would care to share a divided responsibility of the kind in question.'[17]

Significantly the fact that she had been offered only half of Dr Bleek's salary was not mentioned as a reason for her reluctance to accept the appointment. Her ability must have been highly regarded for an official approach of this sort to have been made to her at all.

Her reluctance was obviously overcome and she began working at the

Library in October 1875. The appointment was continued until the end of 1880. During this time she worked on various projects in the Grey Collection and edited material collected by Bleek (*DSAB* 1968,4:315), but throughout this period she continued her own work with the Bushmen, later extending her research to include the !Kung dialect.

On 3 August 1876 Lloyd wrote to Professor Ernst Haeckel:

> ... you can imagine our anxiety to see the Grey Library in scholarly, & safe keeping, again, as well as, that one so highly recommended by Prof Max Muller[18] as is J. Jolly should come out to continue (as far as this is now possible) dear Wilhelm's philological work. And to speak of a comparatively very minor matter, I shall be most thankful to find myself safely able to leave off my copying-work at the Grey Library, (undertaken chiefly as a kind of small safeguard, while there is no fitting curator) & to have my whole time free for the Bushman work at home, which my daily absence hinders.

In the event, Jolly did not in fact come to take over the work, and it was not until 1880 that the Library Committee decided to appoint a professionally qualified philologist as custodian. Dr Theophilus Hahn was selected and took up this post in December of that year. Lucy Lloyd appealed to the Trustees of the Grey Collection against her dismissal. The Trustees supported her and the whole matter eventually reached the Supreme Court for judgment. Apparently the case could not be decided there, and when Hahn resigned in 1883 no further appointment was made to the post of custodian (*DSAB*, 4:315). Lucy Lloyd played an active part in the South African Folklore Society, and for a time acted as secretary. She took a prominent part in the establishment of the *Folk-lore Journal* in 1879. This journal, although sadly short-lived, is important as it was the first in South Africa devoted to ethnography (*DSAB* 1968, 4:315; *SESA* 1973, 2:58).

From her papers it is not easy to trace Lucy Lloyd's activities, and one is left with only tantalising glimpses. She left Cape Town for Europe in the mid-1880s (it has not been possible to establish a more accurate date), and lived for many years at various places in England, North Wales, Germany and Switzerland, before returning to the Cape between 1905 and 1907.

When G W Stow, the geologist and ethnologist, died in 1882, Lucy Lloyd bought his drawings of rock art and his unpublished manuscript of *Native Races of South Africa* from his widow, and published it, with the assistance of

G.M.Theal, in London in 1905. Some of the original drawings as well as receipts for her payments to Mrs Stow, have survived in the collection.

Lloyd's report, *A Short Account of Further Bushman Material Collected* was published in London in 1889; and *Specimens of Bushman Folklore* in 1911, also in London. In 1912 the University of the Cape of Good Hope[19] conferred an honorary doctorate of literature on her. She was the first woman in South Africa to be honoured in this way. She died at Charlton House, Mowbray, Cape, on 31 August 1914 and was buried in Wynberg.

Among the wealth of information left by Lucy Lloyd, much still unpublished, are also notes on Bushman medicines and the words and music of Bushman songs which she had recorded.

---

Dorothea Frances Bleek was born on 26 March 1873, and was thus barely two and a half years old when her father died. She was at that time the youngest of his four surviving daughters, but a younger sister was born four months after her father's death.

In 1883 Jemima Bleek took her five daughters to Germany for their education. They attended schools in both Germany and Switzerland, and Dorothea later trained as a teacher in Berlin where she also took a course in African languages at the University of Berlin (*DSAB* 1968, 1:80) and later attended the School of Oriental Languages in London (Scott, personal communication).

Dorothea returned to South Africa in 1904 with her mother and two of her sisters. On 26 October 1909 Jemima Bleek died while staying with her daughter Helma (Wilhelmine) and son-in-law Henry Hepburn Bright, at their farm 'Greystones' at the foot of Sir Lowry's Pass. Jemima was very probably buried in the cemetery at Somerset West (Scott, personal communication).

Dorothea Bleek took a teaching post at the Rocklands Girls High School in Cradock in 1904, and taught there until 1907 (*DSAB* 1968,1:80). She had been exposed to the Bushman language as a child and would have heard it spoken by her father and aunt, as well as by the Bushmen who were staying with them. Her interest obviously endured and when one of her colleagues in Cradock, Helen Tongue, went on expeditions to copy the rock art in the area, Dorothea accompanied her. They went to the Eastern Cape, Orange Free State and Lesotho. In 1908 Dorothea accompanied Helen Tongue to England where the latter's paintings were exhibited at the Anthropological Institute in

London; some of these paintings were published in 1909, with notes on the Bushmen by Dorothea Bleek and her sister Edith (Tongue 1909).

When Dorothea returned to Cape Town from London in 1908, having given up her teaching post in Cradock, she devoted all her time to studying Bushman life and languages. She assisted her aunt in the preparation of *Specimens of Bushman Folklore* for publication, and also edited and published much of the research of her father and aunt, for example, *The Mantis and his Friends* (1924), and a series of articles which appeared in *Bantu Studies* during the 1930s.

Her continued interest in rock art is reflected in the collection in various ways. For instance, in 1929 she arranged for the Stow drawings, purchased by her aunt, to be published as *Rock Paintings in South Africa*, after carefully checking many of Stow's original sites in the Eastern Cape and the Orange Free State herself (Stow & Bleek 1930). In 1932 Dorothea employed the sisters, Mollie and Joyce van der Riet, to copy rock paintings in the Grahamstown, Humansdorp, Oudtshoorn, George and Knysna areas. Their letters to her describe where they found the paintings and how they copied them. Eventually a hundred and fifty sheets of watercolours were sent to London, and there is detailed correspondence with the publishers Methuen regarding their publication in *More Rock Paintings in South Africa*. Those watercolours not used in the book were sent back to South Africa on board the *City of Simla* in 1941. Unfortunately the ship and all its cargo was lost as a result of enemy action. Undaunted, Dorothea used the insurance money (£222.12.6) to have the drawings recopied. These paintings, by James Eddie and others, are in the collection.

There are 32 notebooks, kept between 1910 and 1930, which have been preserved in the collection and serve as a record of Dorothea's extensive travels in southern Africa in search of information about other Bushman dialects. She made field trips to the Kalahari, Botswana, Angola and Tanzania, and recorded vocabularies, genealogies, notes on rock art and lists of the photographs she took. In the diary she kept in 1913 on a trip to Botswana, she describes the weather, the countryside, the people they met and what they did, but does not reveal any of her own feelings or thoughts. All her other notebooks are devoted entirely to the languages and the stories she recorded. Many of the photographs taken on these travels have been preserved in the collection.

From her notes it is clear that Dorothea also recorded Bushman speech on wax phonograph cylinders, about which she reports:

> The value of the phonograph for reproducing songs and showing the intonation is very great, but for giving the language it is a failure, because of its inability to record the majority of the clicks and its bad reproduction of gutturals.[20]

From 1923 to 1948 Dorothea Bleek was Honorary Reader in Bushman Languages at the University of Cape Town and she also helped the staff of the South African Museum with their researches into the life and language of the Bushmen.

The publication of the *Bushman Dictionary* in 1956, eight years after Dorothea's death, was her major achievement (Bleek 1956) and has been described as '... the culminating point of a "family" research which extended over almost an entire century' (Engelbrecht n.d.). She was encouraged by the German philologist, Professor Diedrich Westermann in 1933 when he wrote to her,

> We have read your researches into the Bushman dictionary with interest, it seems that you are on the right track and that you should continue on this way, and it seems to me better that you should give the translation in English and not German. The Germans know English but it doesn't work the other way round.[21]

There is correspondence from 1944 onwards reflecting the battle she had to obtain funding for the publication of the *Bushman Dictionary*, finally culminating in an agreement signed by Dorothea Bleek and the American Oriental Society in December 1947, six months before her death.[22]

There are no personal documents amongst Dorothea's papers. Like her aunt, Lucy Lloyd, she seems to have been a very private person. In a letter to her, L.F.Maingard, Professor of French at the University of the Witwatersrand, who had become interested in Bushman languages and had helped Dorothea with the Dictionary, showed his high regard for her work: '... I have all along considered it an honour to be allowed to see the Dictionary in the process of being made and a great privilege to be asked to help ...'[23] In the Maingard Papers at the University of South Africa one finds a statement in support of a proposal to confer an honorary doctorate on Dorothea Bleek by the University of the Witwatersrand in 1936. She is reputed to have declined the honour, however, maintaining that there could be only one Dr Bleek.[24]

This hardworking, modest scholar died on 27 June 1948, in Plumstead, Cape.

The University of Cape Town Libraries are proud to be the repository of this unique and priceless collection.

## *ACKNOWLEDGEMENTS*

We wish to thank the staff of the Manuscripts and Archives Department and the African Studies Library, University of Cape Town for their courtesy and help at all times, and Dr K.M.F. Scott, Wilhelm Bleek's granddaughter, whose help was invaluable.

## *NOTES*

1. Professor Ernst Heinrich Haeckel, 1834-1919, cousin of W.H.I. Bleek and friend of T.H. Huxley and Charles Darwin. Professor of Zoology at Jena University, 1862-1909.
2. W.H.I. Bleek to W.H. Cynric Lloyd, Colonial Chaplain, Durban, Natal, 18 Aug. 1862. (BC 151 C6.2)
3. Bleek to Cynric Lloyd, 18 Aug. 1862. The Niger Tshadda Expedition, 1854, was led by W.D. Baikie.
4. Bleek to Cynric Lloyd, 18 Aug. 1862.
5. The exact location of the boarding house has not been established, but it was probably in the Gardens, Cape Town.
6. New Street later became Queen Victoria Street (*SESA* 1973, 9:203).
7. Rathfelder's Inn, famous for its hospitality, was the halfway house between Cape Town and Simon's Town (*SESA* 1973, 9:247).
8. The *SS Waldensian*, an iron screw steamer of 369 tons, was a coaster plying between Cape Town and Durban, carrying mail and passengers. It was wrecked on the night of 13 October 1862 when it went aground on Bulldog Reef at Struis Point, near Cape Agulhas. There were 121 passengers and crew aboard, all of whom were saved, although they lost most of their luggage. Lucy Lloyd was one of the passengers on this voyage and was bringing wedding gifts to Cape Town for her sister Jemima. She managed to save two blue glass vases, which she carried ashore on her lap in the lifeboat. Later she salvaged a set of the works of Sir Walter Scott (also a wedding gift) which had floated ashore, protected by its waterproof packaging. These vases and books are still in the possession of Dr K.M.F. Scott (Turner 1988, *Cape Argus* 21 Oct. 1862; Scott, personal communication).
9. Original letters are in the Killie Campbell Library, University of Natal, Durban.
10. Bleek to Cynric Lloyd, 18 Aug. 1862.
11. Schedule of expenditure up to December 1871 and estimates for 1872. MS (BC 151)

12. Dr Bleek's report, 1871, a MS copy of which is in the collection, was submitted at the request of Thomas Henry Huxley.
13. Bleek and his wife had seven children: Edith, b. 8 Aug. 1863; Ernst Friedrich, 15 July 1868-18 February 1869; Mabel (May), b. 12 Dec. 1869, m. Albert Jaeger, 1 daughter, 1 son; Margaret (Margie) b. 28 June 1871, d. Italy, and her twin Hermine 28 June 1871-23 Aug. 1871; Dorothea (Doris) 26 March 1873-27 June 1948; Wilhelmine (Helma) b. 16 December 1875 (four months after the death of her father), m. Henry Hepburn Bright, 3 daughters, the eldest died in infancy (Scott, personal communication).
14. Dorothea Frances Bleek, the fourth surviving child.
15. Molteno, Sir John Charles, 1814-1886, first Prime Minister of the Cape Colony under responsible government, 1 Dec. 1871-6 Jan. 1878 (*SESA* 1973, 7:496-97).
16. Jemima Bleek to Sir George Grey, 8 Sept. 1875.
17. Ibid.
18. Friedrich Max Muller, 1823-1900, Professor of Comparative Philology, Oxford University.
19. The University of the Cape of Good Hope later became the University of South Africa.
20. Appendix I: List of contents of gramophone records. Dorothea Bleek's notes on Bushman songs. TS p.74.(BC 151)
21. Professor D. Westermann to Dorothea Bleek, 14 Aug. 1933, from Stellenbosch. Signed TS. Translated from the German by A. van den Heever. (BC 151)
22. R.F.M. Immelman to Professor H.M. Robertson, 2 Feb. 1956, requesting him to enquire about the proposed publication of the *Bushman Dictionary*, which had been accepted in 1947 by the American Oriental Society, together with a deposit of $4 007,50 paid by Dorothea Bleek, assisted by the South African National Council for Social Research and by the University of Cape Town (UCT Library records).
23. L.F. Maingard, Professor of French at the University of the Witwatersrand, to Dorothea Bleek, 26 Aug. 1944. (BC 151)
24. Maingard, motivation proposing Dorothea Bleek for an honorary doctorate (Maingard Papers, Unisa).

*Dr Lucy Lloyd, photographed on receiving her honorary doctorate at the University of Cape Town in 1913.*
*Reproduced by courtesy of Dr KMF Scott.*

# Lucy Catherine Lloyd 1834-1914

Sigrid Schmidt

Wilhelm and Dorothea Bleek acquired a reputation during their lifetimes. But 'the part she (his sister-in-law and helpmate, Miss L C Lloyd) played has perhaps never received adequate recognition' (Engelbrecht 1956:2). For the general public she remained but his assistant, but the conjunction of her name with his in the theme of this book gives her her rightful place in a study of their work.

In aiming briefly to outline the life and work of this remarkable woman I found that the sources for a biography are scarce. I owe a certain amount of information to W D Maxwell-Mahon's article on Lucy Lloyd in the Dictionary of South African Biography but, based as it was on family traditions, it lacked accurate information as to her scientific work. I have verified as much as I could and filled in gaps where possible.

On 'December 20th 1834, Lucy Catherine, daughter of William Henry Cynric and Lucy Anne Lloyd' was baptised by her father, the rector of St Peter's Church, Norbury, Staffordshire. He also added her date of birth, 'born Nov 7 1834', an unusual extra (Edwards, personal communication). When Lucy Lloyd was eight years old her mother died. Her father soon married again, and in addition to the four daughters of the first marriage four sons and nine daughters from the second marriage were born. In 1849, when she was fourteen years old, the family – her parents, the six sisters and a brother – emigrated to Natal, where her father played a prominent role as first colonial chaplain and later as archdeacon of Durban. As he was involved in the Colenso controversy he was temporarily removed by Colenso from his post as rector of St Paul's (1856) (Sellers 1977:530).

These were the main events which must have had special impact on her youth. There is no direct evidence for her training. From family records she appears to have been privately educated in England and South Africa. She became a schoolteacher but could not work in this profession because of chronic ill-health (Maxwell-Mahon 1981). The education of the Lloyd

*The rectory of St Peter's, Norbury, Staffordshire, where Lucy lived until she was about fourteen.*

daughters must have been at a level far above the average of girls of that time. Her sister Jemima's letter to Sir George Grey about Bleek's death (Spohr 1962:39-42) shows a remarkable mastery of the written word, and the fact that Lucy Lloyd 'having learnt Italian', translated for Bleek the letters of an Italian scientist (draft of letter WHI Bleek 18 June 1871; Spohr 1962:47; letter F Finzi, 15 Oct. 1869; Spohr 1962:53) is further evidence of a broad education. As Italian is the language of musical notation, one might guess that Lucy Lloyd had some musical training and consequently a fine ear which provided her with the fundamentals for her future scientific work.

Bleek married Jemima Lloyd, Lucy's younger sister, in 1862, after seven years of engagement (Spohr 1962:22). According to Louw (1976:83) 'they had met in Cape Town in 1861', and Lucy Lloyd became a member of the household at Mowbray. This move was probably caused by the prevailing financial strain on both sides; it offered Lucy Lloyd a home and her sister an aid with the upbringing of her children; from the Bleeks' marriage seven children were born.

The decisive point in Lloyd's life was when the first Bushman was taken into the Mowbray home in August 1870 and Bleek started with his investigations. She must soon have joined in this work. In the five years until Bleek's death – actually until the printing of the Second Report, in May 1875 – Bleek himself had written down only somewhat 'more than one third' of the texts (Bleek 1875:5). That means that Lucy Lloyd was responsible for two-thirds of the text recordings up to that date. As early as 12 April 1871 Bleek mentioned to Sir George Grey that 'Miss Lloyd' spent more time on the Bushman studies than he himself could do (Spohr 1962:50), and similarly in the letter of 21 April 73 that Bushman folklore was mainly in her hands (Spohr 1962:51).

Bleek concentrated on the *Dictionary*. He was handicapped because he had to work in the Library to earn their livelihood while suffering from recurring illness. In addition to the text recordings, Lucy Lloyd helped him with the *Dictionary* (Spohr 1962:41), and on the construction of genealogies (Bleek 1875:113-14) and went with the Bushmen to the Museum to learn the Bushman names of animals and to elicit further information on them. Bleek, therefore, did not consider her his assistant but spoke of 'their joint Bushman studies' (Spohr 1962:14).

When Bleek died in August 1875 the two sisters decided to carry on the work: 'I,' Jemima wrote, 'to keep up the household & manage the practical matters connected with having Bushmen on the place, & Lucy to continue [their studies] & work well out' (Spohr 1962:41). They immediately addressed Sir George and the Grey Library asking whether Lucy Lloyd might possibly succeed Bleek in the curatorship (Letter to Grey, 8 Sept. 1875, Spohr 1962:46). The library committee appointed her his successor on half-pay of £125 per annum (Maxwell-Mahon 1981). In 1880, however, the committee gave her notice and favoured Dr Theophilus Hahn because he had a university training as an ethnologist. Hahn, a person of rather controversial character (Trumpelmann 1976; Schmidt 1982b) had supposedly instigated this dismissal. The dispute was taken to the Supreme Court for judgment but could not be decided there (Maxwell-Mahon 1981).

At the time of Bleek's death Dia!kwain was staying in Mowbray. He had returned of his own free will after his sentence had terminated and had been living in Mowbray for fourteen months. He longed to go home but was persuaded to remain until 7 March 1876; during this period Lucy Lloyd was able to take down numerous additional texts from him, especially about customs and beliefs (Lloyd 1889, all entries marked V).

Later, from 10 January 1878 to December 1879, that is for nearly two years, //Kabbo's son-in-law, /Han≠kass'o, joined them. He turned out to be an excellent narrator (cf. E. & D. Bleek 1909:42) and informant, dictated a substantial number of new stories and information and added considerable information to clarify and supplement the accounts given by the former Bushmen. Lucy Lloyd published a summary of this work as the 'Third Report' in 1889.

So it was that Lucy Lloyd gained first-rate texts and recorded them in a first-rate way. Furthermore she tried to continue Bleek's work collecting any possible items on spiritual and material Bushman culture. She contacted a musician, Charles Weisbecker, and had him write down the music of many of /Han≠kass'o's songs. These were later investigated and published by Kirby (1936), and they offer a unique insight into nineteenth-century Bushman music. She induced the Bushmen to draw, had them photographed and painted, and encouraged them to produce implements and to describe precisely the manner of their production (Bleek and Lloyd 1911).

Because of the reputation gained by Lucy Lloyd's work on the /Xam folklore, her further efforts and achievements are usually overlooked. In 1879 a Bushman family was sent to her from Kimberley. It turned out to be a Korana family whose language was totally different from that of the /Xam. Now Lucy Lloyd began to learn the !Kora speech and to take down texts in that language. Unfortunately Piet Links was no great narrator, but nevertheless these texts belong to the very few existing ones in this language and since it has practically died out by now Lloyd's !Kora texts, edited by Maingard in 1962, are especially important.

Bleek had already tried to learn something about the languages of the Northern Bushmen. For several months in 1877 a boy from the neighbourhood of Lake Ngami stayed with Lucy Lloyd, and in May 1878 a young woman visited from the same place (Lloyd 1889:5). In September 1879 Palgrave brought with him from his political missions in South West Africa two !Kung boys from the territory on the further side of Damaraland. Six months later two decidedly younger !Kung youths came. All four boys spent several years with Lloyd, it was not until March 1884 that she parted from the last of them (Bleek & Lloyd 1911:xii-xiii). If one looks at their photograph (Bleek & Lloyd 1911:276) one can guess what a demanding job it must have been for the two women to keep these four youngsters, three of them still quite childlike, in their home – boys from the undisturbed Bushman world of northern South West Africa. Dorothea and Edith Bleek describe some of the problems the boys had, and some that the women had with the boys (1909:42-43). Lucy Lloyd took great pains to master their speech, which, according to Köhler (1975:321) is West-!Kung. She was the first person ever to study a Northern Bushman language and the first to convey it into writing. With infinite patience she tried to learn from the boys about the life and lore of their people and to bring them to the point of dictating their texts. It was extremely difficult because these youngsters knew all too little about the spiritual world of their elders and as narrating is usually an occupation of elderly people they were untrained narrators. In spite of various restrictions, however, these !Kung texts of Lucy Lloyd are a unique testimony and of unique value beyond merely being pioneer work.

'Besides the informants already mentioned, material has been taken down from a good many other Native sources; including several Natives who were with us for short periods only,' Lucy Lloyd stated in her Third Report (1889:5; see also E. & D. Bleek 1909:43-44). One was 'an old Bushman woman ... taken, at Salt river ... She was with us, for a little while in 1884; but could not make herself happy at Mowbray. She longed to return to her own country, so that she might be buried with her forefathers' (Bleak and Lloyd 1911:xi). For Lucy Lloyd, who later wrote about it in these few scanty words, these must, however, have been weeks which cost endless patience and persuasion – and resulted in nothing but buried hopes.

In my opinion, what the Bleek family and later the two women alone did deserves far more attention from the human point of view. The Bushmen of that time were by no means 'the harmless people'. The men staying with them were not sentenced 'for eating part of a stolen ox, I believe', as Edith or Dorothea Bleek declared (1909:39). Right on the next page they described Dia!kwain as 'their father's pet murderer' who had killed a white farmer in self-defence (see Deacon 1986). And //Kabbo, whom the sisters, at least Dorothea, only knew from hearsay and depicted as 'the gentle old soul [that] appeared lost in a dream-life of his own' (1909:39) was a member of a notorious robber gang (A. Traill, personal communication). On the other hand, many whites hardly regarded the Bushmen as humans, or at least only as mentally comparable with European children of five or six years. When the Bleek family succeeded in persuading these men to stay with them for years, even of their own free will, and to open their hearts to share their own traditions, they must have expended an enormous amount of love, open-heartedness and understanding, as well as showing a readiness to accept these men as full personalities in their own right.

Lucy Lloyd's merits are not restricted to the achievements of /Xam, !Kora and !Kung investigations. She took a prominent part in the South African Folklore Society, served as its secretary and was connected with the publication of the two volumes of its journal, the *Folk-lore Journal*. After Stow's death in 1882, she bought his manuscripts and rock painting copies from his widow, and with the help of Theal she ensured that *The Native Races of South Africa* was published (Maxwell-Mahon 1981).

Owing to their precarious financial situation Jemima Bleek and her five daughters left the Cape in order to live in Berlin, Germany, the home town of WHI Bleek. In 1887 (University of the Cape of Good Hope 1912:110; Burne: 1915) Lucy Lloyd went to Europe, too, living for a while in Rhyl, North Wales (with relatives of her fathers?), but mostly with Jemima in Berlin. During these years she had two further achievements which were significant for posterity. The first was the editing of the *Specimens*. After having prepared the manuscript there was a long and discouraging search for a publisher. 'When at last a publisher was found, Miss Lloyd unfortunately fell ill and it was only by dint of patient exertion, resumed often after long intervals of weakness, that her great work *Specimens of Bushman Folklore* was brought to completion and published...' (University of the Cape of Good Hope 1912). *Specimens* appeared in 1911 in London. It became the fundamental work of Khoisan research and of great value for African studies in general.

Her second great accomplishment was to introduce her niece Dorothea, who at the time of her father's death was only two years old, to Bushman research and to make her familiar with the /Xam language and her methods of study so that later on Dorothea was able to continue the work on the Dictionary and with editing the texts.

In 1912 Lucy Lloyd returned to South Africa. By that time the value of her work had been recognised. It was acknowledged by the conferment of an Honorary Doctorate by the University of the Cape of Good Hope on 22 February 1913. She had 'won the unstinted praise of all students of South African folklore and philology' (University of the Cape of Good Hope 1912). In South Africa she was the first woman to receive such a distinction.

On 31 August 1914, at the age of seventy-nine, she died at Mowbray, the place where her greatest labours in Bushman research were carried out.

'To the quiet dignity of an old-fashioned English gentlewoman she added the painstaking accuracy of the truly scientific student', C.S. Burne stated in his obituary (1915:99-100). Posterity owes to her the preservation of an important cultural inheritance. Even more than her contemporaries we, the later generations, are aware of her achievements in her pioneer work and appreciate her accomplishments as a scientist, a woman, a human being, especially when these are seen against the background of her time.

## *ACKNOWLEDGEMENTS*

I gratefully acknowledge the support in my investigations of the late Professor R.F. Lawrence, Grahamstown, who had personal relations with the Bleek family; of Mrs E. Edwards, Norbury, Stafford, who made copies for me from the old records of St Peter's and furnished me with photographs of the church and rectory; and of the library staffs of the University of Cape Town and Unisa for information and copies.

The photograph of Lucy Lloyd was given to Janette Deacon by Lucy's grand-niece – and WHI Bleek's granddaughter – Dr Marjorie Scott (née Bright) in Grahamstown, to whom grateful thanks are due.

# PART II

# RESEARCH IN THE 1990s

# Attempting to Contextualise /Xam Oral Tradition

Mathias Guenther

> The text, of course, is extremely important, but without the context it remains lifeless. The stories live in native life and not on paper, and when a scholar jots them down without being able to evoke the atmosphere in which they flourish he has given us but a mutilated bit of reality ... Folktales must be lifted from their flat existence on paper, and placed in the three-dimensional reality of full life.
>
> Malinowski 1926

> It is a world outside the song – performance, style, social usage, individual personality of the performer, community world view and local history, as well as the long tradition shaping the conventions – which create the meaning of a song.
>
> Caraveli 1982

One of the most popular analytical approaches to the study of folklore over the past two decades has been the contextual approach, in which the focus is less on the text of a narrative than on the performance event and its placement within its wider cultural, social and historical setting. This approach has been used creatively and fruitfully in contemporary folklore studies by students who have taken the paradigm to the field with them and have used it in the course of their ethnographic studies and their subsequent analyses (for instance, Caraveli 1982; see Limon and Young 1986 for a review of other such studies). What I will attempt in this paper is to identify certain contextual elements of the /Xam collection and suggest how they might affect one's interpretation of the texts. Such an enterprise might strike some as an exercise in futility, in view of the disappearance over a century ago of the performers and the audience, and the fact that what one works on are not living performances but a fossil oral record, not of native live performances but artificial, stilted dictation sessions. Yet, as I hope to show, a number of contextual elements can be identified, and to a degree their effects on the texts that were collected by Bleek and Lloyd can be ascertained. Moreover, by knowing what these contextual elements are and how they intrude on and distort the text that was presented at these clinical recording sessions, it becomes possible partially to reconstruct the texts, as well as performance events, as they might have been amongst the /Xam.

## *THE CONTEXTUAL APPROACH IN FOLKLORISTICS*

Over the past two decades the focus of a number of American folkorists[1] has shifted away from the texts of oral traditions and other genres of 'artful uses of folklore' to the performance of such texts. What these students of folklore are preoccupied with are 'performance events' that encompass the interaction between narrator and audience, both parties engaged in a communicative event that is situated within a yet wider social and cultural milieu which will also leave its social and symbolic imprint on the performance.

Dan Ben-Amos, one of the architects and leading proponents of the 'new folkloristics' put it thus:

> In the real habitat of all folklore forms there is no dichotomy between processes and products. The telling is the tale; therefore the narrator, his story, and his audience are all related to each other as components of a single continuum, which is the communicative event. (Ben-Amos 1971:10)

With the 'communicative – or performance – event' as the basic unit of observation, storytelling is treated 'holistically rather than atomistically'; its essence lies 'in the doing, not in the artefact as a structural entity' (Toelken [1979: 147], paraphrasing Georges 1969). Not only is a text 'lifeless' without context – as Malinowski observed decades earlier – but one's understanding and interpretation of the texts themselves is liable to become seriously distorted were context to be bracketed out by an overly text-orientated folklorist (Murphy 1978:125).

The obvious theoretical connection of the contemporary contextual paradigm to Malinowski is generally acknowledged by its practitioners (Murphy

1978:123-24 and Limon and Young 1986:438), specifically his general concept of the sociological context of 'myth in primitive psychology' (Malinowski 1926) and the more precise concept of 'context of situation' he proposed for the analysis of language use (Malinowski 1965:11). Regarding more contemporary theoretical currents, the affinity of this branch of folkloristics with sociolinguistics, especially the 'ethnography of speaking' (*à la* Dell Hymes and his associates) and ethnomethodology, is fruitfully explored and exploited by a number of the new folklorists (such as Paredes & Bauman 1972; Darnell 1974; Bauman & Sherzer 1974, 1975; Bauman 1975; see also Murphy 1978:131 and Toelken 1979:51,87,147,235), who all contribute to, or draw from, one or another of these fields. Moreover, by identifying the 'notion of intentions' as a critical contextual element, that is, the narrator's 'communicative intent' and the 'rhetorical strategies' with which to formulate and negotiate a desirable social setting, the new folkloristics has also situated itself within the discourse of the 'new (reflexive, experimental) ethnography' (Murphy 1978:124-32).

In identifying the contextual parameters for the style and meaning of narrative texts folklorists have been guided by sociolinguists, specifically Dell Hymes (1967, 1972) whose catchy and comprehensive SPEAKING model of the interaction of language and social setting has been adopted by some of them (such as Sherzer & Darnell 1972; see Bauman and Sherzer (1975:100-01); see also Murphy 1978:125-31 and Dundes 1980). Adapting this model to oral literature, one can list the following as key elements of context:

### *Physical Setting*

The immediate surroundings, the time of year, weather, features of the landscape, flora, fauna, the shape or size of the moon or the configuration of the stars above, and so on, all could dictate the contents of stories that are told. This contextual element could be set by either cultural dictates – for instance, the winter, among the Navaho, is the time for coyote stories and string games (Toelken 1979:94, 169) – or contingency – for example, a certain species of insect flying by, a bird call or an erupting thunderstorm.

### *Social Setting*

Whether or not a performance event takes place in an informal conversation, an *ad hoc* storytelling session, or in a formal setting, such as the interview hut or room of the researcher, or a ritual, would significantly affect style and content. Giving just one example, Kirshenblatt-Gimblett's much-cited study (1975) of parables among Toronto Jewish immigrants, it is seen how one and the same parable can assume different meaning and style when narrated in a sermon as against a conversation. It is expansive, exhortative and exegetical in the ritual context, while in the secular context it is truncated and metaphorical, delivered as a comment or gloss on an issue arising in the conversation or social interaction.

### *Participants*

Such things as the number, composition, age, kin and social relationships, temperament, background and life histories of the narrator(s) and his/her (their) audience will each and all affect the selection, style of delivery and content of the stories told. With respect to the narrator, his or her sources and experience as well as narrative competence will influence the substance and style, quality and quantity of the narratives that are presented. Included within the body or personnel is the researcher whose presence and participation within the performance event might affect the choice and presentation of materials on the part of the narrator, as well as the reaction of the audience, its size and its composition (Haring 1972; Darnell 1974; Toelken 1979:50-51, 101-103; Murphy 1978:131).

### *Ends*

The goals or purposes and the outcomes of the narrator, the aforementioned rhetorical intent, and the strategy that she/he brings to the narrative task, are potent factors affecting the narrative's style or content. A narrator may wish to teach or exhort (and tell a cautionary tale to an audience of children), explain customs (and dictate an aetiological tale into the pencil or microphone of the outside researcher), advance his own interests (and cite the appropriate proverb at the tribal court), engage the supernatural (and recite a myth at a clan ritual), enhance her/his enjoyment of social life (and tell, or listen to, the old stories or family memorates). The variations on these themes are endless.

### *Key*

The tone, manner or spirit informing the narrative performance would include such metalinguistic elements as gestures and body language, as well as voice and inflection. The latter may alter meaning, making a statement a command or a question, or, as shown by Dundes (1980:29), a narrative, a proverb or a riddle. Another factor is the degree of narrator-audience involvement; the extent to which it is high or low might affect the choice, as well as the style of presentation, of a narrative. Some narrative genres (such as epics) require little audience interaction, others (such as riddles) cannot be told without the interactive component. Charting the emotional dimension of the performance (laughing, excitement, gesturing, repetition, etc.), within narrator as well as the audience, may help identify the 'value centre' of the 'emotional core' – 'that central clustering of actions and concerns that characterise the main idea of a tale' – of the narrative (Toelken 1979:106).

### *Norms*

The norms of interaction – decorous and formal, boisterous and relaxed – will affect style and substance of narrative. A tale genre that readily illustrates the point is the joke: one's choice of material, or how to edit and deliver the punch-line, would be set by the normative context of the performance event (Dundes 1980:26-27).

### *Cognitive Orientation*

Whether or not narrator and audience share a common set of beliefs and values will affect narrative performance. Within a 'high context' group, one sharing knowledge and attitudes extensively and implicitly, storytellers are likely to use language that is more connotative, metaphorical and idiosyncratic or (sub)culture-specific (Toelken 1979:51-71, 202-206). An audience cognitively attuned to the story that is being told may, in fact, be given a narrative that is quite different from the one that would be presented to a person who stands outside such a common frame of reference. Thus Degh and Vazsonyi (1976), working with the legend genre, report that in the context of an attuned audience the narration of the story is likely to be more parsimonious and fragmented as explanations, details and embellishments are left out of the story. Considered extraneous by the cognitively attuned audience, all such textual and textural features would be included within the narrative delivered to the outsider, altering the story's style and content.

In operationalising a contextual approach, folklorists (such as Tedlock [1972] or Toelken [1979:94-101]) have developed techniques for transcription that carefully document, in side-by-side format, both text and context. The sample page (Figure 1) from Toelken's transcription of a Navaho narrative performance illustrates this technique. In moving from transcription to

| | |
|---|---|
| "Come back to my sockets!<br>Come back to my sockets!<br>Come back to my sockets!<br>Come back to my sockets!" | *much giggling* (Ma'i is carrying his example to excess.) |
| | [pause: two seconds] |
| And they came back to his sockets. | |
| | [pause: four seconds] |
| He did it again.<br>He threw them way up.<br>He could see all around the countryside while they were up there.<br>He said, "Come back to my sockets!<br>Come back to my sockets!<br>Come back to my sockets!<br>Come back to my sockets!"<br>Ma'i said. | *narrator slows down, sounds nasal and almost tired* (Ma'i has "committed himself" to the usual fourfold pattern, totally ignoring Golízhí, totally carried away by his own pleasure.) |
| | [pause: two seconds] |
| They came down and got caught around the branches of a tree. | *extended laughter, lasting seven seconds* |
| Everything got dark for him.<br>He couldn't see.<br>He groped around all over and finally found the tree.<br>It was an old tree with pitchballs all over it.<br>He could feel them with his hands. | *narrator laughs so hard that these lines are distorted* |
| He pulled two of them off and put them in his eye sockets. | *laughter* |
| | [pause: two seconds] |
| He couldn't see very well with them, | |

**Figure 1.** *Contextual transcription. (Source: Toelken 1979:99)*

interpretation the information recorded on both sides of the page – content and context – are taken together.

Which of the contextual parameters listed above can be ascertained from the Bleek and Lloyd collection that is housed in the archives of the Jagger Library? Can the transcriptions on the notebook pages written by Bleek and Lloyd over a century ago be complemented with relevant contextual notations?

## *THE CONTEXT OF /XAM NARRATIVE PERFORMANCES*

Not one of the storytelling sessions participated in by Bleek and Lloyd's informants was a live performance; all were 'clinical', conducted in Bleek's home in Mowbray, by himself (until his death in 1875) and by his sister-in-law, Lucy Lloyd, thereafter. Storytelling sessions were drawn-out affairs that were evidently quite tedious and confusing for some of the informants, especially at the beginning (Lewis-Williams 1981:27, 29-30). One of them, !Kweiten ta //ken, the only female narrator to give more than a few fragments of text, never got used to the format of the sessions and it remained an obstacle to her effectiveness as a narrator throughout the six months she worked at Mowbray (Hewitt 1986a:135). The performance events did not really consist of story*telling* but of story-*dictation*, tediously, methodically, sentence by sentence or word by word, taking days or weeks to complete one narrative. After translating the same, days, weeks, months or even years later, the researcher would read the text back to an informant for corroboration and additional information. Not infrequently this second round would use the services of a narrator different from the original one, rendering the text the more complex and confusing, as well as enhancing its richness and nuance. The narrative flow was thus generally extremely slow and stilted and only three of the six informants appear to have adapted well to the new and foreign narrative style their European hosts imposed on them.

As regards the native performance context, within the /Xam narrator's traditional social setting up in far-away 'Bushmanland', I would agree with Hewitt's appraisal – 'very difficult' – of the task of extrapolating from the Bleek/Lloyd corpus anything on the live performance context of pre-contact times:

> ... because the narratives were collected outside their native context everything is lost to us in the way of dramatic presentation, gesture,

> facial expression, narrator/audience interaction – indeed most of what characterises narrative in performance. (Hewitt 1986a:51)

Nevertheless, he does tackle the problem in a short introductory chapter – to a masterful structuralist study of /Xam narratives that is essentially text-orientated – drawing his clues from the narrative styles and explanatory comments of the various narrators. The few things he feels able to suggest on this score seem quite plausible. Concurring with Dorothea Bleek's observation that visiting, talking, listening and storytelling is an everyday activity amongst the /Xam Bushmen and the prime mode for filling the many hours of leisure time their relaxed foraging way of life affords them (Bleek 1929:311), he correlates the extensive use of dialogue and the shifting perspectives and narrative voices within a narrative with this highly vocal, speech-resounding element of /Xam social life (Hewitt 1986a:46). Adults formed the audience in such storytelling sessions; however, given that mothers[2] were frequently cited by Bleek and Lloyd's informants as the source of their stories, Hewitt suggests that another social context might have been women socialising, or comforting, their children (Hewitt 1986a:50). However, he does not suggest that storytelling was necessarily the province of women, especially with reference to an adult audience. For the latter storytelling and listening were predominantly expressions of sociability, amongst members of a band or when visiting, or being visited by, members of neighbouring bands. Gestures were used extensively, especially mimicry and 'speech' of animals as the animal kingdom provided most of the protagonists of /Xam stories (Hewitt 1986a:51-53; Bleek 1936b). Animals were also closely observed and understood by these hunting peoples, constituting for them the 'significant others' of their lives and imagination (Guenther 1988, 1989:31, 86-88). As shown by Janette Deacon (1986) another contextual feature relating to the natural world were such topographical features as mountains, pans and valleys. At the end of this article, when drawing some conclusions from the contextual elements examined at the Mowbray sessions, I will complement Hewitt's reconstruction of the native live performance *context* by suggesting that the *text* as well might have been different when narrated to a /Xam audience.

Returning again to the /Xam at Bleek's home, we note that with respect to the physical and social settings, the Bushman narrators in the Bleek household at Mowbray could scarcely have been on more foreign ground. They were a long way from their own home land – in the northern Cape – and in an alien sociocultural environment (all, however, it would seem, having had some previous contact with Europeans). Socially, the Bushmen were in a subordinate position to the two researchers. Indeed, in addition to being storytellers for their European hosts, they were also their house servants; they were not 'particularly good' at the latter task, however for, as

> you can imagine, a Bushman who has not even learnt to live in a house, and who knows nothing about cultivating the soil, did not make a particularly good house-boy. (Bleek, in Rosenthal and Goodwin 1953: 12f, quoted by Hewitt 1986a:13)

Three (possibly four [Deacon 1986:147-48]) of the /Xam informants to live at Mowbray, /A!kunta, //Kabbo, ≠Kasin (and, perhaps, Dia!kwain), were living at the Bleek household on sufferance from the Cape prison authorities, who had agreed to give custody over these Bushman convicts to Bleek on condition that they be locked up at night (Bleek and Lloyd 1911:xxvii). Bleek had requested this arrangement of the Governor of the Cape Colony as his initial attempts of collecting information from the Bushman convicts at the Breakwater jail had proved unfruitful (Lewis-Williams 1981:26). On the advice of the prison(?) chaplain, Bleek had selected these two /Xam men in 1870 out of some twenty-eight Bushman convicts then working at the breakwater. The first, /A!kunta ('Stoffel'), was chosen because he was the 'best-behaved boy' of the lot (Bleek and Lloyd 1911:443). However, some four months later, after Bleek found that he was a most inept storyteller, //Kabbo ('Jantje Tooren' or /Hui ddoro) came to join Bleek's household because of his storytelling ability.

The other /Xam informants joined the Bleek household in subsequent years. Bleek and Lloyd were anxious to get more informants in order to expand their growing store of linguistic, folkloristic and ethnographic data. A total of seventeen Bushmen lived at Mowbray over a fourteen-year period (from 1870 to 1884) and there was not a year at which the Bleek household did not entertain at least one Bushman house guest (see Figure 2). At one time, in 1874, the /Xam visitors consisted of an entire small band, consisiting of Dia!kwain ('David Husar') and his sister !Kweiten ta //ken ('Rachel') and her husband ≠Kasin ('Klaas Katkop'), along with their four children.

Eleven of the Bushmen to reside at Mowbray, for periods ranging from a month to four years, were /Xam who hailed from two dialectically distinct regions of the northern Karoo, the Strandberg ('Flat Bushmen') and the Katkop Mountains ('Grass Bushmen'). Although some two hundred and forty kilometres distance separated these two places and groups, they were

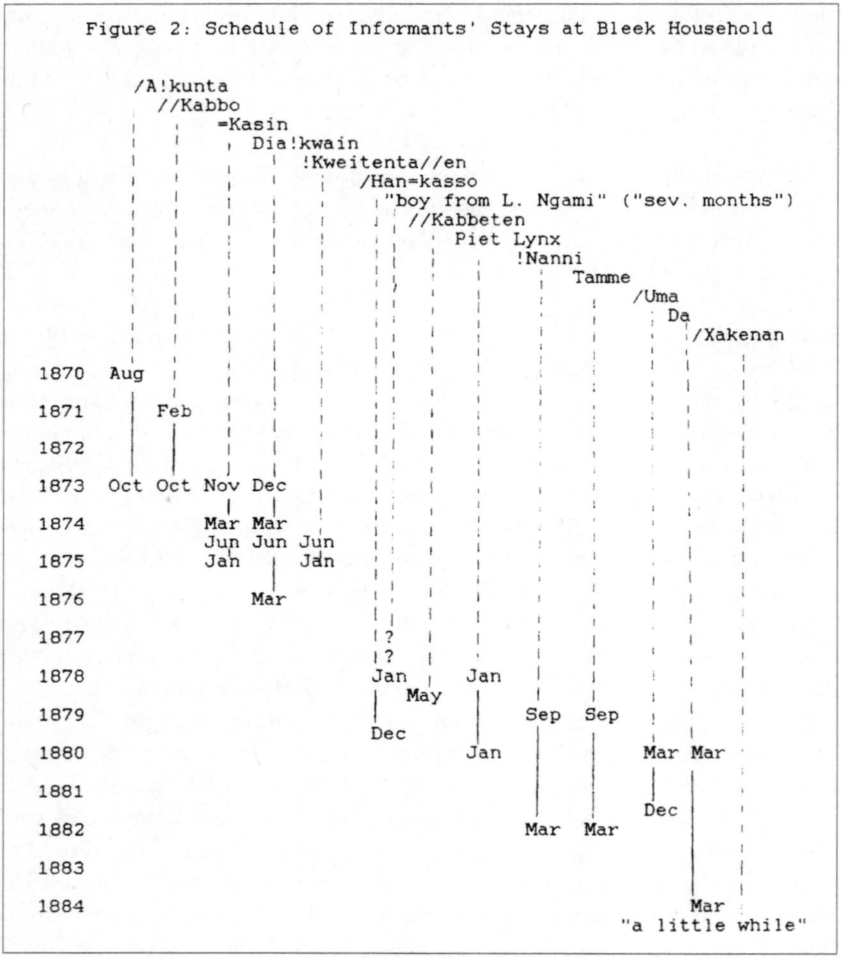


***Figure 2.*** *Schedule of informants' stays at Bleek household*

connected by bonds of kinship, thereby further enhancing the similarity between the two sets of narrative material collected. Both these points were made explicitly by Dia!kwain when Lloyd read back to him for comment and clarification the complicated text of the key myth about Anteater's Laws that she had collected from //Kabbo almost two years before. In the course of this exercise he remarked that this *ko kkumi* (story) was 'just what his mother used to tell him. She came from the same part of the country as Jantje Toorn, to whom she was related' (L II-3., p.421). The rest of Lloyd's Bushman household residents were !Kung (four boys) and 'Bushmen from the neighbourhood of Lake Ngami' (a boy and a young woman). In addition to these Bushman guests a Khoikhoi family (headed by Piet Lynx) also stayed with Lloyd for one year.

There is no reason to suggest that the many Bushman house guests and servants were treated with anything other than kindness, civility and respect. Nevertheless, one must assume that, given the elevated and lowly status of Europeans and Bushmen within nineteenth-century colonial Cape society, that the /Xam narrators 'knew their place' and, presumably, their deportment towards European benefactors, masters and interviewers contained elements also of wariness, distance, self-consciousness, servility and muted hostility.

Another feeling was homesickness, coupled with culture shock and worries about kin back home. These feelings were held by all the /Xam informants, more or less intensely. Bleek reported how both /A!kunta and //Kabbo worried about the whereabouts of their wives and left for this reason, despite entreaties to stay longer (although the 'promise of a greatly longed-for reward' had enticed //Kabbo to stay through the winter) (Bleek 1875:5). //Kabbo's sense of homesickness and alienation – amongst 'people of another place [who] do not possess my stories ... [nor] talk my language' – reverberates through his lengthy, nostalgic musing to Bleek, about returning home and about the old days (Bleek and Lloyd 1911:199-217):

> Thou knowest that I sit waiting for the moon to turn back for me, that I may return to my place. That I may listen to all the people's stories when I visit them; that I may listen to their stories ... Then, I shall get hold of a story from them because they (the stories) float from a distance; while I feel that I must altogether visit; that I may be talking with them, my fellow men. For I do work here, at women's household work ... For, I am here; I do not obtain stories; because I do not visit, so that I might hear stories which float along; while I feel that the people of another place are here; they do not possess my stories. They do not talk my language; ... As regards myself ... I am waiting that the moon may turn back for me; that I may set my feet forward in the path. For, I verily ... think that I must only await the moon; that I may tell my Master ... that I feel this is the time when I should sit among my fellow men, who walking meet their like ... for, I work here, together with women; and I do not talk with them; for, they merely send me to work ... I must wait

> (listening) behind me, while I listen along the road, while I feel that my name floats along the road; they (my three names) float along to my place; ... Therefore, I must sit waiting for Sunday on which I remain here, on which I continue to teach thee ... I do not again await another moon, for this moon is the one about which I told thee. Therefore, I desire that it should return for me. For I have sat waiting for the boots, that I must put on to walk in; which are strong for the road ...

Similarly, the next two informants, ≠Kasin and Dia!kwain, could not be persuaded by Bleek to stay beyond a certain date, because of 'their anxiety to rejoin their families' (Bleek 1875:5). After returning for a second time Dia!kwain was driven home yet again, by the same concern, to Lloyd's consternation. The last of the key narrators, /Han≠kass'o ('Klein Jantje'), also left Lloyd, to her 'great regret' as he had 'proved to be an excellent narrator', to return to 'Bushmanland', because, recently widowered, he was concerned for his only surviving child (whom, unsuccessfully, Lloyd had tried to have brought to Mowbray) (Lloyd 1889:3). Finally, there was /Xaken-an ('Mikki Streep'), 'an old Bushman woman', who allowed herself to stay for only 'a little while ... but, could not make herself happy at Mowbray. She longed to return to her own country, so that she might be buried with their forefathers' (Bleek and Lloyd 1911:xi).

The social and emotional tensions and strains marking the relationship between the researchers and narrators presumably left their mark on the narratives that were presented. One of the effects may have been that they induced within the servant-interviewees an inclination to meet expectations they perceived their master-interviewers to hold. Expressing her doubts about the veracity of Dia!kwain's report that his father had been an engraver (Bleek and Lloyd 1911:xiv) because this art form had already died out in that region at that time, Rudner suggests that this informant might have been 'carried away by months of relating legends and myths to the researchers' (Rudner 1970:153, cited by Lewis-Williams 1981:30). In examining the narrative style of the same informant, one might wonder with Hewitt (1986a:246) whether the presence of so stern (and small) an audience as listened to his tales may have influenced his choice of narratives and mode of delivery. What he presented were not outrageous trickster stories but semi-factual, legend-like accounts, frequently of people with lions, told in serious, somewhat stolid and suppressed fashion. Underscoring Hewitt's observation is the fact that apparently he dwelled, perhaps more than the others, on the didactic role of the stories 'told by our fathers', so that 'we might ourselves know things – how to feed ourselves, look after the orphan children after the parents had died. … Through the stories', Dia!kwain continues in his lengthy musing on the matter (L V-6, pp.4411rev.-19rev.), 'our fathers educated us about them[selves] when they were still alive. … When we asked a person for a thing, he should listen to the stories which the person would speak.'

As regards the effects of the social context of the performance events at Mowbray on the contents of /Xam oral literature, one might wonder about the evident prominence that the two collectors assigned to sidereal tales – about the moon, sun and stars. That Bleek deemed this to be the core element of /Xam mythology is evident from the thumbnail sketch he wrote on the Bushmen a year after starting his /Xam researches: after listing the people's identifying economic ('a hunting race') and sociopolitical ('strictly monogamous, without chiefs') features, he defines their idiosyncratic religious trait as 'worshipping moon, sun and stars' (Bleek and Lloyd 1911:435). One must ask whether Bleek's Müllerian predilections, and, consequently, his likely *a priori* theoretical bias regarding early religions, may have been picked up by the narrators who, in the interactive and socially unequal performance process may have obliged their interviewer-*baas* and presented him with an unrepresentative selection of such material, much of it in the form not of actual stories but observations, notions and beliefs. I ask this question because in other, more recent and decidedly post-Müllerian, Bushman text collections, such as Megan Biesele's (1993) among the !Kung, Thomas's (1950) among the Hai//kom or my own among the Nharo (Guenther 1989), such tales are low in number and rather incidental in substance. This impression is confirmed if one looks at Khoisan folklore in general, a task that can be readily performed, thanks to Sigrid Schmidt's 'Catalogue' (Schmidt 1989). Of the 2 399 tales listed in this superb, comprehensive and extensively cross-referenced 'field guide' to Khoisan oral literature, only 69 are about stellar bodies, the majority having been collected by Bleek and Lloyd, or '*Nacherzählungen*' thereof by other writers (a number of whom have, over the years, published retold, and often unacknowledged and thus plagiarised, versions of the /Xam collection [Schmidt 1982a]). In fact, even looking at the actual number in the /Xam collection, one finds 'that the actual number of [sidereal] narratives – as opposed to beliefs and superstitions – is extremely small indeed: of the 100-plus distinct stories collected, only nine dealt with celestial bodies' (Hewitt 1986a:91).

Another, perceived expectation on the part of the subordinate narrators *vis à vis* their superordinate interviewers may have applied to moral standards. As

I have suggested elsewhere (Guenther 1989:22), the nineteenth-century Prussian and Victorian sensitivities of the two researchers – who were, to boot, one a theologian's son and the other a minister's daughter – may have been communicated more or less explicitly to the narrators. It was, possibly, in deference to these sensitivities that the narrators may have resorted to circumlocution whenever erotic, menstrual or scatological elements entered a story. Thus, menarche, a key theme in /Xam mythology, is referred to as 'when a maid becomes a maid', or 'she went to lie down' or simply 'the new maiden'. Stories featuring male characters whose actions in a Nharo plot setting would more than likely have been raw lust, are talked about 'being in love' with a maiden, 'carrying her off because he wanted to marry her' or 'feeling that her husband he was'. Two examples are the Lynx carrying off the springbok maiden !Khauko (L II-2. pp. 323-56; see Guenther 1989:323-56) or the Baboon, watching a girl in the act of painting – a baboon – who becomes so smitten with her that he 'goes about weeping with longing', and eventually, after her menarche, he abducts her (L VIII-18, pp.7608-25). Another story, featuring sibling incest, the action of the brother towards his elder sister is, again, referred to as 'marrying her'. In referring to this tale Hewitt (1986a:110) describes the event of the story as 'having sexual intercourse with his elder sister', thereby, presumably, calling a spade a spade. In addition to the impressionistic reason stated above – that these Bushman stories 'don't quite sound right' – there is one other and more concrete reason for my reluctance to take these stories about 'pure love' at face value. It is the presence in the /Xam corpus of a certain widespread, perhaps pan-Khoisan trickster tale which, in most of the other recorded Bushman and Khoi versions, is decidedly lascivious. It is the story in which Trickster, upon seeing the approach of one or several nubile girls, places himself into their path in the form of a dead game antelope. The girls, excited about this windfall of delectable meat, proceed to cut up the carcass and either prepare it for cooking or walk off with it carrying away parts of the antelope-Trickster. The latter now starts to have his fun with the girls and, eventually his way, as certain of the severed parts enter the girls. Such is the outcome of this lusty tale in the !Kung, Dama and Nama versions (Schmidt 1989:115-16). Not so, however, in the /Xam case (Bleek and Lloyd 1911:5-9): /Kaggen's actions here are merely good, clean fun, restricted to his severed hartebeest head whispering and winking at the girl that carries him and later on scaring her and her mates by suddenly reassembling himself and chasing them a distance. That the researchers were themselves uneasy about whatever immodest story elements their narrators presented to them, which, as seen above, were few enough, is evidenced also by the fact that they might leave untranslated, or only partially or incorrectly translated, the meaning of such passages. The unsavoury character Foulmouth, who is reported by the narrator to have broken wind (L VIII-29, p. 8528, 8529), is seen to 'hiccough' in the published book about the trickster Mantis (Bleek 1924). More tellingly, we find, in Lloyd's transcription of a /Kaggen tale she collected from /Han≠kass'o in 1878, the following comment on the stock passage '*I /ke-ten !khwaiten !khwaiten. !kui ha i*: 'Of these words of the Mantis (which frequently appear in stories concerning him) the narrators were not able to furnish a sufficiently clear explanation, so the original text is given' (Bleek and Lloyd 1911:31), Given that its meaning, is, apparently 'Our name is Penis! The man has done it!' (Hewitt 1986a:238), one wonders whether, in the interest of decorum, the male narrator refrained from providing his lady interviewer with a translation.

Thus we see that with respect to the the 'moral' tenor of the /Xam texts, as presented and transcribed and translated by the /Xam narrators and their interviewers, the contrast between texts by contemporary Nharo and !Kung, as well as other Khoisan groups, is striking indeed. Sex and excretion are talked about unabashedly, with ribald and earthy language, and constitute a pervasive element of the key of these other Khoisan collections. The comparative civility or restraint of the /Xam corpus suggests that the narrators may have presented their tales selectively, leaving out the racy stuff, or, if such were contained in a story, were careful to present it in edited form. It should be stated, however, that it is also possible that the narrators were themselves by inclination decorous and restrained. For instance, notwithstanding the Decameronesque quality of Nharo folklore in general, a couple of my dozen or so informants were of puritanical bent and not one of the stories I collected from them was explicit about, let alone dwelled on, the excretory or erotic element the story contained in other versions (Guenther 1989:22-25). Furthermore, had I obtained narratives from women – the reverse situation that Lucy Lloyd was in – the norms of interaction for such inter-gender discourse would, once again, have precluded the inclusion of saucy plot elements.

Quite a different element of key or tone is the wistfulness and melancholy that can be sensed in a number of the narratives and which, as suggested above, may be a function of the emotional state of mind of the /Xam members of the Bleek household. This is in evidence especially in accounts about the old days and personal lives of the narrator, such as //Kabbo's musing about home and going home, or Dia!kwain telling Bleek about his mother's recollection about the abundance of gemsbok before the Boers came (B.XXVI, p.2492). More rarely and more subtly expressed, nostalgia and good-old-days longing for home and for the freedom and the game prevailing there and then, can be detected in many a tale or fable. This is what I sense in ≠Kasin's story about Jackal-Trickster, who in one of his rare benign and helpful moods and modes, bests the bullying Lion and protects the Bushmen and their children from his rapaciousness. As I have suggested elsewhere (Guenther 1989:149-51), one might be tempted to see 'Klaas Katkop''s story as an implicit form of oral 'protest literature' in which the weak but wily Jackal-Bushman is seen to get the better of the strong but obtuse Lion-Boer. In looking at this tale in this way I follow the lead from the Nharo whose oral traditions contain numerous such stories and the parallels between Jakkals and Lion and *Boesman jong* and Boer-*baas* is explicitly drawn in a number of them.

Stories of modern cast are quite rare in the /Xam collection, however. Most of them have very much a 'traditional' ring, especially the tales of the trickster Mantis (or /Kaggen) which 'show no trace of the Bushman's struggle for existence in later times' (Bleek 1924:vi). Moreover, the addition by some of the narrators (especially //Kabbo) of large amounts of ethnographic information, in the form of commentaries on elements of the story, situates the narratives squarely within traditional, pre-Boer or pre-Koranna /Xam society. These narratives create the mistaken impression that the narrators were themselves 'traditional' veld Bushmen. It is doubtful that they were that; each of the narrators was a 'Colonial Bushman', for whom life as a free-roaming hunter or gatherer had ceased a generation ago (Dunn 1873; Theal 1911:xxv-xxvi; Bleek 1924:vi,vii and 1932b:326, 328; Lewis-Williams 1981:28; Hewitt 1986a: 22-24; Guenther 1989:17-20). This was so despite the fact that, given the isolation and thus relatively late settlement by Europeans of the northern Karoo, stretches of this inhospitable land remained, until the last decades of the nineteenth century, where some /Xam groups were able to continue their lives as hunter-gatherers (Dunn 1873:32-36; Deacon 1986:136). Bleek and Lloyd's informants were not of that kind, however; in their case the old foraging life had been supplanted by frontier farm life, consisting of farm labour or squatting at or around Korana, Baster or white farms. The latter, largely in the southern periphery of Bushmanland (at Victoria West, Schietfontein and Fraserburg), had been allotted to the white settlers some decades before and were, by the 1870s, places alive with the 'bustle and stir' of Dutch farmers (Dunn 1873:38; also see Theal 1911:xxxv). Similar in many ways to the situation of the farm Bushmen in Ghanzi in Botswana almost a century later

(Guenther 1989:17-18), hunting-gathering had become either a recent memory or a non-viable supplementary or emergency subsistence strategy (Guenther 1976, 1986). At least one of them (Dia!kwain) had been employed by a white farmer and had witnessed the beating to death of a fellow Bushman farm labourer (Lewis-Williams 1981:28). He also recounted the story of a /Xam 'sorcerer' or shaman who, in the guise of a lion, had killed a 'Boer ox', been pursued by a Boer commando in retaliation, and wounded (while also routing the Boers) (Bleek 1936a:132-33). Moreover, as suggested by Janette Deacon (1986:147-48) there is also some evidence that suggests that the same narrator killed, and was in turn killed by, a Boer farmer (see Dunn 1873:60-62 for accounts of other Bushmen attacking Europeans in /Xam country).

All Bleek and Lloyd's narrators had European names in addition to their /Xam ones, and all spoke smatterings of Dutch and even English, not infrequently resorting to either, or a combination, of these languages when explaining to their interviewers a point in the narrative. In fact, some of the earliest narratives recorded by Bleek, found scattered amongst his language exercises in his first notebooks, were given to him by his informant (/A!kunta) in a language that was an almost half-and-half blend of /Xam with Dutch and English. While attesting to the originality and cultural integrity of the narratives he collected from his /Xam informants, Bleek does admit the possibility of some European influence, specifically on /Kaggen himself, whom some narrators (such as //Kabbo) occasionally refer to as 'the Devil'. Bleek suggests that this distorting misidentification resulted from Dutch-speaking Bushmen or /Xam-speaking farmers trading stories and beliefs and in the process putting on the /Kaggen figure the garb and guise of the Christian devil (Bleek 1875:8-9).

Speculating, and once more following the lead from the situation of the Ghanzi farm Bushmen (Guenther 1975, 1975/76, 1986), I would suggest that the alienation and oppressiveness of the narrators' lives in colonial Cape society may have evoked a sense of the integrity of their own culture and stimulated a revitalisation of some of its features, in particular ritual and certain elements of belief. Consequently, the stories that were told amongst the /Xam of the days back in the north-western Cape may thus have had less of a traditional ring than those they told at Mowbray to their European interviewers who wanted 'old stories'. In their own social setting the /Xam narratives would likely have addressed, to a much greater degree than in Cape Town, the commandos of the recent past, the raids by the Korana, the encroachment of frontier farmers and cattle, the theft of land and loss of game, the labour rendered, by force or necessity, on the Boers' farms and the like. All this is the subject matter for a large number of the Nharo stories that I collected. Directly or obliquely, they weave all the features of their new existence into their oral traditions, physical ones like wagons, ploughs, kraals, gardens, houses, chickens, 'dams', oxen, butter, cream; social ones like *baas*, *miessis*, boss-boy, employment, wages, school, Christmas; and moral ones like injustice, oppression, exploitation, despair or rebelliousness. Furthermore, actual stories and motifs from the folklore of the settler groups have also found their way into the corpus. While likely less extensive because of fewer years of exposure to the new settlers, it would be surprising if /Xam folklore of the late 1800s did not also contain these contemporary elements and, in addition, had not been as dynamic and responsive to the new economic, social and political conditions as were the narratives of the Ghanzi Bushmen a century later.

The performance style and competence of the individual narrators, and their influence on the narratives' content has been examined perceptively by Hewitt (1986a:239-46). After presenting brief biographical sketches of the six /Xam narrators,[3] /A!kunta, ≠Kasin !Kweiten ta //ken, Dia!kwain, //Kabbo, and /Han≠kass'o, Hewitt focuses on the last three. They had provided most of the texts and were the most skilled storytellers. After identifying some of the common rhetorical elements – such as opening a story with a terse statement about the central character and his or her action at a certain time or concluding a narrative in mid-dialogue – Hewitt turns to the three narrators and shows how each of them uses his own idiosyncratic narrative techniques, with differing effects on the story's texture and text.

Starting with //Kabbo, Hewitt (1986a:239-42) identifies as this narrator's most distinctive rhetorical trademark a high degree of narrative skill. It is exemplified, among other things, in his shift of perspective, or point of view, over to another character, once or several times within the same narrative. He adds drama and colour to these shifts by adopting a distinctive voice (including special clicks) for some of the characters, such as Ichneumon, Jackal, or the Moon (reminiscent of Tweety Bird of American fakelore). He brought enthusiasm to his delivery, shown, for instance, in his absorption in ancillary plot elements. The resulting, often very lengthy, tangents, usually on practical matters and the old days, were frequently at the expense of the narrative's unity. He would leave a story incomplete, having dealt only with the 'centres of activity' he found most interesting. The foremost of these were the outrageous actions of /Kaggen. //Kabbo was the most knowledgeable of all of the informants, partly because of his advanced age, partly because he seems to have been a *!gi xa*, a medicine man, in possession of certain arcane knowledge, for instance, rain-making (Bleek 1936a:143; Lewis-Williams 1981:27). His maternal grandmother, who 'made springbok come and helped sick people etc.' (LII-37, p.3338rev.), had been a *!gi xa* as well.

/Han≠kass'o's (Hewitt 1986a:242-44, see also pp. 83-86) special rhetorical skill lay in his presentation of coherent, well structured and rounded stories which did not digress or jump ahead of the plot as did those of some of the other narrators. He had a 'strong sense of narrative shape', suggesting to Hewitt that he might have been a seasoned storyteller. He used repetition, always five times, to good effect, and enriched the texture of his narratives by using chanted phrases and songs. Another narrative device was his occasional use of a 'hook', by opening a story with a dream and not letting the audience know about this beguiling plot element until well into the story. Unlike his father-in-law //Kabbo, he used little dialogue, but he shared with the other accomplished narrator a strong interest in trickster stories. However, when telling these narratives his plot dealt not so much with the outrageous antics of /Kaggen but with his creativity and helpfulness.

As suggested earlier on, Dia!kwain (Hewitt 1986a:244-45) was the most restrained of the three key narrators. He drew on a great store of stories; he used this knowledge, however, not to tell a story for its own sake but as a means for demonstrating one or another feature of belief (another manifestation of his abovementioned didactic penchant). His narratives tended to be serious and somewhat matter-of-fact in tone and showed a preference for legend-like stories featuring lions. The best of these, about the young man who was carried off by the lion, with dramatic and tragic consequences for both parties, was published by Bleek and Lloyd (1911:174-91). His narratives were interspersed with chants but he used little repetition.

## SUMMARY AND CONCLUSION

I have attempted to identify some of the contextual elements of /Xam narrative performances, as these unfolded, by the hundreds, on the porch or in the living room at the Bleek home in Mowbray. The performance sessions were initiated by Bleek or Lloyd, in terms of their own schedules, rather than the seasonal, social and ritual dictates of /Xam culture. The interviews were conducted on a one-to-one basis, that is, involving one interviewer and one narrator at a time, resulting in a minimalist audience, of one.

As alien to the narrators as the physical and performance settings of the narrative events that they had become thrust into was the social context.

They stood in a subordinate relationship to their interviewers, who were also their benefactors and employers and, in three cases, their probationary officers. The employment relationship was cast in a master-servant mould as the narrators also worked as servants, or 'house boys', in the Bleek household. The two interviewers, probably somewhat stern, if kind and well-intentioned Victorians, were influential middle-class members of colonial Cape society. The informants, themselves 'Colonial Bushmen' with various degrees of exposure to European frontier culture and each bearing a Dutch name, had closely similar or identical cultural backgrounds, came from the same or nearby places from a far-away frontier region and were for the most part kin-related.

The narrators displayed a wide range of narrative competence and three of them, all men, were highly competent as storytellers, each employing his distinctive set of stylistic devices – repetition, chanted refrains, songs, shifting perspective, voice imitation and others – and holding his own preference as to story genres, plot development or explanatory commentary. In consequence, the thousands of notebook pages of narratives they delivered varied in terms of text and texture. While extending co-operation with their interviewers and regaling them with generous amounts of text laboriously dictated word by word, none of the narrators seemed at ease in the performance and social settings they found themselves in. Indeed, there is more than a little evidence to suggest that they were unhappy, feeling lonely, homesick, worried and culturally alienated. What they seemed to want more than anything was to go home.

The status difference between audience and narrators, the absence of a common cognitive orientation, and the anxiety and nostalgia of the narrators may have shaped the storytellers' narrative intentions and the 'key' of their performances. The social and emotional context may have created a text-book case of the most basic and classic of fieldwork problems: the informant's responding to perceived expectations of the researcher and, for his or her own reasons, 'feeding him a line'. While we cannot know these personal reasons, we can assume that some of them had to do with the employment relationship with the informants' master-interviewers. Each time a Bushman, say //Kabbo, told a story he would suspend his role as servant and the longer his narrative and the more wide-ranging its tangents the less 'women's household work' he would have to do. Other motivating factors were doubtless the dread of being sent back to jail and the toil at the breakwater, and the desire to be allowed, as soon as possible, to be relieved of their tour of duty at the Bleek household and return home. Finally, they may also genuinely have appreciated the kindness their hosts were showing them.

One might expect all these contextual elements to have left their mark on the style and content of the texts that were presented to Bleek and Lloyd. The inhibited, if not altogether seized up, narrative style of some of the informants (Dia!kwain, /A!kunta, and especially the two women !Kweiten ta //ken and /Xaken-an) was probably a result of this self-consciousness and unease. The ponderous length of so many narratives and their extensive explanatory comments, the frequent use of Dutch or English words, the emphasis on sidereal tales, the absence, as elements of tone or plot, of sex and excretion, and the traditional and static quality of the narratives generally may have been the effects of the performance context on content. Another important distortion is the gender-bias of the narrative corpus collected by Bleek and Lloyd; women, having at one time or other provided the narrators with over ninety per cent of the sourced material, are all but muted in the Mowbray collection.

Having identified the contextual distortions of the narratives' text and texture that were created through the artificial and strained setting in which they were performed, we may be in a position to speculate somewhat less gratuitously than would have been possible before, about /Xam oral tradition in its native context, back at the Bitterpits or Katkop, amongst contemporaneous fellow-/Xam. There, the stories would probably have been more racy and earthy. The tales that were told were possibly less conservative and, instead, more reflective of the life situation that had been created by the aggressively encroaching white settlers. The narratives would perhaps have been less lengthy, as explanatory commentary to provide background information would become redundant amongst an audience attuned to the same cognitive orientation as the narrator. The prominent story themes would not be stellar bodies but people, both of the 'early race' and contemporary ones. With respect to their gender, girls and women would have a high profile, as well as menarche and marriage, the more so because female performers would unrestrainedly join into storytelling sessions and bring to the narratives the female perspective which is so prominent in other bodies of Khoisan oral literature (Guenther 1983/84, 1990). Back in their own natural and social landscape and climate, at their respective farm settlements or within what was left of the traditional social patterns of hunting and gathering, seasonal dispersal and aggregation, band and inter-band social life, exchange, marriage, ritual and dance, the context would be provided not only for telling the stories from each band's established narrative repertoire but for constantly adding to it. Oral materials to be generated from a social life that is vibrant and 'high context' would be such things as hunting stories, stories about ranchers and farm work and life, stories about places or features of the landscape, and stories especially about people as each generation adds to the store of family memorates it holds, drawing on the events and experiences that happen in the course of its everyday life.

One element that the narratives told to Bleek and Lloyd would certainly share with those related to fellow-/Xam back in the northern Karoo would be /Kaggen. The Trickster, in his many guises, is the central figure in Nharo folklore and, as evidenced by Schmidt's catalogue, of Khoisan folklore in general. His magical powers, outrageous antics, foolishness and earthiness would amuse and beguile the home audience. His occasional helpfulness and protectiveness, championing the case of the weak and vulnerable and his wiliness, as well as defiance and manipulation of others, especially beings stronger than he is (such as the Lion/Boer) might become the elaborated attributes of the Bushman Trickster within the new social and political reality of life in the Colony.

When we remove the contextual elements that intruded on the narrative performance at Mowbray and distorted the style and substance of the stories as they were told in an authentic context, we see the /Xam corpus to be in line with Bushman oral tradition in general. The special status some might want to ascribe to the myth and lore of the /Xam Bushmen – for instance, Schapera (1930:398) who deemed the Southern Bushmen to 'stand apart from the rest' – is seen to dissolve and the fact that Bushman expressive and religious culture does indeed constitute one unit (Guenther 1989:33-36) becomes the more apparent.

## *NOTES*

1. For a recent critical but sympathetic survey of the field throughout much of its twenty-year existence see Limon and Young (1986). Another useful, if dated, position paper was presented by Murphy (1978). Barry Toelken (1979) has written a comprehensive text book that is squarely based on the context-performance approach.
2. Hewitt's parenthetical observation on this matter is corroborated by my own sample of tales, derived in part from what is published in *Specimens* (Bleek & Lloyd 1911) and from the fifty-five narratives I obtained from the Archives at the Jagger Library. In forty-three of these the narrators identify the source of their tale. The sources break down as follows: mother (39, 72%); grandparents (9 [6 grandmother, 3 grandfather], 21%); father (1); and 'female relation' (1). By gender, women were the source of as many as thirty-nine (just over 90%) of the narratives and men of only four (just under 10%).

3. These sketches can be supplemented with the biographical information that is found in the two annotated reports on the collection published by Bleek (1875:5-6), Lloyd (1889:3-5) and Bleek and Lloyd (1911:x-xv). Other writers who have recently compiled biographical sketches on these key informants are Lewis-Williams (1981:27-29), Deacon (1986:136-39, 148-49) and Guenther (1989:27-29).

# The Relevance of the Bleek/Lloyd Folktales to the General Khoisan Traditions

Sigrid Schmidt

The Bleek/Lloyd collection of /Xam texts gained popularity among a wider public because of the considerable number of folktales included. They were regarded as the core of the collection. Generally it was believed that they were unique in every respect. As recently as twenty years ago a specialist assured me that the tales stand completely apart from the folklore of any other African peoples. It is true to say, however, that a considerable number of /Xam texts have variants among other Khoisan folklore. The aim of this study is to trace this relationship, to treat it from various angles and to go beyond the mere enumeration of common topics.

The character of the /Xam narratives was described by Hewitt (1986a). In his outstanding and sensitive treatise he analysed the tales as to their structure, meaning and relation to /Xam life and belief; it is not necessary, therefore, to embark on another study of the /Xam stories.

The majority of /Xam tales can be grouped into four sections: stories about the origin of the present world, tales about the trickster /Kaggen, magic tales, and legends.

## *THE PEOPLE OF THE EARLY RACE*

A general trait of the /Xam traditions is the conception of 'the people of the early race'. It was assumed that in a remote time the world did not have its present form. In those days neither the celestial bodies and the mountains and rivers in the landscape had their current positions nor did men and women have the same appearance as they do today. The people of the early race were nearly like men and women but many had animal names and some animal characteristics. When at a certain point the old world changed into the present one, those people became the animals whose names they possessed, and men and women became real human beings. This turning point is to be regarded as crucial for the world view of the /Xam, for it means that at that moment the laws that govern the present world were installed. At that point death came into the world; before that people did not die, but from then on they became subject to the laws of nature, of birth and death. Human beings were separated from the animals and became real people by obtaining fire and all their other cultural possessions (Bleek 1924:33-34). They also received new laws of social life which were mainly symbolised by the laws of marriage and of food (Hewitt 1986a:116-20, 1986b; Guenther 1989:83-85).

This conception was not built into a straight philosophical system but rather appears in protean forms. It can be traced as a red line in /Xam folklore but in the lore of other Khoisan peoples too (cf. Stow 1905:129; Vialls 1908: 303; Schmidt 1980:26; Guenther 1989:42).

It is noteworthy that the tales about the origin of death and the acquisition of fire are by far the most popular folktales of the Khoisan peoples. I indexed fifty-seven variants of the origin of death story (KH 197) and twenty-eight of the stories about the acquisition of fire (KH 261,1 = 1 var.; 265 = 11; 266,2 = 1; 267 = 8; 268 = 3; 270 = 3; 215 = 1). A closer look reveals how firmly this complex of tales was anchored in the old Khoisan lore. The Nama tales of the origin of death were connected with male initiation for they were told in order to explain why men who had passed the initiation ceremonies were no longer allowed to eat hares (Schmidt 1980:243; Winter 1988:173). On the uppermost level the acquisition of fire meant the acquisition of facilities for cooking and warming. On a deeper level it stood for human culture (cf. Bleek 1924:33). And it meant much more: generally fire was stolen from the animal-people of the early time and this loss of fire caused their transformation into present day animals (Vialls 1908:303-304). Fire, then, not only has cultural and social connotations but contains the very essence of humanity, namely having a human form. It symbolises even the life force: when the trickster Dima of the Sekele !Kung in Angola had stolen the fire of his friend, the bird Txikungulo, 'he now could create the African land, trees, rivers and finally man, too' (Almeida 1957:554-55).

In the /Xam tales, the new social laws were installed by the Anteater. This has parallels in !Kung, Hei//om, Damara and Nama tales. There these new marriage and food laws are added in the same manner as a kind of coda to very different tale types, even to tales of foreign origin, and proclaimed by a variety of tale characters. Usually they appear in one of several variants of a tale only, thus showing how loosely this episode was linked to the stories. This comparison leads to the question as to what extent the 'Anteater's laws' really were 'Anteater's' laws and might not have been put into the mouth of another actor in another /Xam tale. In most cases we find that we have to regard this episode as a more or less independent unit which the narrator might add to the stories of the early time when he felt it appropriate.

This basic group of tales about the change of the primeval world into the present world was discussed in more detail in an earlier paper (Schmidt 1988).

## *THE TALES ABOUT /KAGGEN, THE TRICKSTER*

### */Kaggen in Tales and /Kaggen in Folk Belief*

The conception of the 'early race' is very pronounced in the tales about /Kaggen. But before turning to these /Kaggen tales we have to outline briefly some of the characteristics of this figure. We have to distinguish sharply between the /Kaggen of the tales and the /Kaggen of folk belief, who was present in the daily life of the /Xam. He lurked in the neighbourhood to see whether people obeyed the laws of hunting, initiation and treatment of animals. He tested the young hunter severely and punished a woman who stepped over the head of a hartebeest with the death of her little child. The attitude towards this figure therefore was one of awe and fear. In contrast, the /Kaggen of the tales is remote and set amidst the people of the early race. The character of this /Kaggen oscillates between having supernatural abilities on one hand and being stupid and greedy on the other.

A contradictory personality identical to this possesses the tricksters of those Khoisan peoples for whom we have a sufficient number of traditions available. The protagonists of folk belief and the protagonists of tales are not to be reconciled. The same !Kung who hardly dared to talk about their ≠Gao!na to Lorna Marshall roared with laughter when they told about ≠Gao!na's pranks. They timidly whispered the deity's name into her ear but pronounced it without hesitation in the tales (Marshall 1962:227).

The Nama and Damara prayed at the 'graves', the cairns, to Heitsi Eibib or Haiseb, and the more one goes north the Namibian Damara will remember that Haiseb was 'their Jesus' or 'God' before their forefathers became Christians. But they tell the most hilarious stories about Heitsi Eibib's or Haiseb's foolishness. The names of these figures are the same in folk belief and in tales, and informants stress that they are the same persons, but the characters are completely different. Therefore the outsider has to watch carefully to which of the two sides of the personality the informants refer: to belief or to tale.

No doubt there are obvious regional deviations in the descriptions of the protagonists of folk belief. Yet the representations of the heroes in the *tales* show amazing resemblances. The /Kaggen of the tales irritates the reader because of his kaleidoscopic character: in some tales he is nothing but a fool, in others the trickster *par excellence* who outwits the beings around him, in others again the benefactor, and again in others the tragical hero. To irritate the reader even more, in the same story /Kaggen may turn from one personality into another. /Kaggen, beaten and humiliated by his adversaries to the utmost, may suddenly turn out to have supernatural abilities ('The Mantis makes an eland', Bleek 1924:1-9, 'The Mantis takes away the ticks' sheep', Bleek 1924:30-34).

The same colourful picture is offered of the trickster in the tales of the other Khoisan peoples, Cagn of the Maluti Bushmen, Heitsi Eibeb and Haiseb of Nama, Damara and Hei//om, ≠Gao!na of the !Kung and Pisamboro of the Nharo and G/wi. He may be nothing but a fool, or a benefactor, or a player of tricks, but he may change his character – and thereby the character of the story – to a remarkable degree within one text. In one popular Nama/Damara tale greedy Haiseb takes too much honey from the Bees. They punish him by biting off part of his skull. Haiseb tricks his niece, the Dassie, to come near, kills her and makes a hood of her fur to hide his open head. In one version it is said explicitly that this was the first hood in the country (Thomas 1950:5-8). Haiseb wears this hood permanently. But his wives succeed in pulling it off by a trick. Now, in his deepest humiliation, overcome by the Bees, his wives and his little son, standing there with his open skull, he suddenly turns into the great culture-hero: he seizes his brains, scatters them into the landscape and shouts: 'A good place shall be here, a bad place shall be there!' And the brains turned into the staple *veldkos* !han, the uintjies, of which there are two kinds, one sweet and the other bitter (Lebzelter 1934:173; KH 318).

A detailed comparison of the individual tricksters of the tales would probably reveal more common traits than are known today. In one story /Kaggen does not use the right click (Bleek & Lloyd 1911:8-9, notes); a few Damara narrators represent Haiseb in a similar way. Lebzelter (1934:172) mentioned that he only used the alveolar click ≠. One of my informants explained that Haiseb's speech corresponds to that of a child who has not yet mastered the clicks. /Kaggen's wife often told him that 'he was not like a grown-up person'

(Bleek 1924:46). The successor of the Nama Heitsi Eibib, the Jackal, sometimes has a 'hasty, clumsy and stumbling way of expression' which is intentionally employed by the narrators to produce comical effects (Schultze 1907:417). The !Kung trickster Kauha lisps (Biesele 1975:I,82). At another place /Kaggen exclaimed words for which the narrators were not able to furnish a sufficiently clear explanation though they frequently appear in stories concerning him (Bleek & Lloyd 1911:31). This reminds me of the *njiranjajoa* which one Damara narrator inserted again and again in Haiseb's speeches (it was one of those narrators who also had Haiseb speak without proper clicks). These words, she declared, did not mean anything; they were just Haiseb's typical words. Maybe the /Xam exclamations have to be understood in the same manner.

## */Kaggen in the Form of a Hartebeest*

### The Tricky Trickster

*Specimens of Bushmen Folklore* opens with 'The Mantis assumes the form of a Hartebeest': /Kaggen turns into a dead hartebeest and has himself found and cut up by a group of girls. While they are transporting the meat home, the head carried by the youngest girl starts to whisper and asks her to remove the thong from its eye. The other girls do not believe the little girl when she tells them about it. When, however, the head speaks again the little girl drops it to the ground. The head scolds the girl aloud. Now all the girls drop their loads of meat and flee. The parts of /Kaggen join again, he turns into a man and chases them. But the girls reach home and are told by their father that they had cut up /Kaggen (Bleek & Lloyd 1911:2-17; KH 280). Von Wielligh's version is very similar: here the family of a man by the name of 'Ga carries the parts of the dead antelope home, and at the end the parts spring together and the antelope runs away alive (1917 – 1921:I, 12-14).

In these two versions /Kaggen just tricks the girls for no obvious reason. The main emphasis lies in the disappointment of the people that the meat which they were happy to have found disappeared in such a frightening way. The story was also noted down among the Nama (Schultze 1907:494-95) and among the !Kung (Biesele 1975 I,115-16; II,51-53). I myself heard it from a Damara man (Schmidt 1980:19-20). These three versions shift the focus: the trickster turns himself into a dead antelope because he wants to win a certain girl who had rejected him. He either cohabits with her while she is carrying him on her back (!Kung), or his private parts which the girl is preparing for food spring into the girl (Nama/Damara). I still see before me the narrator's sparkling face while he was telling about Haiseb's victory and was shouting triumphantly: 'Oh, I have tasted the girl that nobody had tasted! I have tasted her!'

Such a similarity, but also such a difference, in the /Xam version raises a number of questions: did the South African Bushmen really tell the tale among themselves in the way they told it to Bleek? It does, after all, represent a coherent whole and Von Wielligh published it in a closely related form. Or did the narrators, who usually have fine feelings of tact, change the stories for their Victorian audience sensitive to sexual items? How far can we speak of 'myths'? Or are these tales nothing but trickster adventures? How far can we stress the importance of details and analyse them as symbols? I think mainly of the hartebeest in the /Xam story. Does it really stand in mythical relationship to /Kaggen here? Or is it just an antelope which is highly esteemed as food like the springbok or kudu in the Nama, Damara and !Kung variants?

## *The Mantis makes an Eland*

### /Kaggen, the Tragical Hero

Another /Kaggen tale which has drawn much attention is the story of how /Kaggen created the eland out of a piece of leather. /Kaggen put a piece of his son-in-law's shoe into a pond, and a tiny eland developed from it. /Kaggen fed it daily with honey. But his family who no longer got any honey sent his grandchild to spy on him, and when the boy reported what he had discovered the family killed the eland. When later /Kaggen came to feed it he called in vain. He found the bloodstains and wept (Bleek 1924:1-5, 5-9; Hewitt 1986a:216; Lewis-Williams 1983:45; KH 207).

Here /Kaggen is a tragical hero, and the reader greatly pities him. The audience probably reacted in the same way. There are three /Xam versions dictated by the three main informants; the story must have been familiar to the different Bushman groups to which these men belonged. But the story was spread much further. Ten years ago an elderly Nama woman told me a unique story: The Jackal kept six motherless lambs in a kraal and fed them with honey-water. Every time he came back from collecting honey he sang: 'Six little sheep, six little sheep that drink honey-water!' Then the lambs came out. But while the Jackal was away his neighbour Lion drove them to his house and killed them. When Jackal had sung in vain he followed the spoor and saw the pots filled with meat cooking at the Lion's house. He took revenge in a manner called by folklorists 'The false beauty-doctor' (AaTh 8A): he enticed the Lion to let himself be shaved as beautifully as he was shaved himself and during the shaving killed him. Then follows the typical ending of Nama magic tales: the Jackal set the hearts of the six lambs into calabashes, and from these they grew again into their former shape (KH 713).

When you know that in Nama folklore the Jackal has completely replaced old Heitsi Eibeb as a trickster you easily recognise that the first part of the story is a variant of the /Xam one. Unfortunately it was not possible to discuss the story with the narrator and her audience, so I discussed the tape later with other people. When listening they were deeply moved and felt concerned for the Jackal. It was only after some discussion that they realised how unrealistic and contrary to the standards of Nama folklore was this image of a jackal feeding sheep with honey. I suppose that this is why the story did not survive in Nama tradition after the trickster role had been handed over from the anthropomorphous trickster to the animal trickster.

Far in the north, among the !Kung of East Ovamboland and West Kavango, Heikkinen (1985) recorded versions strikingly similar to the /Xam stories (KH 259,4+5): 'A man rears an eland calf' and 'Huwe rears a roan antelope'. The trickster kept the antelope calf in the veld. As he did not bring home any honey, or only honey of inferior quality, his son or sons were sent to spy on him. He ordered them to go to sleep but at least one of them watched what he was doing. His family, however, was not content to have killed the eland or roan calves and to see the man weeping. In both versions a further revenge was carried out.

A closely related tale is very popular mainly among the Hei//om (KH 208). There it is not a little antelope calf which is fed with honey by the trickster but the trickster's sweetheart. This sweetheart is usually an oryx woman. Though the motifs are nearly the same as in Bleek and Lloyd's /Xam and Heikkinen's !Kung variants, there is a shift of meaning. In Thomas's version this is clearly pronounced: at the end of the story the mother proclaims that from now on oryxes should be game and should no longer be married to humans (Thomas 1950:17-19). In other words, the early time has ended, the world has changed into the present world with its new laws. We are reminded of the Anteater's laws again.

The idea of the separation from the animal world is central to a story which is different in content but related in spirit: the trickster is married to an elephant woman. His brother kills the elephant wife and convinces the trickster that he was only married to meat. In this tale the forceful separation of early man and animals is stressed: after the elephant wife is killed her family tries to avenge her. But in the end the trickster's side wins (KH 209). In Jantunen's !Kung version the trickster saved himself by fleeing. But his brother blew on his whistle and announced that the elephants should become animals and subsist on twigs. His band came and they all ate the meat of the dead elephant. We have to add: And this was the ceremonial introduction of elephant meat as food (Jantunen 1967:133-36).

The stories in which the trickster is mainly a tragic hero focus on the death of somebody very dear to him: the eland he is creating, his sweetheart, his wife. In another cluster of tales it is his son or his sons who die. In all cases it is killing and murder, not natural deaths or accidents. This topic must have been of special concern to the old Khoisan peoples, for it was handed down in thirteen texts stemming from Maluti and /Xam Bushmen, Damara, Hei//om, !Kung of Namibia and !Kung of Botswana; that is to say from the far south-east to the far north-west of the Khoisan area, from the Bushmen of the southern, central and northern language groups as well as the Nama-speakers (KH 240-43).

Lloyd's text, '/Kaggen's young son met the baboons', is as far as I know, the only text in the /Xam collection dealing with this topic. They asked him where he was going. The son told them that he 'must fetch for his father sticks that his father might take aim at the people who sit upon their heels'. One baboon after the other was called to listen to the boy's words. The fifth realised that they themselves were meant. They beat the boy until an eye sprang out of his head and the boy died. /Kaggen dreamt what had happened, and when he saw that it was true he wept. While the baboons were playing at ball with the boy's eye he joined them, snatched the eye and hid it. The baboons beat him severely but he managed to fly away with the eye. He put it into the water and after a while the boy grew from this to his former state (Bleek & Lloyd 1911:16-37). The boy's name is !Gaunu-tsaxau, which, according to Dorothea Bleek's *Dictionary*, is '!Gaunu's eye' (1956:379). !Gaunu, on the other hand, is the Great Star, 'which, singing, named the Stars' (Bleek & Lloyd 1911:78-81).

The episode of how the eye of the slain child is used as a ball for playing is unknown to all the other versions except Von Wielligh's (1917-1921:I,129-36). In Orpen's Maluti version the stress is laid on Cagn's revenge: he fixed sticks on to the backs of the dancing baboon people, turned them into animals and chased them into the mountains (Orpen [1874] 1919:149). The stories of the !Kung, Hei//om and Damara (KH 240) tell how the sons of Lion and

Trickster hunted or played together. The son(s) of the Trickster were killed by the young Lion(s) and usually buried under the stomach contents of the eland or giraffe they had killed. The Trickster wept. But then he avenged the death of his son(s). This was done during a dance, as in the Maluti version. In the Hei//om-Damara tradition Haiseb danced together with the Lions, enticed them to stretch their necks and then threw the axe which he had made from the shoulder-blade of the animal killed by the sons. This axe cut off the heads of all the Lions.

If ever a story may be called myth, it is this group of tales about the murder of the trickster's son. What is most striking is the number of correspondences to different elements of the old system of belief and rites. The /Xam obviously connected the story with astral lore, the Maluti with the central idea of the change of the old world into the present one and the turning of people of the early race into animals. In one of Biesele's !Kung variants, the institution of several rites is described: !Gara tries to find out which bones of the eland have to be hung in the tree so that a thunderstorm might be called; the neckbones do not work but the horns do. !Gara and his companions dance that it may rain. He wants to cleanse himself from murder and tries to find out in which way trance could be achieved: coal burnt in the eland's foot does not work but eland fat and coal in the shell of a tortoise does. For this purpose he has to kill the tortoise – though he is called his nephew (Biesele 1975:I,178-82). So here the introduction of rain dances, of cleansing from murder, of trance and the equipment for trance stimulation are connected with the theme of the murder of the trickster's sons.

In a Damara variant Young Lion celebrates the feast of his first kill in spite of the fact that he was not entitled to do so because he could not kill the giraffe without Young Haiseb's help. There are quite a number of items with deep symbolic meaning: the stomach contents under which the boys are buried, the magic shoulder-blade of the animal, the spittle blessing by which, in Heikkinen's Hei//om text, the son is revived. In the centre there is the trickster who weeps. There is room for much speculation about how this death of his son, sweetheart, wife or eland in the state of creation might be interpreted. Death and rebirth may be seen in connection with the change of the old world into the present one, of human life or nature in general, of boys' initiation. There is no direct proof for any one of these possibilities. But I believe that something of all this underlies the texts, thus radiating extraordinary fascination.

## */Kaggen and Eyes-on-his-Feet*

### The Interrelatedness of Tales and Folk Belief

There is another /Kaggen tale known in variants from South Africa to the north of Namibia and Botswana: /Kaggen and Eyes-on-his-Feet. /Kaggen meets a stranger in the veld and starts a fight with him. This stranger has no eyes in his face but behaves like a normal person and even manages to beat /Kaggen severely. The second part of the story follows a favoured pattern of /Xam /Kaggen tales using standard motifs. After having learned from his son-in-law that the man has his eyes on his feet /Kaggen instigates a second fight with the stranger; he applies his son-in-law's advice, throws sand into his eyes and thus wins (Bleek 1924:13-15).

Who is this figure that, according to Bleek (1875:7), is 'one of the most interesting to the Bushman mind'? When editing the story, Dorothea Bleek introduced the name of Will-o'-the-wisp because one of the names of this being seemed to suggest such a translation (Bleek 1875:7). But, in fact, in the whole tale there is not the slightest hint of such an identity.

There are two clusters of tales around this figure: first, the /Xam texts (KH 256), their four variants among the Nama and the Damara in the Witbooi area of Gibeon and Mariental (KH 845), and perhaps the fragmentary Nharo tale (Guenther 1989:118), and second the tales of Nama, Damara, Hei//om, Nharo and !Kung, in the sixteen variants of which the trickster and Eyes-on-his-Feet sit together at the fire and roast some food. And though the stranger generally has done nothing but take the best food for himself the trickster triumphantly blinds him (KH 257).

But why did he blind him? I suppose we get some clues from looking at the general treatment of characters in different genres. It is a basic trait of jests that the dupes suffer serious calamity; in animal jests they may often even be brought to death though in the story itself they have done nothing bad. Their only 'sin' is not being as clever as the hero. We have to look for other evidence to gain the full meaning of the image which they represent in the story. The lion, for instance, is greatly feared in real life both as dangerous in the veld and because of his relationship to sorcery. In the jests, however, he has committed no crime but is tortured and killed to the delight of narrator and audience alike. The jests, from ancient animal stories to modern political jokes, counterbalance physical, psychical or social suppressions with psychohygienic effects. I suppose, therefore, that at least some of the Khoisan trickster tales had the same role. In order to know more about Eyes-on-his-Feet in the tales we have to look at what counterbalances this figure in folk belief. And in fact, in the records of the nineteenth century we find Eyes-on-his-Feet definitely connected with the life-threatening forces. He is closely associated with the man-eating ogres (Schmidt 1986b).

The story is an outstanding example of the interrelatedness of Khoisan folklore. I mentioned that in southern Namibia there are side-by-side variants of the /Xam type of story and of the type told in the north. In addition, in South Africa the Khoisan figure of Eyes-on-his-Feet was assimilated into Afrikaans folklore. In 1823 Thompson met a 'matron' who had learned in her youth that cannibals had eyes in their legs (Thompson 1968:128). This testifies that Eyes-on-his-Feet must have turned into a figure of Afrikaans folk belief by the latter part of the eighteenth century. Today he is still a popular bogey but of course only living in the world of children (Grobbelaar *et al.* 1977:70). This Afrikaans figure, in his turn, must also have influenced the Nama figure. For if the Nama tell about him in Afrikaans they do not translate their own name ≠Ailgêmûchab (Foot-back-eye-man) but generally use the Afrikaans name Voetoog.

Thus the Nama tale complex on the first layer is connected with the /Xam variants, on the second with !Kung-Nharo-Hei//om-Damara variants, and on the third with Afrikaans folk belief. If we add that the Afrikaans component was grafted on to another Cape Khoisan tradition, we realise that we must also consider the trickster stories, the essence of Khoisan tales, in the time dimension, as not only synchronous but also diachronous, and as something dynamic and by no means static.

## *THE MAGIC TALES*

Few people would expect magic tales in the sense of German *Märchen* or English fairy tales in the /Xam collection. There are, of course, no fairies, and we have to know some basic elements which distinguish the /Xam stories from what are generally accepted as magic tales. The most important distinction of /Xam magic tales is that they are set in the early time and that the actors are very often 'animal-people' – people with animal names. This, on the one hand, has to be taken as a device to remove the tale from the realistic world into the world of fantasy, in the same way as 'Once upon a time …' introduces an English-speaking audience into the particular realm of this genre of tales. On the other hand, it is related to the old belief systems.

This device is not restricted to /Xam tales. It is used by the !Kung according to Biesele's collection (1975:II,1-11), the Nharo (Bleek 1928b:45-46, cf. KH 972), and especially among the Nama and Damara. In Nama/Damara tradition many a heroine – and many an antagonist – has an animal name and is regarded as a person of the early days. Heroes, or more commonly heroines, are connected with antelopes and small creatures, ogres with carnivores or such dangerous animals as elephants and snakes. But this rule is only a very rough one. Even such a gracious animal as the springbok can appear in the role of the ogre provided the heroine is still smaller: in our example she is a steenbok (KH 932).

As we have Nama/Damara records from the beginning of the nineteenth century we can study this device over time: It can be shown that in the older variants of some tales there are more animal names than in later ones. In Schultze's early version of a very popular magic tale, for instance (1907:514-19), it is a fly, in later recordings usually a woman, who is married to an elephant (KH 925). The rule is that animal heroes have gradually been replaced by humans, but the antagonists remain animals or they turn into the *khoe-oreb* (literally 'man-eater'), the anthropomorphous ogre.

So it can definitely be said that the /Xam tales represent an earlier form of a general Khoisan device.

## *The Young Dog*

### The Characteristics of Khoisan Magic Tales

I have chosen to use this less well-known /Xam tale in order to discuss further characteristics of Khoisan magic tales.

Probably it received its title of 'The Young Dog' because the first sentence runs: 'The Young Dog married into the Quaggas'. But the Quagga woman is the heroine and the Dog as the carnivorous and often detested animal the antagonist:

> The Quagga wife fed her children by secretly giving them pieces of her own liver (probably a symbol for raising her children according to her own tradition amidst a strange world of threatening in-laws). The Tortoise snatched a piece of the liver and let the Jackal, the Hyena and the Blue Crane taste it. They persuaded the Young Dog to kill the Quagga. He struck poisoned pointed bones under her bed and the Quagga was

> hurt. Weakened by the poison she tried to get to the water pool, while her children sang that she might reach it in order to drink. But she died at the pool. The Jackal traced her; he and the other adversaries cut her up and started to feast on her meat. Meanwhile her children sat in the tree. When their tears dropped on to the pots in which the meat was cooking, all the pots burst and nothing of the meat could be eaten. After a while the Young Dog wanted to marry the sister of his wife. Her parents agreed. But in the (wedding?) dance they trampled the Young Dog to death (Bleek 1936b:180-86; Guenther 1989:98-100).

The character of the tale becomes much clearer when we compare the /Xam text with the three Nama and the three Damara variants. In these the heroine is a young giraffe woman, a zebra woman or a Nama woman. The antagonists are either the Jackal, the carnivorous animal, or the ogre Khoe-oreb, the Man-eater (KH 940). A juxtaposition of the different variants also illuminates several general particularities of /Xam as well as Khoisan magic tales.

Occasionally the heroine is a young girl who finally marries a prince or a chieftain's son; more often she is a young woman already married, having one or more children. The end of a magic tale does not correspond to the cliché of our fairy tales. This /Xam tale represents the type in which the happy ending consists of the revenging of the heroine's death. In the Nama and Damara versions (Schultze 1907:530-32; Schmidt 1980:113-15) the harmony is regained by the second type, the restoration of the woman. Nama/Damara tales have a standard episode for this process: the restoration in the calabash. The details of this process still hint at the people's different economic systems. In magic tales of the Nama – the herders – a part of the dead hero or heroine, usually the heart, is put into a calabash together with milk, and from this the person grows again. In the magic tales of the Damara – the hunter-gatherers – the heart is put into a calabash and set into a warm place; milk, however, is not mentioned. In /Xam texts, the dead heroes are revived by putting a part of them into water (cf. Schmidt 1989:I,312-13 *Wiederbelebung*).

Another difference between Khoisan and European magic tales is the concept of magic. In Khoisan (and also other African) magic tales heroes and heroines sometimes have supernatural abilities. Generally this is not mentioned at the beginning of the tale, but in a critical situation the hero can suddenly perform miraculous deeds. In keeping with the true style of magic tales these deeds are not regarded as miracles by the people in the tales but only by the reader or listener (Lüthi 1962:29). While a considerable section of the

European magic tale is devoted to how the hero achieves magical aid from old men or women or animals, those parts which influence character, contents and structure of the tales, are usually absent in Khoisan narratives. In the /Xam variants the tears of the children supernaturally destroy the meat pots, while the little daughter of the Damara variant throws magical sticks into the pots to make the meat inedible. Nothing is said about where and from whom the girl received the sticks. In the other variant the woman asks the tree to become smaller so that she may climb into it. The tree obeys. Nothing is said about why it does so. The super-normal abilities of the heroes, however, are restricted and do not keep them out of danger or even from death.

## *The Wife of the Dawn's-Heart Star*

### Khoisan and International Magic Tales

It has been noted before that some of the /Xam narratives are also known outside the Khoisan area. The most famous example is that of the All-devourer (Bleek 1924:34-40). A huge monster approaches and swallows everything in its way. It swallows the food with its containers, bushes, a whole herd of sheep and then asks where the food is to which it had been invited. It swallows everybody except a woman with her two young boys. This monster creeps around in the folktales of many of the Bantu-speaking peoples and has instigated much discussion (Dammann 1961; Werner 1968:206-21; Paulme 1976: 277-313; Hewitt 1986a:225-33). It is remarkable, however, to what extent this tale, probably introduced by Bantu-speaking neighbours, has turned into a /Xam tale. It is totally adjusted to the /Kaggen stories and to /Kaggen's character. I believe, therefore, that it must have been absorbed some time before it was recorded.

The story of 'The kwai-kwai bird, the Mantis and the children' (Bleek 1924:45-46) has also some supposed connections with the favourite story of the Nguni and Tswana peoples in which the ogre carries away a child in a drum or other container. The relationship, however, is so distant and the majority of motifs so changed, that this connection has become rather vague.

The story of 'The wife of the dawn's-heart star' is, however, definitely related to further Khoisan as well as to international oral traditions. It is the /Xam representation of the tale of the Substitute Bride. According to the /Xam tale, the young wife went to dig ant chrysalids. A female hyena came and poisoned the chrysalids so that, after eating of them, the young woman gradually turned into a lioness. She hid in the reeds, and as long as she felt like a human being she allowed her little sister to bring her baby for nursing. The Hyena meanwhile tried to take her place with her husband. Later the little sister informed him, but the Hyena was able to escape from his revenge. Next day they prepared the salvation of the wife, who by now had turned completely into a lioness. The little sister called her, and the lioness sprang on to the goats which had been put there as bait – and as a remedy. For the people who had hidden up to this moment killed the goats and rubbed the lioness with their stomach contents until she became a human being again. They only left tufts of hair on the tips of her ears, the characteristics of the lynx, for later this woman of the early race turned into a lynx (Bleek & Lloyd 1911:84-98).

The remedy in this tale, the stomach contents of the *goats*, shows some direct influence from outside the /Xam world. The contents of the stomachs of antelopes had symbolic meaning for the Bushmen in life (Lewis-Williams 1981:60) and in tales it was described above how the sons of the trickster were buried under the stomach contents of the eland or giraffe which they had killed. But here goats are used for the restoration of the heroine and indicate relations with the herders of the neighbourhood. In fact, the whole ceremony echoes widespread rites of the Bantu-speaking peoples. The stomach contents of sacrificial animals (the goats in this tale are not killed by the lioness but by the people who want to redeem her) are mainly a symbol for ritual cleansing (Gutmann 1909:133; Junod 1912: I,101; 1913: II,393-95, 427-28; Dornan 1925:304; Berglund 1976:129-30). Another Bushman group with Bantu contact also uses this remedy today. Thus among the present-day Nharo '... unspecific illnesses may be washed away with the contents of a goat's stomach rubbed on the patient's body' (Barnard 1979:69).

The tale of the 'Substitute Bride' is one of the most popular in many parts of the world (AaTh 403 IV, 450 IV, 533). It is a special favourite of the Nguni peoples. There an animal ogre, the *mbulu*, forces the heroine to change places (Hammond-Tooke 1977; 1988; Kuper 1986:183-94). The scene where the young girl goes to the heroine 'in the otherworld' so that she may nurse her baby is well known among Xhosa (Theal 1910:323-27; Scheub 1975: 386-91) but also among other peoples in Africa, for example, the Balese-Efe (Vorbichler & Brandl 1979:182-85).

Apart from the /Xam form, the 'Substitute Bride' story is very popular among other Khoisan peoples, the !Kung, the Nama and the Damara (KH 972 A-C). Their versions form clearly distinguishable subtypes in which characters, setting and motifs differ considerably: the !Kung versions tell about the python girl, the Nama/Damara versions about a Nama or Damara woman; the impostors are represented by the jackal in the !Kung, the frog-woman in the Nama and, probably due to Herero influence, a ghost woman in the Damara versions (cf. Dammann 1987:70-81). In addition, there are several forms of the story which the Nama adapted some generations ago from Europeans. These are similar tales added as episodes to 'Cinderella' and other heroine stories in order to portray a second calamity which befell the heroine after the happy marriage (AaTh 403). And to conclude the summary of variations, I recorded a version of Grimm's 'The Speaking Horsehead' (AaTh 533) which had been skilfully reshaped from alleged oral tradition (KH 972D).

All these adaptations of the 'Substitute Bride' are considered by the narrators as the ancient heritage of their forefathers. Yet we can clearly recognise variants of recent and fairly recent adaptation, and, on the other hand, those redactions which have really turned the tale into expressions of the narrator's world and world-view. Not only are the scenery and equipment completely changed into the local ones but the fundamental ideas of Khoisan folklore are in place. Here the /Xam and !Kung texts stand foremost. Both have been set into the 'early time', and heroes as well as imposters receive animal names.

The !Kung texts even end with the basic topic of Khoisan lore: the change from the primeval to the present world (Biesele 1975:I,220-21, II:7). We know that this cannot be original because the story must have been absorbed from foreign sources at a certain time. But this ending fits perfectly into the present state of the text. For the text now is a real Bushman text and certainly it must have been so for a long time. The same is true for our /Xam text which, as a further element, shows the /Xam peculiarity, the connection with astral lore. I suppose, therefore, that these texts were adapted quite a number of years before or, more likely, generations ago. They are testimony of early contact with Bantu-speaking peoples.

## *LEGENDS*

The /Xam had only one word for stories and did not distinguish any genres. The word *kum* (pl. *kukummi*) even included conversation and news (Hewitt 1986a:47). The Nama and Damara, however, speak of */oro /garuben* (old stories) or *isede* (things that happened) respectively and set them apart from reports on present-day life. It happened repeatedly that people who told stories to me emphasised: 'But what I am going to tell now, that is not an old story, this really happened!' And they told something extraordinary which, nevertheless, I would have classified as a folktale: a legend or an anecdote. These people distinguish between tales which tell of a far-off past and tales of the present or recent past. The first group includes myths, tales of anthropomorphous and zoomorphous tricksters as well as magic tales; the second group includes legends and anecdotes. Roughly speaking, the first group is considered as fiction, the second as possible fact. This is a very rough generalisation. Some myths certainly were truth to people in former times while many of the jokes and anecdotes are mere fiction. There are tales that in some variants are told as fact and in others as fiction.

Legends comprise a broad spectrum of subjects. A main theme is confrontation with the numinous world. While in the stories of the early time and in magic tales the conflicts are set into a faraway realm, legends describe how the numinous, demoniacal forces penetrate into the human world. In most cases this confrontation leads to a victory of these forces and human beings either perish or have a narrow escape. The atmosphere in the tales of the early time is light, and in the end harmony is achieved; the atmosphere of legends, however, is usually gloomy. The reaction of the audience to the former is delight, to the latter fear and awe.

I want to discuss only two items: The first deals with a cluster of tales told only by the /Xam, based, however, on beliefs that were common to several ethnic groups in southern Africa. The second is devoted to the question of whether the /Xam actually knew the general laws of legend-telling, and to what extent the interpretation of legend texts might depend on the observation of these laws.

## *The Cautionary Stories about !Khwa*

### The Interrelatedness of Beliefs

A considerable number of /Xam tales report on girls who violated the rules of first menstruation. They tell about the awful consequences for the girls themselves, and also for their community, brought forth by their disobedience. These tales are remarkable in several ways.

In the first place it is their large number within the /Xam repertoire which points to the importance and popularity they must have had. This contrasts sharply with their absence in the other Khoisan groups. There is only one rather confused account which the missionary Schmelen noted in his diary after an interview with Namib Bushmen in 1815: The ocean was made by a girl during her first menstruation. She angrily mixed the sweet and the bitter waters so that from then on the sea water has been undrinkable (Schmelen 1815:15; Schmidt 1979a:61-62). This story is proof that in the Central Language Group of Khoisan tales beliefs of this kind probably also existed. Though I asked many Nama and Damara women who had passed the first-menstruation ceremonies in obedience to the old traditions, they all denied that during the seclusion there was any instruction by such cautionary tales, and none of them had ever met with tales of this kind. The second remarkable feature is that many of these /Xam tales are set into the time of the early race, and, similar to the Namib Bushman version, the creation of stars and animals resulted from the girls' wrong behaviour.

The group of /Xam tales set in the present world includes !Khwa, the personified Rain or Water. He is the bogey who punishes the misdeeds of the girls. In the tales themselves it does not become clear how this figure has to be visualised. At other places, in tale and in folk belief, he appears in the form of a bull. This Rain or Water Bull is said to live in the deep water but to leave the water at night in order to graze outside. It was a task of the rain medicine men to catch this animal with a thong and to lead it around the country so that rain may fall there (Bleek 1933b: Orpen [1874], 1919:155). How this ancient image was adapted to the trance visions of the medicine men was meticulously described by Lewis-Williams (1979).

Moreover, the /Xam said that the Rain Bull was in the clouds (Lewis-Williams & Dowson 1988:204). This belief of the Rain Bull or Cow that stayed in a deep pond or in the rain clouds was alive in large areas of southern Africa. The Lake Chrissie Bushmen talked about a bull in the fountain (Potgieter 1955:31), the Nama of Alexander's time did the same (1838:II,198). Present-day /Khobesin of Namibia know Turos, the Rain Cow, that comes down from the clouds during heavy rains in order to live in deep places of the Fish River (Schmidt 1979b:205), and even today in the home country of the Bleek informants, the 'Khoekhoe' are said to believe that there is the Water Bull in the clouds which works together with the lightning: if you look up it enrages the Water Bull, and then lightning will kill you (Van der Merwe 1987:28). The *Waterbul* or *Waterbees* has penetrated into Afrikaans folklore and was recorded from Higgshope, Hopetown and Aurora (Coetzee 1960:38-39).

This figure of South African folk belief cannot be regarded as a heritage of the Bushmen alone. It is only understood when it is seen in relation to further folk belief regarding water and weather personifications. Side by side or even intermingled with the water bull or cow are real snakes, mythical giant snakes, but also water kudu and other antelope, as well as their various blended forms. They must date back to early humankind. The image of the *bull* as a personification of water and of weather deities is found in other parts of the world, too. It is best known from the ancient Near East, and most likely the Bushman image was also related to this concept.

Thus this group of legends about !Khwa has two faces: the stories are restricted to the /Xam, but the underlying folk belief is widespread in time and space.

## *A Lion Pursued a Lonely Girl*

### The Laws of Legend-telling

In this section I want to discuss briefly the general basic laws of legend-telling, whether they were known by Khoisan peoples and to what extent they were applied by the /Xam.

The field of legends is usually shunned by anthropologists. Those texts which are obviously not connected with mythical times are especially avoided, for most of them are rather bewildering for a modern Westerner. A typical example of such legends is the account by Dia!kwain about his sister's adventure, which she had told him herself:

When the girl was walking by herself from Kenhardt, she was attacked by an owl. This was a sign for her that a beast of prey was near. She therefore lit a fire so that the animal might think that she was warming herself, but she sneaked away. Soon she discovered a lion. He had looked for her at the fire in vain and was now following her spoor. In order to evade a sudden attack she climbed on to a rock. There the lion lost the spoor of the girl. He called her by name and asked her to pull him up the rock. The girl remembered that lions sometimes put their tails into their mouths and then talk like human beings. In this way they entice people to speak and thereby betray their hiding-places. The girl, therefore, remained silent and was able to save herself (Bleek 1932a: 47-50).

This is evidently a true story from the point of view of the narrator, but the reader has certain doubts as to its actual reality. A closer look reveals that the narrator uses the typical devices commonly applied in legend-telling. His aim is to tell the story as a true story. It is set, therefore, in his own neighbourhood and exact place-names are inserted: the girl went away from Kenhardt, the lion was sitting on the Brinkkop hill. Generally legend-tellers also like to give precise information on the time of happening. As time, however, was not considered of equal importance among the hunter-gatherers, no reference to time is given here. The third device of legend-telling in achieving credibility is to attribute the adventure to a person of one's acquaintance or family. This is carried on even in Western contemporary urban legends which are usually told as experiences of a 'friend of a friend'. Dia!kwain depicted his own elder sister as the heroine. I doubt whether she really met a lion! But I am sure he had heard strange things that lions are sometimes capable of doing.

The device of attributing such reports to people of one's own social group is known from other Khoisan areas as well. A !Kung informant portrayed how he himself went to the people without knees and watched how they slept by leaning against the forks of trees (Thomas 1988:146). An inhabitant of Gibeon assured me that it was the person himself who had lived among the baboons that had given him the information (Schmidt 1977). A Bondelswart woman even described to me that her sister was caught by the Great Watersnake, lived with him under the water, bore him several children but was then freed by her father. The audience is probably used to such devices and tactfully abstains from further questions.

The contents of legends are mainly based on folk belief. The connection of the owl with carnivorous animals and the ability of the lion to talk like a person as soon as he puts his tail into his mouth seem to be such elements of folk belief. They can easily be understood when the links of owl and lion as night animals and lion and sorcerer are considered. In addition, there is the popular tale motif of the lion or hyena who greedily wanted to be pulled up a rock in order to get the meat that the jackal trickily offered (KH 473). Bleek's narrator himself used the same motif extensively in his tale 'Jackal and Hyena' (Guenther 1989:147-49).

This observation of general laws of legend-telling and the indication of their validity for the /Xam legends are a warning for those who study similar texts. Was it really Dia!kwain's aunt who visited them in the shape of a lion (Bleek 1935a:43-47)? Was it the friend of Dia!kwain's grandfather who in the shape of a lion killed the Boer's ox (Bleek 1936a:131-34)? Did //Xabbiten//xabbiten tell his adventure with the baboons to Dia!kwain? Did he really experience this himself (Bleek & Lloyd 1911:254-59)? Von Wielligh told the same story in a manner which hints at its existence as a common joke in the area (Von Wielligh 1917-1921:II,61-66).

The few /Xam stories which treat the tense relationship with the Korana have to be grouped in the same category: they are represented as 'true' reports of actual happenings in connection with Korana raids. But most likely they are legends that clad traditional narrative material in a local garment. The story of the little boy who was left alive by his enemies and warned his family is the best example (KH 1570). Besides the /Xam text there are a Nama, a Hei//om, two Damara and two Nharo texts (Guenther 1989:152-56) available. Each is adapted to the last raids the group had experienced and each is realistically depicted. Yet even the element that the boy gives his warning in a song is represented as the centre of the story in the /Xam, the Nama and one of the Damara variants.

The /Xam tales, however, are bewildering in that they are 'true' tales and at the same time are set in the world of the early race; this would involve those legends which had been told to the narrators more or less as tales and not as folk belief.

## *CONCLUSION*

The /Xam tales are deeply imbedded in the general Khoisan folklore. It was my intention to give some examples of this relationship. Many of the /Xam tales not only share topics with other Khoisan tales but share numerous other elements too.

The underlying concept is the idea of the early time in which the world was different from now and in which animals were still people. This is known to all Khoisan peoples but its presence varies in the tale genres. The trickster tales are set in the early time by all Khoisan peoples: the magic tales by the /Xam totally, and by other Khoisan peoples to varying degrees. The greatest difference becomes obvious in the treatment of legends. Though a number of /Xam legends apply the general devices of legend telling in order to stress 'truth', a certain number are mixed with the elements of the early-race conceptions. The Nama-speaking peoples, on the other hand, distinguish more clearly between tales of the early time and those of the present and near past.

Another element common to the folklore of all Khoisan peoples is the different treatment of certain topics in folk belief and folk tale. This is most prominent in the representation of the trickster in belief and the trickster in tale. Common to the folklore of all Khoisan peoples is also the diverging evaluation of characters in the individual genres: the lion of belief and legend is frightening in the extreme, and in the animal trickster tales he is the dupe of whom fun is made. Jackal and Hare are celebrated heroes if they act as protagonists of trickster tales (under foreign influences?), but in the ancient Khoisan magic tales they represent life-threatening forces.

There are, however, notable differences between the /Xam and the remaining Khoisan narratives. The /Xam tales contain a number of characters with animal names which, neither by intellect nor by emotion, can Westeners fit into the hero-opponent pattern of folk tales and are thus unable to understand or to identify with them. I think of the Blue Crane, the Frog, Ostriches and various birds. In the /Xam area there are favourite motifs and tale patterns, especially in the /Kaggen tale cluster (/Kaggen's flight into the water, the order to his equipment to go home by itself, /Kwammang-a's admonitions given via the Ichneumon, /Kaggen's dreams and their realisations); they are absent in other areas altogether. On the other hand, tales and motifs which are popular in other Khoisan areas are missing in the Bleek and Lloyd Collection. The Jackal and Hyena tales, the favourites in present-day Namibia, appear only in a negligible number. This leaves us with the question which has to be put again and again: did the collectors not record them because they considered them borrowings from a foreign culture or had the tales not yet penetrated into the region?

The juxtaposition of /Xam and other Khoisan tales and a comparison of variants helps us to understand the /Xam texts better. It illustrates many a character, motif or device. It opens up the path for considering tales and their spiritual background in a time dimension and demonstrates their durability. But it also warns us not to overemphasise particular elements of an individual variant.

# 'A Visit to the Lion's House'

## The Structure, Metaphors and Socio-political Significance of a Nineteenth-century Bushman Myth

J D Lewis-Williams

On 18 September 1871 //Kabbo, one of Wilhelm Bleek's and Lucy Lloyd's most prolific /Xam Bushman (San) informants, began a long narrative about the trickster-deity somewhat misleadingly known as the Mantis (/Kaggen; for discussions of this name see Schmidt 1973; Lewis-Williams 1981:117-26; Hewitt 1986a:140-42; Barnard 1992:84-85). Using a phonetic script developed by Bleek, Lloyd took down the narrative verbatim in the /Xam language; the dictation of the tale continued, with breaks, until early October 1871 (L.II.4.482-86; 489-529; 5.530-624). Despite the time involved, the rather tedious way of recording the informant's words and, for //Kabbo, the unnaturalness of the circumstances, the story is remarkably structured and never seems to ramble; many of //Kabbo's narratives wander quite considerably.

When Dorothea Bleek prepared the narrative for publication in 1924, she divided it into four separate tales, *The Mantis makes an eland*, *A visit to the Lion's house*, *The Mantis and the cat* and *The Mantis and the tortoise* (Bleek 1924: 2-5, 15-18, 19-21); the last of these (L.II.5.565-624) remains only partially translated and unpublished. Bleek gave no indication that the published parts were narrated consecutively. Her breaking up of the narrative was, however, not entirely without justification because each of the sections can stand as a complete story and was no doubt performed separately.

Moreover, each section has a ternary form that, I argue, derived from the /Xam world-view and from a set of metaphors that came out of the most profound experience open to the /Xam. Indeed, the ternary structure of each of the sections may be, at least in part, a product of this experience and therefore lie at the heart of /Xam thought and belief. The various ways in which //Kabbo elaborated manifestations of this experience in each of the three published sections point to his manipulation of the narrative for his own socio-political ends. Instead of ascribing any rigidity to structure, we should think of it as an elastic resource that could be stretched in many different ways to suit the narrator. Its reproduction in broad terms in every performance facilitated contact between narrator and auditors, but, at the same time, each performance was a conscious transformation that recursively modified the structure.

This tension between structure and performance can be discerned in *A visit to the Lion's house*, of which I give a summary; the other two published sections of //Kabbo's narrative will be dealt with elsewhere.

## *THE MYTH*

> /Kwammang-a, the Mantis's son-in-law, told the Mantis's family that the Lions, relatives of his, had killed a quagga, and that he and his son, the Ichneumon, would go to the Lions' camp. The Mantis wanted to accompany them, but the Ichneumon warned him that he would be afraid of the Lions. The Mantis, however, got his way, and they set off.
>
> When they came across the Lions' spoor, the Ichneumon identified the individuals to whom they belonged. Then they saw quagga's blood on the ground, and /Kwammang-a exclaimed that they would surely soon be eating quagga meat. They continued following the Lions' spoor until they came to a waterhole where they found the Lions.
>
> The Mantis was at once afraid and asked the Ichneumon to hide him in his bag so that the Lions would not see him. He also asked the Ichneumon to place an ostrich eggshell of water in the bag so that he would be able to drink, to leave the mouth of the bag open so that he would be able to see what was happening, and to cover him with a kaross (antelope skin cloak).
>
> Soon the little Lion spotted the Mantis looking out of the bag and went crying to his mother because the Mantis was whispering in the bag. When he saw the Mantis a second time, he ran to his mother again, and begged her to take what he saw as a little hare out of the bag. When the little Lion went to the bag a third time, the Mantis winked at him and said that he would like to poke out his eye. The little Lion again ran back to his mother.
>
> The Lioness, angered by what the Mantis was doing to her child,

> came up to the bag and tried to stamp on the Mantis to crush him. But the Mantis jumped out of the bag, got feathers and flew up into the sky. The Ichneumon threw him up into the sky. As he went, he called upon his bag, shoes, quiver, kaross and cap to follow him. Boasting that no one was his equal, he dived into the waterhole. Coming out of the water, he called upon his possessions to wait for him until he had dried himself. His possessions wanted to leave him, but he commanded them to remain there. After the feathers had been washed off and he had dried himself, he returned to his own camp.
>
> There he deceived his wife, the Dassie, and his adopted daughter, the Porcupine, telling them that the Lions had eaten /Kwammang-a and the Ichneumon. But when they saw the two coming laden with quagga meat, they realised that the Mantis had deceived them. While /Kwammang-a sat in silent anger, the Ichneumon lectured the Mantis on good behaviour.

In a passage Dorothea Bleek omitted (L.II.5.536-534) from her 1924 publication, the Ichneumon retells much of the story for the benefit of the Dassie and the Porcupine.

Before examining the narrative structure of this myth and the metaphors embedded in it, I consider two interlocking cosmological axes that constitute, as it were, the stage on which the action is played out.

## COSMOLOGY

A reading of the Bleek and Lloyd Collection suggests that the /Xam cosmos may be understood to have been structured on two intersecting axes, horizontal and vertical. Each axis was divided into two major areas with a shared transitional zone between them (Figure 1). Nevertheless, all realms of San cosmology interdigitate; the bi-axial schema is an analytical construct.

The extremities of the horizontal axis were the camp and the hunting-ground, or open veld. The camp comprised a number of grass dwellings. The /Xam word *//nein*, translated in the title of the tale as 'house', means an individual dwelling but was also used to mean a camp comprising a number of dwellings. The *//nein* was where the norms of society were dramatised and reinforced; here were the people to whom one was most closely related and whom one knew best; here the meat sharing and curing rituals were performed. It was an essentially social context with associations of safety, dependability and co-operation.

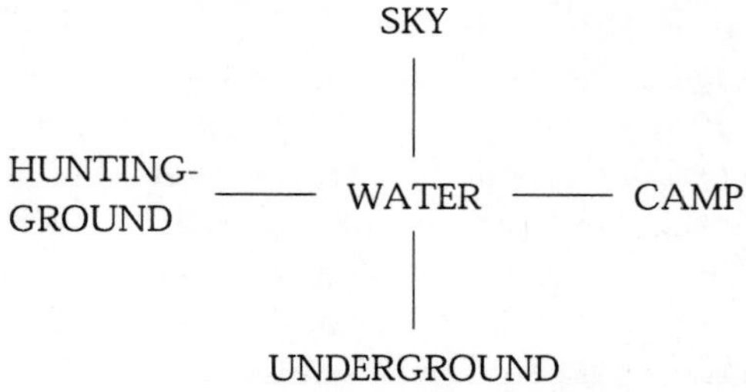


***Figure 1.*** *Diagram showing the two intersecting axes of /Xam cosmology.*

The hunting-ground was in direct opposition to the camp: it was characterised by strangers and essentially anti-social associations. It was an area of danger and uncertainty, the domain of the tricky and unpredictable situations of the hunt. This uncertainty extended to the people who lived out there: they were unfamiliar, sometimes threatening. The animal which most typically characterised the hunting-ground was the 'angry' lion.

Between the camp and the hunting ground was the waterhole. Groups established their camps up to a mile and more from a waterhole to avoid frightening away the game which, like the people, depended on water in the inhospitable, semi-arid terrain south of the Orange River. The waterhole was thus the meeting place of people who may have been camped some miles apart; Heinz (1966) specifies the waterhole as the place of social contact between members of a !Kõ band nexus. Moreover, in many of the tales water plays a transformative role. For instance, an ostrich feather, placed in a waterhole, was said to grow into an ostrich (Bleek & Lloyd 1911: 137-45). At the same time, the waterhole was the place where people and the dangerous animals of the hunting-ground met, sometimes with frightening or tragic results. While the associations of the camp were positive and those of the hunting ground generally negative, the intermediary water was ambivalent: positive because it provided life for both people and animals and because it was regenerative, but also negative because of the dangerous encounters that could take place there, again with both people and animals.

Less is known about the vertical axis, perhaps because it was more especially associated with supernatural things (cf. Biesele 1978). Ordinary people lived exclusively on the horizontal axis, but shamans could also traverse the vertical axis. It comprised a realm above, the sky, and a realm beneath the surface of the earth. So far it has not been possible to differentiate these extremities as clearly as those of the horizontal axis.

The realm below seems, none the less, to have been associated with the dead. //Kabbo told Lloyd that the dead – Bushmen, Boers and animals – all walked the same path to one great hole in the ground where they continued to exist (L.II.6.669 rev.). Beliefs about the dead and an afterlife do not, however, seem to have been well developed or formalised, and ≠Kasin gave a slightly different account. He said, 'Our thoughts ascending, leave us, while our bodies are those which are in (or lie in?) the earth' (L.IV.1.3445; Lloyd's parenthesis). Dia!kwain, on the other hand, said that his mother had told him that the crescent moon carried the dead, though this belief seems to have been more associated with omens, because she went on to say that the 'hollow moon' meant that the people would soon receive news of a death (Bleek and Lloyd 1911:399).

Apart from this belief about the moon, the sky – the realm above – was associated with spirits, shamans and the Mantis. Dia!kwain said, 'When a sorcerer [*!gi:xa*, shaman] dies, his heart comes out in the sky and becomes a star.' He added that a shaman's 'magic' [*!gi:di*, literally, deed of supernatural potency] made the star so that his body could 'walk about' (Bleek 1935a:24). Because the rest of this passage is clearly not about physical death, it seems likely that Dia!kwain was using 'dies' in a common metaphorical sense to mean that the shaman was entering the spirit world (trance). In addition to stars, lightning was said to be caused by two men, one of whom was a rain-shaman, fighting with each other (Bleek & Lloyd 1911:113-19). The Mantis was also associated with the sky. Arbousset and Daumas (1846:253) found that he was known as 'Chief in the sky', and /Han≠kass'o told Lloyd that the Mantis and /Kwammang-a together constituted the rainbow: the Mantis was the yellow part, while /Kwammang-a was the red part (Bleek 1924:66). Similar beliefs were recorded by Dornan (1909:443) and Potgieter (1955:29).

As on the horizontal axis, the extremities of the vertical axis – the underworld and the sky – were mediated by water which both wells up in waterholes and falls from the sky. As we shall see, shamans spoke of entering a waterhole, travelling underground and then climbing up into the sky where they confronted god. Biesele (personal communication) found similar notions among the !Kung. The place of water in the bi-axial schema is emphasised by the /Xam word *!khwa* which means both rain and water. Water was the point of intersection between the two axes; shared by both, it derived some of its power from its unique position at the point of articulation.

## *NARRATIVE STRUCTURE*

The narrative structure of *A visit to the Lion's house* is built on these intersecting axes, with water providing access from one to the other. Three episodes may be discerned (cf. Hewitt 1986a:182). In the initial episode, the myth starts in the Mantis's camp and moves out to the hunting-ground via the waterhole. The central episode is characterised by movement on the vertical axis: the Mantis dives into the waterhole, flies up into the sky and then comes down to the ground to dry off. In the third episode, the action returns to the camp.

### *Initial Episode*

At the beginning of the myth, everything in the camp is normal and well ordered. The manifest motivation is introduced when /Kwammang-a announces that they will go to the Lion's house to obtain quagga meat. Numerous early travellers who met the /Xam in the eighteenth and nineteenth centuries were impressed by the way in which meat was invariably shared. Lichtenstein (1930(2):63), for instance, described the arrival of people after a large kill, a circumstance which vividly recalls the visit to the Lion's house: the visitors came 'without any ceremony, or waiting for an invitation to partake of it'. The same apparent magnanimity still obtains in the Kalahari where sharing rules have been documented. Among the !Kung, for instance, an animal belongs to the person who owns the fatal arrow; he is often, but not necessarily, the man who discharged the shot; sometimes the owner is a woman (Marshall 1961; on the relationship between San ethnographies see Lewis-Williams & Biesele 1978; Lewis-Williams 1981). It is this person's responsibility to see to the equitable distribution of the meat according to rules informed by the kinship system; symbolic statements made by meat-sharing are statements about kinship. Although we cannot be sure that identical rules operated among the /Xam, it is likely that at least a broadly similar sharing pattern ensured that everyone received a portion. So it seems probable that the Mantis's access to the Lions' quagga meat was through /Kwammang-a. The owner of the meat, one of the Lions, would have handed a portion to their relative, /Kwammang-a, who would have passed some of it on to his father-in-law, perhaps via his son, the Ichneumon; the Mantis would not have enjoyed direct access to the meat. Furthermore, his fear of the Lions and his subsequent behaviour suggest that the relationship between him and his affines was strained.

No such tension characterises the Ichneumon's response to seeing the

Lions' footprints near the water: he and his father are evidently eager to join their consanguinial kin. The Ichneumon's recognition of the tracks left by individual members of his father's family suggests that he knows them well; the !Kung are still able to recognise the footprints of individuals (Marshall 1960:336; see also Heinz 1966).

## *Central Episode*

All the events so far have been 'normal' in the sense that they could have happened in any Bushman camp. By contrast, the central episode comprises a set of 'non-normal', preternatural events, and the social order falls apart when the Mantis offends the Lions. Hewitt (1986a:182,189) explains the supernatural events in terms of 'magic', but I argue that each of the events is in some way related to trance experience and Bushman shamanism; it is the activities and experiences of shamans that explain the otherwise bizarre central section of the myth. Because these non-sense happenings hold the key to an understanding of the whole myth, each must be analysed in some detail. As Freilich (1975:211) remarks, 'Other things being equal, the 'madder' the non-sense, the more hidden meanings it contains' (cf. Hammond-Tooke 1977).

The non-sense events start when the Mantis gets into the Ichneumon's bag. Bags are, of course, made of animal skin, usually that of a small antelope. Silberbauer (1981:132) points out that for the G/wi Bushmen of the central Kalahari the sharing of some noun stems by artefacts and the raw material from which they are made suggests that the G/wi feel that the process of manufacture does not destroy the essential identity and nature of the material used. Whether Silberbauer is right or wrong about this linguistic point, the /Xam Bushmen seem to have entertained a similar idea. An arrow, for instance, was *!nwa*, the same word for reed, the raw material from which arrows were made (Bleek 1956:487; Bleek 1933a:300; cf. Maingard 1937:278 on the /Auni). The /Xam also spoke of quivers made from springbok skin reverting, under supernatural circumstances, to springbok (Bleek 1933a:300). The artefact was never far removed from the raw material. Getting into a bag was thus in some ways like 'getting into an animal' and, I now argue, like entering the spirit world of trance.

In the first place, entry into that world was achieved through the activation of a supernatural potency, or essence, that was believed to reside in, amongst other things, antelope. A /Xam shaman possessed, or owned, the potency of a specific animal or two. Secondly, scent was believed to be a vehicle for the transference of this potency. For instance, the scent of a /Xam shaman's nasal blood was believed to keep sickness away from a person on whom he rubbed it (Bleek 1935a:34). Similarly, the potency of a !Kung shaman is said to be in his sweat and in the smell that comes from his burning hair (ibid.:371). The !Kung also believe that it is the scent of a whirlwind that goes into people and harms them (Marshall 1962:239) and that the potency of medicine plants and supernatural substances is in their smell (Marshall 1969:360, 371). These two points suggest that the act of getting into a bag implied not just 'getting into an animal' but immersing oneself in the scent and the potency of an animal; inside a bag, the scent of the animal from which the bag was made is strong. It therefore seems probable that the Mantis was absorbing an animal's potency, the first stage of effecting his entry into the spirit world of trance experience.

The concept of transformation that this action implies is further developed by the Ichneumon's placing of a kaross over the Mantis in response to his request. Karosses, like bags, were made from antelope skin, and the /Xam believed that they could revert to antelope under certain supernatural circumstances. An 'angry' rain, for instance, was said to turn karosses back into springbok (Bleek 1933a:300). Karosses were, moreover, sometimes associated with the activities of shamans:

> A man who is a sorcerer will not lay down his kaross, even if it is hot, because he knows that the place will not seem hot to him, for his inside is cold. Therefore if he puts the kaross down, he would shiver, he would be cold. For the doings of sorcery [*//ke:n-ka didi*, literally, 'the deeds of supernatural potency'] are not easy. (Bleek 1935a:13)

These beliefs about karosses are expressed in rock paintings that depict shamans partially transformed into antelope: the shoulders and head are of an antelope, but lower down the body there is the clear edge of a kaross (Figure 2). Both the paintings and the ethnography thus suggest that putting on, or being covered by, a kaross could, under certain circumstances associated with shamanism, be akin to taking on not only the potency but also the form of an antelope.

While the Mantis was covered with the kaross and hidden in the Ichneumon's bag, he frightened the little Lion in three ways. I consider each in turn.

First, he was 'whispering' in the bag. The /Xam word here is *kweiten kweiten*, which the *Bushman Dictionary* (Bleek 1956:112) gives as 'to whisper, speak softly', but it seems to have been associated with conspiratorial circumstances.

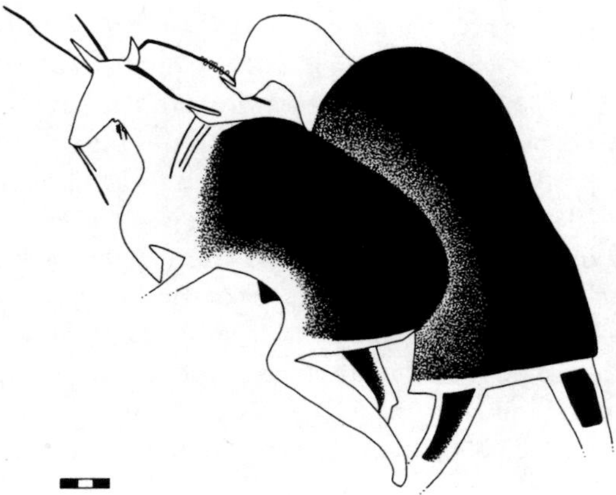

***Figure 2**. Drakensberg rock painting of shamans transformed into eland; now in the South African Museum, Cape Town. Note lower edges of the karosses.*

For instance, in *The Mantis makes an eland,* the Ichneumon, /Kwammang-a and the Porcupine plan to trap the Mantis in the act of stealing honey: 'They were plotting together; the Ichneumon whispered, Kwammang-a also whispered, the Porcupine whispered' (Bleek 1924:3; L.II.4.503 rev.). It may have been this conspiratorial connotation of *kweiten kweiten* that first frightened the little Lion.

The second time, the Mantis causes trouble by turning himself into a hare. The little Lion springs back and goes crying to his mother: 'O mammy, take out for me the little Hare, which is in the Ichneumon's bag!' It is not entirely clear here whether he is afraid of the hare or whether he simply wants the hare, though his crying out and jumping back do suggest fright. Hewitt (1986a:189), on the other hand, suggests that the Lions may have mistakely believed that the hare was a 'token gift' and that the resulting confusion emphasises the 'anti-socialness of what actually did occur'. Be that as it may, hares have specific associations in /Xam myths and beliefs. The Mantis was believed to possess certain hares which distracted hunters who were after gemsbok, one of his favourite creatures. He also turned himself into a hare so that if he were killed by the hunter who had wounded a gemsbok, the gemsbok would recover from the poison and escape (Bleek 1924:12). The hare was thus one of the Mantis's 'anti-social' manifestations, a creature that he used in order to thwart human endeavour.

Lastly, 'the Mantis shut one eye and winked [*dabba*] at him'. In the Ichneumon's recounting of the incident we are told that the little Lion 'thought the Mantis was bewitching [*tsweiten tsweiten*, a word not given in the *Dictionary*] him when he did this' (L.II.5.539). Clearly, 'wink' is not an appropriate translation of //Kabbo's word *dabba*. The *Dictionary* lists the verb as 'to wink, blink, twinkle, open and shut eyes'. Only one example of its use as a noun is given: 'a person who seems to be dying, his eyes' blinking is there' (Bleek 1956:20). A development of the connotation of death is found in an account of dreams and rain that Dia!kwain gave to his wife: 'Then father's eye blinked [*dabba dabba*] at me ... it acted as if rain were going to fall.' Dia!kwain continued:

> You did not look when I told you that I had been dreaming of father, you did not see that someone's eye was blinking [*dabba dabba*] there. It was the eye blinking [*dabba dabbaken*] of a person who seemed to be dying. Because of that you are going to see rain water which will pour down like this. (Bleek 1932c:327-28)

*Dabba* is thus associated with dying, causing rain to fall (or foretelling it) and 'bewitching'. All these ideas are linked to shamanism. When Bushman shamans enter trance, they are said to 'die' (Katz 1982); they make rain (Bleek 1933b); they foretell the future; and they can harm people (Bleek 1935a:29). We can now see that the 'winking' incident ties in with the other four elements of the central episode, getting into a bag, covering with a kaross, 'whispering' (conspiring) and transformation into a hare, in that it too is in some way associated with shamanism.

Together, these five elements have set the stage for an important element in Bushman shamanistic beliefs: conflict in the spirit realm. Although the Lions are the Mantis's affines, there is evidence suggesting that they are, at the same time, another category of being, shamans in feline form. When a /Xam shaman became very violent in trance, lion's hair was said to grow on him

(Bleek 1935a:2); in other words, he began to change into a lion. Similarly, a !Kō Bushman claimed that a shaman in feline form is able to 'mix with' a pride of lions without fear (Heinz 1975:29). In this way shamans are believed to be able to drive off threatening lions and thus protect people at night. A !Kung shaman described such people as 'lions of god' and added that 'they were real lions, different from normal lions, but no less real' (Katz 1982:115). Indeed, the !Kung use the word for 'pawed-creature' (*jum*) to mean 'to go on out-of-body travel in the form of a lion' (Biesele personal communication). They say that hostile shamans maraud in leonine form (Katz 1982:227). So powerful was a man in the form of a lion that the nineteenth-century /Xam believed that a lion that did not die when it had been shot was in reality a shaman (Bleek & Lloyd 1911:187). These ideas inform Bushman hallucinations of battles between beneficent shamans and evil, feline shamans: 'The great healers [shamans] went hunting as lions, searching for people to kill. Then someone would shoot an arrow or throw a spear into those healers who were prowling around as lions' (Katz 1982:227).

In view of the setting created by the non-sense happenings, it seems likely that the Mantis's threat to poke out the little Lion's eye may be seen in terms of this kind of preternatural shamanistic conflict. The poking out of the eye may not have been simply infliction of blindness and, perhaps, physical death, but the destruction of the little Lion's shamanistic ability to 'see' into the future and to far away places; shamans are seers. After having 'winked' and having turned himself into a hare, it was the Mantis's explicit threat of injury that provoked the Lioness to retaliate: she stamped up to him and stood on him 'to crush him' (Bleek 1924:16). Here the Mantis seems to be conceived as an insect, a *mantis religioso*, that can be stamped on, a transformation that follows his becoming a hare. We are moving further and further away from the 'realistic' Bushman that the Mantis was at the beginning of the tale.

The insect transformation is not, however, indicative of vulnerability; instead it facilitates his escape, for he then 'got feathers' and 'flew up into the sky'. This change may refer to a praying mantis's ability to transform itself from what is apparently a stick into a flying creature with large, spreading wings. In any event, flight is a universal image of trance: all over the world shamans interpret the sense of weightlessness and changes in perspective that certain altered states of consciousness create as flying to distant and strange realms (see, for example, Eliade 1972).

By flying and what flight implies, the Mantis leaves the horizontal axis of /Xam cosmology and moves along the vertical axis. Having gone up into the sky, he descends into the water. Being underwater is, like flight, a Bushman metaphor for trance: both conditions entail weightlessness, difficulty in breathing, affected vision, a sense of being in another world, inhibited movement and, eventually, unconsciousness (Lewis-Williams 1980; Lewis-Williams & Dowson 1989:54-55). Indeed, his descent into the waterhole seems to be closely linked to his flight because the Ichneumon, in his retelling of the incident, says, 'The Mantis was in the water, *because* [he] had flown through the sky. *Therefore* he went into the water' (L.II.5.540-541; emphases added). The same set of ideas, though in a different sequence, was expressed by a !Kung shaman who spoke of going underground, entering a stream, and then climbing up into the sky until he reached the god's dwelling (Biesele 1980:54-62). In other words, by switching from the 'realistic' horizontal axis to the 'supernatural' vertical axis, a change facilitated by shamanic powers, the Mantis escapes from the Lions and is able to return home.

## *Final Episode*

When the Mantis arrives at his home he causes his wife and daughter great distress by telling them that the Lions have killed /Kwammang-a and the Ichneumon. In the published version this deception appears to be another example of the Mantis's antisocial behaviour. No doubt that is partially true, but in the Ichneumon's unpublished retelling of the story and in a sentence Dorothea Bleek unfortunately altered in the published version the Mantis explains why he deceived them: 'I wanted them to come carrying quagga meat' (L.II.5.536 and 544). The apparent contradiction here is probably explained by the Bushman customs of responding evasively when asked if they have made a successful kill and of deliberately underestimating the amount of meat on an animal. A /Xam man returning from a successful eland hunt did not say to the people in the camp, 'I have shot an eland'; instead he told them 'that a bush must have pricked his foot' (Bleek 1932b:236). He also avoided telling them that the eland he had shot was fat: 'He tells the people that the eland is lean, and does not tell them that the eland is fat' (ibid.:239-40). The Kalahari Bushmen similarly speak slightingly of an animal they have shot; to speak positively is thought to jeopardise the quality and quantity of the meat (Lewis-Williams & Biesele 1978). The Mantis's mendacity may therefore have been a result, at least in part, of a Bushman custom.

Then, when /Kwammang-a and the Ichneumon have put down the quagga meat, /Kwammang-a sits in silence because, in accordance with Bushman avoidance customs, he would not address his father-in-law directly. The Ichneumon, on the other hand, is able to speak directly to his grandfather. He retells the story, and condemns the Mantis's bad behaviour at the Lion's house and, given the custom of evasiveness, somewhat contradictorily, the way he deceived his family by telling them that the Lions had killed /Kwammang-a and himself.

## *STRUCTURE AND MEANING*

The ternary narrative structure of the myth is now clear. It starts in the camp and moves out to the hunting-ground where, in the central episode, the supernatural conflict with the Lions takes place and the vertical axis is breached. Finally, in the third episode, the action returns to the camp and the values of good behaviour and meat-sharing are emphasised. As the narrative moves along the horizontal axis, it goes from the order of the Mantis's camp to conflict and confusion at the Lion's camp and then, after the central episode at the waterhole, returns to the order of the Mantis's own camp and the Ichneumon's assertion of social values.

On one level, these values centre on meat-sharing, the manifest motivation for the myth. On another level, meat-sharing symbolises kinship relations. One of the dilemmas the myth addresses is how to exist in amity and to share scarce resources with people to whom one is related by marriage, but with whom one is still to some extent in competition for those resources. The link and associated tension between affines is expressed in the myth through the practice of meat-sharing. That the Lions should retain the quagga meat would be natural; that they should share it would be a response to imposed cultural norms. Put in Lévi-Straussian terms, the myth presents both a denial and an assertion of affinal relationships and concomitant responsibilities. The Mantis denies the relationship when he provokes the Lions to anger and violence; /Kwammang-a affirms affinal relationships by bringing the (symbolic) meat back to the Mantis's camp.

This contradiction, or dilemma, created by the need to share scarce resources with affines, cannot be resolved; it is inherent in Bushman social structure and economy. But it can be mitigated. To understand the kind of mitigation presented by the myth we return to the vertical axis of Bushman cosmology and the point where it intersects with the horizontal axis.

As I have shown, the non-sense happenings of the central episode are related to trance performance and shamanism. They are, moreover, a specifically /Xam manifestation of universal shamanistic experiences. In his extensive survey of shamanism Eliade (1972) defines what he calls 'three cosmic zones': sky, earth and underworld. These three zones are connected by a central axis, the *axis mundi*, that links them by passing through a 'hole': 'It is through this hole that the gods descend to earth and the dead to the subterranean regions; it is through the same hole that the soul of the shaman in ecstasy can fly up or down in the course of his celestial or infernal journeys' (Eliade 1972:259). The 'centre', in Eliade's phrase the 'site of a possible break-through in plane' (ibid.), is variously conceived in different shamanistic societies. In this /Xam myth the centre is the waterhole: it is at this point that the shaman can escape from the horizontal, mundane, axis and break into the vertical, supernatural *axis mundi*. Among the /Xam, 'this break-through in plane' was achieved principally, but not exclusively, at a communal trance dance. The shamans' hallucinations carried them, flying, up into the sky and also down into the realms below the earth, transcendent experiences conveyed by the cluster of metaphors in the central episode of *A visit to the Lions' house*.

These transcendent experiences bring us to the mitigation posited by the myth. The social efficacy of the trance dance does not escape the Bushmen: they recognise that the dance dissipates tensions. Indeed, they contrive to have men between whom there is animosity to dance one behind the other so that rhythmic unity can establish emotional amity (Biesele personal communication). Marshall (1969:374) describes a fight that was interrupted by the women, who started singing a medicine song in full voice: 'In minutes, two of the men from [one] group and one from the other group went abruptly into frenzied trance and soon fell unconscious.' During the actual curing, shamans remove from people whatever has been causing tensions, supernatural 'sickness' that can be seen only by shamans and which they cast back into the spiritual realm whence it came.

Meat-sharing is a frequent situation in which ill-feeling, such as that described by Marshall, can be generated; if people feel they have been slighted by receiving a niggardly portion, arguments erupt. The kinship ties which meat distribution celebrates become strained and, if the strain is unchecked, it jeopardises the survival of the social unit. It is therefore no coincidence that a trance dance often follows a substantial kill which attracts visitors, as the quagga meat does to the Lion's camp. The ill-feeling arising from inequitable distribution can be reduced by a trance dance.

By presenting access to the *axis mundi* as the essence of the central episode, the myth thus points to a way of mitigating a major social dilemma. It shows that shamanism not only links different realms; it also enables people to live with unresolved dilemmas.

## MANIPULATED COMPLEXITY

This analysis of *A visit to the Lion's house* raises some general points about the connection between myth and ritual and the role of this and other myths in Bushman society.

Without wishing to align myself with the view that myth says in words what ritual says in action, I believe it is true to say that *A visit to the Lion's house* cannot be understood apart from the ritual whose symbols and metaphors constitute some of its building blocks. Whether the converse is also true – that Bushman shamanistic rituals cannot be comprehended apart from this and related myths – is a more difficult question, but I am inclined to think that this is the case, but only in a restricted sense. This restriction on understanding would be imposed if we were to follow the school of thought that considers myth and ritual to be two sides of the same coin. A better, though still not ideal, metaphor may be the six sides of a die. We must avoid taking the metaphor too far, but two of the sides may be said to be myth and ritual, the rest being other beliefs and social practices. In the case of the Bushmen, one of these other sides was the making of rock art, a practice that used, in its own peculiar way, some of the same metaphorical, symbolic and experiential building blocks as myth and ritual (Lewis-Williams and Loubser 1986). Another side of the die may be taken to represent myths that do not appear to have anything to do with trance (or other) rituals. Beliefs about trance rituals and experiences are, as I have shown, embedded in a bi-axial cosmology that links them to other, apparently unrelated, myths; these tales stand in need of detailed analysis. Yet another side of the die may be taken to represent shamans' accounts of their experiences in the spirit realm. Using some of the same building blocks as myth, shamans tell how they both fly and enter waterholes, how they travel to god's place, how they converse with him, how they see his animals and monsters, how they capture rain-animals, and so forth. People listen to these accounts with great interest because they believe they are hearing about ultimate reality (Biesele 1978). In some admittedly restricted senses, shamans' reports of the spirit world are impromptu myths that have not become part of the social patrimony.

The wider, multifaceted complex suggested by the die metaphor does not, however, prevent the analysis I have given of *A visit to the Lion's house* from seeming limited and inadequate – as indeed all such analyses must be. Clearly, much more work needs to be done to uncover further 'meanings', such as gender relations and the range of other tensions inherent in Bushman social structure. Nevertheless, a number of significant points have begun to emerge. One of these concerns the ternary narrative structure of the myth (camp-waterhole-camp) and the two interlocking cosmological axes. As I have shown, the myth moves from normality to bizarrerie and back to normality. I now suggest that this narrative structure is informed by the experience of profoundly altered consciousness. Such experiences start in the normal world, move into a world of fantasy and hallucination that is in some sense on a different axis and to which different rules and limitations apply, and finally return to normality. The structure of the myth is thus not simply homologous with the cosmos as it is experienced by shamans and expressed in the structure of their narrations of trance experience; the human experience of moving between states of consciousness, some 'normal', some 'abnormal', may, moreover, have engendered this particular bi-axial view of the cosmos and, perhaps consequently, the structure of some myths.

But we can go further. Bushman shamanistic rock art evinces a comparable structure: the viewers stand in the world of normality while the art leads their experience through the rock face to the spirit world that lies beyond it (Lewis-Williams and Dowson 1990; Lewis-Williams 1991). Here it is paintings made by specific shamans that carry the viewer, at any rate vicariously, through to another realm. In other circumstances and in other ways this vicarious journey is achieved by certain myths and by shamans' first-hand accounts of their experiences. Ultimately, however, it is individual shamans, and only they, who actually travel the ternary route and experientially confirm its existence and, by extension, the validity of the cosmos as they and other people have come to conceive it: they know that there is an *axis mundi* because they have travelled along it.

By emphasising the transformative experiences of the *axis mundi*, the actual performance of myths at specific times and by specific people, and the execution of specific rock art images by specific artists, we are moving away from Lévi-Strauss's view that myths think themselves through the minds of people. He argues that myths are anonymous: 'When the myth is repeated, the individual listeners are receiving a message that, properly speaking, is coming from nowhere' (Lévi-Strauss 1970:18). On the contrary, myths, whatever impersonal deep structure they may have, are created by people and are reproduced by people in specific social circumstances at specific times for specific purposes; they do not come from 'nowhere'. The existence of numerous versions of myths points not only to a diversity of circumstances but also to diverse personal and sectional interests. As each artist drew upon and manipulated the received resources of rock art for his or her own purposes (Dowson, in prep.), so too the performance of myths was recursively implicated in social circumstances and individual interests.

Some of those interests, as they existed for nineteenth-century Bushmen in the central Cape Colony, may be discerned in the way in which //Kabbo recounted narratives. In the first place, there is suggestive evidence to show that he was a shaman who had control of the rain. While staying with the Bleeks at Mowbray, Cape Town, he was required to work in the garden. In October 1871, finding the ground too hard, he caused rain to fall by 'dreaming'. In this state, he claimed, he spoke to the rain, asking it to fall, as he used to do in his own country, and it 'assented'. He also claimed that, in a dream, he went on an extracorporeal journey to his home where he spoke with his wife and son (B.26.625-31). 'Dreaming' was in fact an important feature of Bushman shamanism (Lewis-Williams 1987b). In this connection, it is relevant that '//Kabbo' is the /Xam word for 'dream', and this may suggest that it was a nickname earned by his accounts of what he achieved while in a 'dream'; Bushmen commonly earn nicknames through personal characteristics or experiences (see, for example, L.V.20.5605-7). His other /Xam name was /Uhi-ddoro (Bleek and Lloyd 1911:303), a phrase which may mean 'smoking firestick' (or tinderbox) and may link him to the Mantis, one of whose names was //Kan doro, 'Tinderbox Owner' (Bleek 1956:557), or the one who possesses the ability to make fire.

Another, and for our present purposes highly significant, link between //Kabbo and the Mantis was expressed by /Han≠kass'o: 'My father-in-law //Kabbo has mantises [*/ki /ka/kaggen*], he was a mantis's [*/kaggen-ka*] man.' In the published version of this note (which is given with an incorrect manuscript page number), Dorothea Bleek (1936a:143) has both 'Mantises' (*/ka/kaggen* is a reduplicative plural; Bleek 1928/29:90) and 'Mantis's' with upper case initial letters, but this is not so in Lloyd's manuscript (L.VIII.23.8033). */Ki* means to posses or own, but the word is also used to denote the special relationship between a shaman and the creature he or she was believed to control; there were, for example, 'shamans of the springbok' who could cause them to run into the hunters' ambush. The second part of the statement, where 'mantis' is given in the singular (*/kaggen*), suggests that //Kabbo had some sort of relationship with the Mantis, not just mantises.

Something of what that relationship may have been is implied by the passage that follows. In the published version (Bleek 1924:12), there is no indication that /Han≠kass'o's remarks about //Kabbo were in fact a preamble to his account of the Mantis's special affection for the eland and the ways in which he contrives to allow a wounded eland to escape its hunters. In Lloyd's manuscript, this account is entitled 'Doings of the Mantis when an eland had been wounded', and it is separated from the statement about //Kabbo's being a 'mantis's man' by a short line in the centre of the page (Figure 3); it starts: 'The Mantis does not love us, if we kill an Eland.' No new transcription date is given at this point, so it seems /Han≠kass'o's remarks about //Kabbo led him on directly to speak about the Mantis and the eland. The implication is that //Kabbo's special relationship with the Mantis, here a protecting Lord of the Animals, allowed him to intervene with the trickster-deity and perhaps thereby secure good hunting.

In the light of this evidence, it is of interest to compare //Kabbo's narratives with those of other informants for whom there is no evidence that they were shamans. Unfortunately, we do not have performances of A *visit to the Lion's house* by other informants, but Hewitt's (1986a:240) analysis of many narratives by a number of informants shows that //Kabbo was particularly interested in the Mantis's ability to dive into water, to fly, to cause his possessions to fly after him, and to wash off the feathers that had grown on him. He repeated these parts time and again, sometimes in reported speech, and 'elaborated [them] from every possible point of view' so that they could be appreciated 'from the perspectives of one character after another' (ibid.). Hewitt (1986a: 245-46) concludes that it is unlikely that //Kabbo's interests 'would not also be shown in performance amongst his own people'. In other words, it was to the events of the central episode, the essentially shamanistic one, that he gave special attention in a number of narratives, not just the one I have analysed.

//Kabbo was thus manipulating the myths. Each tale was a resource which he could embellish and elaborate to suit his own interests. //Kabbo's die was loaded. As my analysis of A *visit to the Lion's house* shows, the parts which he particularly emphasised projected the power and importance of shamans. He was thereby emphasising his own importance as a shaman and enhancing his own status as a 'Mantis's man'. Each of his elaborate performances of the various Mantis myths was, for //Kabbo, a potential intervention, not just an entertainment (though they were no doubt that too), a way of negotiating his own status and influence.

//Kabbo's performance of A *visit to the Lion's house* is, in the respects I have

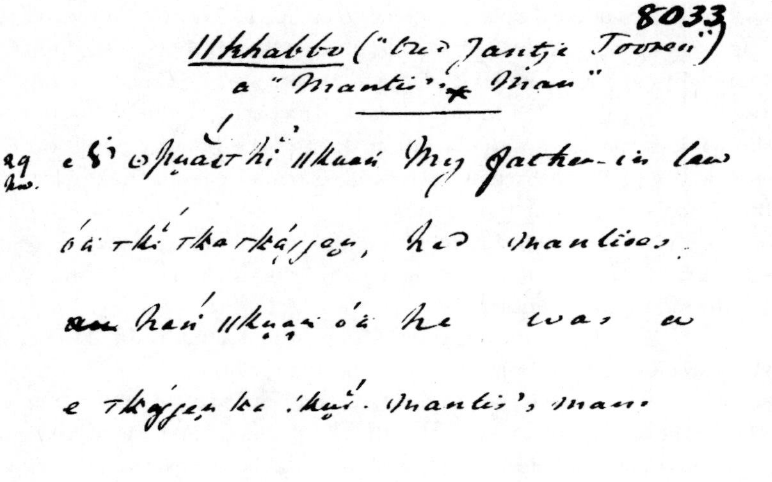
8033

||kabbo ("Oud Jantje Tooren")
a "Mantis* Man"

[29 Nov.] é ẽ ! ǂkuarri ||kaan My father-in-law
ói ‖kaa-||kaugen, had Mantises.
au han ||kuan óa He was a
e ||kaggen ka !kui. Mantis's man.

Doings of the Mantis
when an eland has been wounded

Han yauki kkó- He (the Mantis)
ka i, au i ||kkó does not love us, if
wá. Ta, hannan we kill an eland. For,
||ki i !nuinta, he comes to pinch our
au while ear,

Figure 3. Page 8033 from Lloyd's notebook number VIII.23.

described, a socio-political document, as indeed all narrations of tales may be. In addition to presenting a mediation of social conflicts, myth, with its personal performances and versions, may in some ways have been one of the battlefields on which the struggle to reproduce or to transform society and, moreover, to establish one's own interests was contested. The structure of *A visit to the Lion's House* was not ineluctable; rather, it was a resource which, in performance, could be manipulated to negotiate power and status. Structure is not necessarily conservative.

## *ACKNOWLEDGEMENTS*

I am grateful to those who commented on drafts of this paper: David Hammond-Tooke, Thomas Dowson, Carolyn Hamilton, Anne Holliday, Elwyn Jenkins and Megan Biesele. The Librarian, Jagger Library, University of Cape Town, permitted quotation from the Bleek and Lloyd Collection and publication of Figure 3. The Director of the South African Museum, Cape Town, kindly allowed the rock painting in Figure 2 to be copied. The Rock Art Research Unit is funded by the Centre for Science Development and the University of the Witwatersrand.

# 'He Stealthily Lightened at his Brother-in-law'

## (and Thunder Echoes in Bushman Oral Tradition a Century Later)

Megan Biesele

Magical potency is transferred or used for transformative purposes in Khoisan folklore and ritual in contexts which include illness and its treatment, avenging social wrongs, strained kin relationships, the sharing of resources, control of weather, and the passages of life. It takes forms as various as using lightning, thunder, rain, and meteors as instruments of transfer, magical 'staring' and whistling, finger-pointing and finger-snapping to send forth arrows of misfortune and *n/om* (the healing power), and amniotic fluid that flows away in a river to bring a message of death. Potency may take the form of a whirlwind, burning horns, or drops of blood that blow away in the wind to announce a murder. It can travel in a scent or become activated when a certain kind of person urinates in a fire. It is present in cooking and burning processes, at birth and death, and in medicine smoke from burning herbs in tortoise shells. Bad feelings in the heart of one person can kill another.

When a girl becomes a woman she can charm elands so that hunters can bring them down. Spirits of dead relatives can interfere substantially in the lives of the living. Rock paintings have potency partly because blood, a magical substance, is used to bind them. Antelope horns may be blown to flatten the camps of in-laws who have done wrong. Birds may be tied to a person's head to give early warnings. Body parts can substitute for food in social trickery. Dancing can bring back the 'dead'.

I present these instances of magical transfer in an undigested heap: I want to call attention to the jumble of references we are called on to deconstruct in our work of description and interpretation. The verbs and nouns of potency are intricately embedded in the metaphors of narrative and it is only ethnographic context – or, if we are fortunate, narrators' commentary – which can cause them to stand out as figures against ground. The ways of linguistic embedding are even more various, and we must be even more cunning and well-versed to prize from them gems with real comparability.

Comparability itself possesses no magic. Piling up instances gets us nowhere without the wit and knowledge to contextualise the pile as well: ethnography must also evaluate numerical emphases. In textual analysis as in reading for pleasure, nothing substitutes for background reference. In Ju/'hoan folklore work today, we can profit from the company of Ju/'hoan contemporaries to help us enjoy and understand. No longer 'capering beneath the dining room window', these people, some newly literate, are now participating in the work of analysis. Interactive research is surely some culmination of the reflexive thrust in the social sciences which has characterised recent decades. I suggest that, where possible, people's speculation about their own tradition be enfranchised and their critical faculties be unleashed. If nothing else, this mutuality must convince us at last of the subtlety of the art we try to make a craft by taking it apart into its 'pieces'.

## *≠KAGARA AND !HÃUNU, WHO FOUGHT EACH OTHER WITH LIGHTNING*

They formerly, ≠Kagara formerly went to fetch his younger sister, he went to take her away; he went to take her away from !Hãunu; and he took [her] back to her parents.

!Hãunu gave chase to his brother-in-law, he passed along behind the hill.

The clouds came, clouds which were unequalled in beauty [lit., 'clouds which not beautiful like them']; they vanished away.

≠Kagara said: 'Thou must walk on.' His younger sister walked, carrying [a heavy burden of] things, [her] husband's things. He [≠Kagara] said: 'Thou must walk on; for, home is not near at hand.'

!Hãunu passed along behind [the hill].

The clouds came, the clouds vanished away.

≠Kagara said: 'Thou must walk on, for, thou art the one who dost see.' And he, because the house became near, he exclaimed: 'Walk on! Walk on!' He waited for his younger sister; his younger sister came up to his side. He exclaimed: 'What things can these be, which thou dost heavily carry?'

Then !Hãunu sneezed, on account of it; blood poured out of his nostrils; he stealthily lightened at his brother-in-law. His brother-in-law fended him quickly off, his brother-in-law also stealthily lightened at him. He quickly fended off his brother-in-law. His brother-in-law also lightened at him. He [≠Kagara] said: 'Thou must come [and] walk close beside me; for, thou art the one who dost see that husband does not allow us time; for, he does not singly lighten.'

They [≠Kagara and !Hãunu] went along angry with each other. !Hãunu had intended that he should be the one lightening to whisk away ≠Kagara. ≠Kagara was the one who was strong [lit., 'was not light', or 'did not feel light'], he continued to fend off his younger sister's husband, !Hãunu. His younger sister's husband was also lightening at him; he was lightening at his brother-in-law. Then he stealthily lightened at his younger sister's husband with black lightning, he, lightening, whisked him up [and carried him to a little distance].

His younger sister's husband, in this manner, lay dying; he, in this manner, he thundered, while ≠Kagara bound up his head with the net, he returning arrived at home.

He went to lie down in the hut, while !Hãunu lay thundering; he thundered there, while ≠Kagara went to lie down, when he had rubbed them [i.e. himself and his younger sister] with buchu, buchu, buchu, buchu, he lay down.

### *Note by the Narrator*

My grandmothers used to say, '≠Kagara and his companion are those who fight in the East, he and !Hãunu.'

When the clouds were thick, and the clouds, when the clouds were thick, and the clouds were at this place, and the clouds resembled a mountain, then, the clouds were lightening, on account of it. And my grandmothers used to say: 'It is ≠Kagara, with !Hãunu.'

---

Potency is transferred in this /Xam story (Bleek & Lloyd 1911:112-19) through exchanges of lightning bolts between brothers-in-law. There is explicit anger in this exchange, and an explicit intent to do away with each other magically:

> They [≠Kagara and !Hãunu] went along angry with each other. !Hãunu had intended that he should be the one lightening to whisk away ≠Kagara.

There is also explicit reference to the trance context (see Lewis-Williams 1990a:30):

> Then !Hãunu sneezed, on account of it; blood poured out of his nostrils; he stealthily lightened at his brother-in-law.

The social context appears to be marital unease between in-laws: ≠Kagara is fetching his younger sister from her husband's home in order to take her back to her parents. Yet she is burdened by carrying her husband's 'things'. and they are heavy. So the battle is joined because their progress is slow and hindered by dark clouds. Eventually ≠Kagara vanquishes !Hãunu with 'black lightening', defined by /Han≠kass'o when he told the story in 1879 as '... that which kills us, that which we do not perceive it come; it resembles a gun, we are merely startled by the clouds' thundering ...' !Hãunu lies dying and as he dies he 'thunders'.

≠Kagara returns home and rubs himself and his younger sister with buchu before they lie down. The detail of rubbing with buchu is another instance of potency transfer: it is clearly related to both removing the stain of a ritual battle and the welcoming home of the younger sister after an arduous journey. This gloss on the buchu detail was evidently so automatic to the /Xam storyteller – as it would have been to a Ju/'hoan storyteller with aromatic san powder – that it was not mentioned in the annotation.

There is much more in this /Xam fragment which can also be elucidated by reference to Ju/'hoan oral tradition and ethnography, despite the intervening years, distances, and linguistic differences. Most of what we can learn, however, comes not from mere comparison of details (though this is also revealing, as in the buchu example) but from the way details are embedded in the drama of narration. Picking out comparable 'elements', however defined, becomes a challenging detective game involving much social knowledge and a wide grasp of the themes and plots in the body of narratives. Often a concrete detail, merely mentioned in passing, is enough to give a social clue with enormous ramifications (see Biesele 1993).

A few illustrations of the varieties in Ju/'hoan tradition of potency transfer in the struggle between brothers-in-law in connection with their sister/wife may be examined below (page numbers refer to Biesele 1993).

Heroine stories with affinal symbolic conflict:

1. Husband saved from wife's brothers by entering magically opening termite hill (p.143).

2. Husband saved from wife's brothers by turning into a bird which can perch on the point of a knife (p.143).
3. Husband and his people flattened by effects of magical gemsbok horn blown by wife at behest of her grandmother (p.147).
4. Husband's younger brothers foiled by thorns flung in their path by the heroine (pp.161-62).
5. Husband's younger brothers are foiled by a raincloud magically shot into the sky by the heroine (p.168):

> And the hail broke the strings of Kha//'an's and !Xuma's loincloths, so they just stood there naked. And the bows and arrows they had, with which they had been stalking her, just fell apart, beaten by the hail and the rain.

6. The affinal relationship as a whole is illuminated in the context of murder and vengeance (pp.159-60):

> [The heroine thinks about the insult her child had carried between her mother and her husband and about the murder that had resulted.]
>
> 'Oho! Just you wait,' she whispered to her sleeping husband. 'I'm going to get you! You killed my mother and so I'm going to kill you!' G!kun//'amdima turned these thoughts over and over in her mind.
>
> '*Kuru!*' she said to herself. 'If I take a spear from this pile of short spears he has and try to kill him with it, will I manage to stay alive myself?' She thought the matter over.
>
> Then she pulled out a spear from the pile. But as she did, the spear-heads rattled against each other. Their rattling woke her husband.
>
> 'Yau! What are you doing rattling spears together?'
>
> "Yau!' she retorted. 'What would I be doing with spears? Those spears you hear are my brothers' spears; they are on the move tonight. Why do you think I'd want to have anything to do with spears?"
>
> In this way she meant to soothe his fear so that his watchfulness would no longer hinder her plans.
>
> 'Just wait,' she said to herself, 'as soon as he's off his guard, I'll kill him.' But he stayed awake, and she had no chance of reaching for a spear a second time. Then a fresh thought struck her.
>
> 'There's no point in his going on living when I'm wearing a knife. That's what I'll use to kill him. He killed mother; now I'll do the same to

him!' Then she slowly and carefully drew out her knife and lay it in the fire. It lay there and grew hot. It heated up until it was red-hot. Then G!kon//'amdima did to her husband the same thing he had done to her mother. Yes, she killed him. When his body lay still, she went to sleep.

In the morning, she gathered up her mother's blood into a ball and stuck it in the left side of her groin. Then she gathered up her husband's blood and stuck it in the right side of her groin. She dumped her husband's body in the bush.

Then she came back and fetched her mother's body and dumped it in the bush as well.

When she returned, she found a group of people sitting with her children in the camp. They were eating together.

Her husband's younger brothers had arrived while she was busy in the bush. 'What have my brothers-in-law come for?' she wondered. 'What are they going to do to me?' Just then her little son ran across to one of the men. 'Uncle! Uncle!' he said. G!kun//amdima knew that he was going to say, 'Mother has killed my father! Now you know.' So she grabbed the little boy and turned his attention to something else.

Then the brothers were ready to leave. They told G!kun//'amdima to pack up her things, that she was coming with them. So she packed up all kinds of thorns, morningstar thorns, *g//amiq//ami* (devil's claw) thorns, everything, and was ready to go. But she did it so quickly that she was ready before they were.

The contents of the uneasy affinal relationship touched on in this and the above examples include the fear that the grandparents will not be brought babies and children of the new union for visits often enough to suit them; the fear that the new wife will not be fed properly by her husband and his people; worries about bride service and marital residence in general; and the possibilities for covert insult, real bodily harm, or actual murder to occur in the camp of the affines. The theme of male versus female power is particularly strongly limned, as well, in the affinal context. All this unease and strife is dealt with in multiple manifestations of potency transfer.

In the story of the heroine and her husband's younger brother (Biesele 1993:168), the detail of loincloths broken apart by rain as a magical 'familiar' appears. A similar detail appears in a story collected in 1991, in which the antagonists are not in-laws but rather lions and men. This dyad too participates in an elemental struggle, as we shall see in the following story, presented in full. Potency here is represented as magical power to resurrect 'dead' sons 'buried' in eland chyme, in the form of birds and other animal allies with special abilities; an eland skull and meteor invested with *n/om* and invoked against predators in the creation of the 'first' trance dance.

## METHODOLOGY

What follows consists of the first phase of a computer-assisted approach to Bushman textual materials storage, reference, and manipulation. It shows how this developing approach may physically aid the process of handling large bodies of text in order to arrive at descriptive/interpretive treatments such as the above. Using a single laptop machine for both field and office work, and a single word processing program (Wordperfect 5.1) with some customisation, a high new level of efficiency in textual 'mining' may be achieved. This involves an original Ju/'hoan folktale text and its transcribed translation as prepared and stored within this system, along with a version of the translation which contains annotations and marginal comments to be included or excluded electronically at will.* Document summaries, keywords, and Boolean text searches will enable in-depth investigations and will be revealing precisely because of the large amounts of text processible. An evolving 'Instruction Booklet' for this application was available to interested colleagues at the Bleek and Lloyd Conference as a related piece of 'shareware' for discussion.

### *Kha//'an and !Xuma*

Narrated by /Kunta Boo, /Aotcha, Namibia, February 1991

Sa n!o te ama tju/ho te !aqe. Te g/ae ho n!ang te n/hai, te !xoeha te u tza. Te n!oma te cete gu ha !uh te g!aa. Te cete u te ha !aah, te sa cete !xoe ha, te ka sa !xoe ha, sa !xoe ha te cete u tza. Te n!oma te cete gu ha !uh, //'a n!anga n/a koh tzin caere//'hanga te//'hanga kxaosi gea !hun ha, te//'hanga kxaosi tchoan a sa ko ha. ...

---

* Because of space constraints, only the first few lines of the transcription in the Ju/'hoan language are given. For the same reason, and to avoid duplication, the transcribed translation is given only once, with annotations. – Eds.

Two boys named Kha//'an and !Xuma

> See Lorna Marshall on star lore and names

left their camp one morning to go hunting. They spotted an eland and began to pursue it. They followed it all day and when night fell they slept. In the morning they found its spoor again and tracked it. The eland ran from them, and they followed it. It ran, and they followed it all day and again spent the night. The next morning they took up its spoor again. The eland had turned toward the west: that was where the Owners of the West lived. On the third night they slept close to the Owners of the West. In the morning they again followed the eland and this time went and killed it. The Owners of the West then stole the eland from them.

The men who came and stole the eland from Kha//'an and !Xuma were two men who followed their spoor as they hunted. These two men came up and frightened the two boys so that they died but in fact were not dead.

> This ambiguous statement is common in discussions of illness and the trance state. By extension, it is used in initiatory contexts such as this story seems to be, where boys are buried alive in filth and emerge with the help of their father's magic as men capable of defeating lions, the ancient dark enemies of human beings.

Then those men ripped the eland's chyme from its intestines and buried all this along with Kha//'an and !Xuma. When they were buried, the Owners of the West became the owners of the eland.

The names of the Owners of the West were 'Lions'.

> The West is identified as the direction of death, where the sun dies, where the lesser (more evil) God lives, where strange evil cosmological beings such as 'Those Who Sleep Standing Up' (or the Knees Knees None people) prop themselves against trees because they have no knees or only one leg or only one side of a body, and refuse to share meat with their children. It is also known as the home of the 'Owners of Torment' and of the wife of Tcoq'ma, the terrible woman of the boys' initiation ordeal.

These lions cut the meat off the eland carcase while Kha//'an and !Xuma lay

| |
|---|
| An ambiguous word also meaning 'slept' |

in the midst of the eland's chyme. One of the lions then stayed at the place where the eland had died

| |
|---|
| The phrase 'where (animal) has died' is used invariably as a gloss for 'kill site'. This usage appears to underscore the neutral nature of providence in hunting success and to minimise the hunter's role, which is of a piece with the restraint and modesty shown by hunters at all times as part of social and magical prudence. |

| |
|---|
| *n/ui*: This one word means a kill site. It is a powerful word, connoting all the activities, both practical and ritual, which take place at the site of a kill. |

while the other one went to get water for them.

| |
|---|
| In other versions it is stated the Lions make waterbags from the (variously sized) stomachs of the eland. |

Meanwhile G≠kao N!a'an, the father of Kha//'an and !Xuma, waited three nights for his sons to return. When they did not come back he called for Male Tortoise and Weaver Bird to help him look for his children. Three nights had passed and therefore today he was going to look for Kha//'an and !Xuma.

G≠kao N!a'an and the Male Tortoise and the Weaver Bird followed the tracks of Kha//'an and !Xuma. They came to where the eland had run off. When they came there, G≠kao N!a'an said, 'This is the eland my children were chasing and killed, and other people have stolen it from them.'

So they followed them and found where they had slept. When they came to their sleeping place, the Weaver Bird put his foot into the fire to feel how long ago it had been made. When he had taken his foot out, the Male Tortoise put his head into the fire to feel it. Then they said to G≠kao N!a'an, 'The fire's centre is cold.'

So they started tracking the boys again. Later they came to another place where they had slept. The inside of this fire was warm. They said to G≠kao N!a'an, 'This fire's inside is warm, and if we go to their next fire it will be hot.

So they tracked the boys again. When they came to their next camping place, the Weaver Bird put his foot into the fire and told G≠kao N!a'an and the Male Tortoise, 'The inside of this fire is hot.' And the Male Tortoise put in his head and burned it. He cried out and said,' Why didn't you tell me this fire was hot? I've burned my head off!'

But Weaver Bird said, 'How can you say I didn't tell you? You burned your head yourself!'

So they went on carefully tracking the boys and found where they had turned the eland. They also found the tracks of the Lions. G≠kao N!a'an said, 'This is what I was talking about: strange people are tracking the boys.' Then he said, 'And if strange people are tracking them, they have probably killed them.'

When they went ahead to where the eland had died, they didn't see the tracks that should have been there if the boys had butchered the eland. All they saw were the tracks of the Owners of the West. They looked around and found where Kha//'an and !Xuma had been buried. G≠kao N!a'an opened the burial pit very slowly and carefully and peeped in and saw them. He said to the Male Tortoise and the Weaver Bird, 'Do you see how they have been buried – they're in here but aren't dead!'

Meanwhile, one of the Owners of the West had gone to fetch water and had not yet come back. The other one was resting in the shade. When he saw G≠kao N!a'an and the others he was afraid of them and didn't come to where the eland had died. G≠kao N!a'an said to the Male Tortoise and the Weaver Bird, 'Now, I've found my children, so you two keep watch for us while I make a plan.'

Then he made a certain bird called a *tcxoe* and then made another called a *//auhn//auhn* and then made another called a *koagntchi* and then made another called a *g≠oro*. When he was finished he said, 'You, *tcxoe*, will perch downwind to protect me while you, *//auhn//auhn*, will perch upwind over here. The *koaqntchi* will just stay here in the road. And, *g≠oro*, your mouth is big so you will be here in the south and also keep watch. Now I'm going to do something else.'

Then he took the eland's skull and fixed it and put his *n/om*

> New spelling for *n/um*, magical potency or medicine. The orthographical correctness of this decision has been suggested by G≠kao /kaece of /Aotcha, Namibia, one of the first Ju/'hoansi to be literate in his own language.

into it and hung it up. Then he and the Male Tortoise and the Weaver Bird began to try it out.

They sang and danced under the eland's skull, dancing away from it and coming back to it again. G≠kao N!a'an said to the two others, 'You two go up ahead and dance there, and I'll be behind here dancing, to see whether these things I'm thinking of will turn out right.'

> Note that another skull is used in a similar story context about the origin of a ritual – a wildebeest skull for the origin of Tcoq'ma, the boys' initiation ordeal.

So when they danced past him to dance up front, he slowed down to dance behind. When the two had danced under the eland's skull he looked up at it and it fell down, cutting the strings of his loincloth and piercing his hip.

> Note the detail about magical cutting of loincloth strings. The same detail appears when the heroine in the other stories is pursued by would-be avengers of her husband's death. She magically causes a raincloud to appear in the sky, and when the pursuers are upon her she calls down the rain, which beats on the men, causing the strings of their loincloths to break. This detail is considered comical, but the aggressors are effectively unmanned in both stories.

He took it and hung it up again, saying 'That which you have done to me, won't you later do to another man?'

Then they began to dance again. When they wanted to go somewhere else the skull fell down again and cut the strings of his loincloth. G≠kao N!a'an picked up the skull again and hung it up, saying, 'I've already fully seen how good your work is: a big dance will now start, and when you come down I want you to come down with a meteor.' When he had done this, he told the Weaver Bird and the Male Tortoise 'I'm finished, so let's just wait for the Owners of the West to come so we can start the dance.' He turned and said to the Weaver Bird and the Male Tortoise, 'What I've done may later help us with the people who will come to us. All we have to do now is wait for the Owners of the West.'

When the sun went down the Owners of the West came from downwind and the *tcxoe* saw them and said, 'What is this?'

Then G≠kao N!a'an said, 'That's what I told you would happen.' He also told them 'It's the two of them already coming from downwind. Now you two be clever: my children have been killed and I'm going to see how strong my *n/om* is. Soon we will be carrying my children on our shoulders.'

> Unclear construction: to check with informants.

So the Owners of the West kept walking and when they came up they said, 'G≠kao N!a'an, are you thirsty?'

He answered them, saying, 'I'm thirsty but not too thirsty.'

The Owners of the West gave him the biggest waterbag, but he refused, saying, 'Maybe the others are especially thirsty, so why don't you give them the biggest waterbag and give me the small one to put to the edge of my lip?'

> Informants explained verbally and with gestures that G≠kao N!a'an wanted to keep his vision from being obscured by the big waterbag: he wanted to keep an eye on the lions.

When they had slaked their thirst, G≠kao N!a'an said, 'Now you should cook some meat so we can eat.'

When they had cooked the meat for them to eat, he said, 'Now serve the meat so we can get a dance started. My children have killed an eland, so let's praise it by dancing.'

So they began to dance. And the Owners of the West were surprised and said, 'Now why is this old man saying we should all dance?'

G≠kao N!a'an put the Weaver Bird and the Male Tortoise out in front and told them to begin to dance. So the Weaver Bird and the Male Tortoise came first, and the lions were those which

> This apparently clumsy construction is common in Ju/'hoansi, as it was in /Xam. My decision to leave it this way rather than find a smoother modern paraphrase is a bow to the Bleeks and a nod in the direction of linguistic and narrative commonalities across space and time.

came next, and G≠kao N!a'an came last.

While they were dancing, G≠kao N!a'an said, '*!Aihn tzisi //xan//xan!* (Let there be light!)'

And the lions said, '*G!u noqm noqmsi ku noqm!* (Let the dark of night fall!)'

> The actual words, which occur here and in other versions as unvarying incantation, mean 'Let there be light between the tree trunks', and 'Let the dark darknesses of the night darken'. The opposition between men and lions as beings specialising in daytime vs nighttime activities is clear.

They all danced, moving along beneath the eland's skull. And G≠kao N!a'an took those birds he had fixed and carried them on his shoulder to take care of him. When they had all danced under the skull and turned around to come back, they danced under it again and once again turned around. When the Male Tortoise and the Weaver Bird had danced under the skull again and the Lions were about to go under, G≠kao N!a'an kept close to them but held back from the skull and shouted, 'Why have you (Lions) already caused me pain and you (the skull) not come down?' Then the skull and the meteor fell down together and beat the lions to death.

Then G≠kao N!a'an praised them, saying, 'That's how I wanted you to avenge my tears for what those men had done to me.' He called to Kha//'an and !Xuma, saying, 'You two get up and beat the Lions' feet!'

> The word *jom* means 'clenched paws', like those of carnivores. By extension it is used to mean carnivores themselves, and especially lions. Informants were questioned here and it is clear that it was the lions' feet which were to be beaten by the sons, not the lions themselves. For

Ju/'hoansi, foot form is diagnostic in differentiating animals, particularly carnivores vs herbivores.

The boys jumped out of the pit of eland chyme and stood there and beat the Lions' feet. G≠kao N!a'an said, 'These are the people who caused you such pain that you had died. Now beat these carnivores and avenge yourselves. Then let's leave, let's go home today: we've been in the bush a long time.'

Then they packed up the eland meat and went home to their camp. There was a man there named ≠Ku≠kuri

A bird

who was carrying a lot of the meat. As they were walking back to their camp a man called G!ung!uni

A bird

was the one who said, 'Why is it that ≠Ku≠kuri is so small but has so much meat to carry, and it's even fat meat?'

≠Ku≠kuri just kept quiet. When they had walked along and stopped in the shade to rest, ≠Ku≠kuri just stood there with his meat-yoke over his shoulder, while the others were those who lay theirs down.

G!ung!uni said, 'What is it that you, a little person with small legs, are so strong that you are just standing there with your meat-yoke?'

But ≠Ku≠kuri just kept quiet.

So they started walking again and after they had walked they again rested in the shade. And again ≠Ku≠kuri just held on to his meat-yoke and stayed standing.

And G!ung!uni spoke again and said, 'Here's this man standing around with his meat-yoke on his shoulder again. We've been travelling a long way: shouldn't he be tired and put his meat-yoke down and take a rest?'

At that, ≠Ku≠kuri finally became completely angry. He said, 'Both of us are men even though I'm just naturally small: why is this guy insulting me?'

For 'insult' the storyteller used *≠xui*, which has overtones of racial prejudice. This is also the verb used for bad luck or the negative influence in the '*N!ow*' complex. It can also mean that something doesn't 'go well' with something else.

As he said this he dropped the meat-yoke, because he was a person who had become angry. He grabbed G!ung!uni and spoke and told him, 'This is the person you insulted and said was small who is grabbing you now!' (≠Ku≠kuri was older than G!ung!uni.)

It might be good to check whether the insult was graver since it was made by a younger person about an older person.

He grabbed G!ung!uni and gouged his eyes until the blood ran out. So G!ung!uni's eyes turned red. That's why we say today, 'G!ung!uni's eyes are red.'

Bird identification necessary.

When G!ung!uni got up off the ground he grabbed the meat-yoke and knocked ≠Ku≠kuri's legs out from under him. While this was happening, another man had left the camp and gone out hunting. On his way home he turned around and saw another man coming along behind carrying meat. The man who had gone hunting was named Naqnaqmatagom (Swallow-It-All).

Must check the /Xam for 'All-Devourer.'

When he came up to the man who was carrying the meat,

It is unclear whether this was ≠Ku≠kuri or another man.

the man gave him some of the meat. They parted and he (Swallow-It-All) went and hid the meat. Then he went along his way, but circled wide and went far ahead along the road and stood there waiting. When the man with the meat came up he didn't say anything, so the man took off another bundle of meat strips and gave it to him. When he had given it to him, Swallow-It-All again went and hid it and again circled ahead of him and stood waiting.

The man with the meat set out again with his yoke and soon saw Swallow-It-All and said, 'Here's another man standing in the road.' He again gave him some meat and they parted. Swallow-It-All again went ahead to stand in the road. So the man gave him the last bundle of meat and had only the bare yoke to lay over his shoulder.

Naqnaqmatagom hid the meat and circled around ahead again and stood there. When the other man had walked and again came up to him, he said, 'I bet if I throw this yoke at him he'll swallow it too.' So he threw it and Naqnaqmatagom swallowed the yoke as well. Then he circled ahead and stood waiting.

When the man came up to him, he said, 'I bet if I jump up and turn around he'll swallow me too,' and he jumped up and he swallowed him. When he had swallowed him he vomited him out again along with the meat-yoke. The poor man went to sit down and thought to himself, 'Since this man has eaten all my meat what am I going to do?'

Then he sat and strained

> An informant explained that it was as if he were constipated.

and extruded his anus. Then he cut it into strips like dried meat.

> Yet another instance of the trick sequence between men and women, where body parts are treated as if they were food in order to fool the opposite sex.

He put the yoke over his shoulder and carried it back to his camp. When he got home he hung up the meat-yoke. He chopped poles to make a drying rack, and hung the meat on it.

His child came up and wanted to break off a piece of meat to roast on the fire, but he said, 'If you lay it on the fire the fat will spill.'

His wife said, 'What part of yourself have you brought home that other people are eating meat and you are being completely stingy with yours? Is this your anus you have brought home?' At that his anus gathered itself together and went back where it had come from.

> Great hilarity greeted this detail when it was told: the storyteller waved his arms about as if the anus and attached intestines were flailing about like hoses under pressure as they came back together and went up inside him.

## COMMENT ON METHODOLOGY

The preceding texts show numerous examples of transformation and potency transfer. In some cases they are easy to pick out, such as in the use of the eland skull and meteor to vanquish the lions. In other cases, subtler references must be teased clear, for instance the ramifications of calling the lions 'the Owners of the West'. The whole structure of dancing and doing *n/om* against illness, death, and social problems is a very familiar – perhaps central – dramatic format in Ju/'hoan oral tradition.

These texts have been presented as a working demonstration of an evolving methodology for dealing with large quantities of Khoisan verbal material. The original folktale transcription (not given here in full) is followed by a Document Summary which provides a kind of computerised filecard catalogue to tag, summarise, and store keywords for various text files. Decisions about the most useful ways to name, type and tag a text by storyteller, transcriber/typist, date, and subject are occupying me at present, along with choices of the most effective keyword and abstract strategies. The key in the whole approach is the use of the original language – orthographically standardised – for all searching and mining activities.

Document Summary

| | | | |
|---|---|---|---|
| | Revision date | 08-04-91 | 01:13a |
| 1 – | Creation date | 07-31-91 | 10:50p |
| 2 – | Document Name | justory | |
| | Document Type | Kha//'an | |
| 3 – | Author | /Kunta Boo of /Aotcha, Namibia | |
| | Typists | G≠kao /Kaece, Megan Biesele | |

| | | |
|---|---|---|
| 4 – | Subject | Folktale eland hunt by sons of G≠kao N!a'an |
| 5 – | Account | Told February 1991 |
| 6 – | Keywords | Kha//'an, !Xuma, G≠kao N!a'an, n!ang, zam g!oq, Koq'a tzama, tcxoe, //'hanga kxaosi, n!hai, //auhn-//auhn. |
| 7 – | Abstract | Kha//'an and !Xuma, sons of G≠kao N!a'an, hunt an eland and kill it. It is stolen by the lions, who 'kill' the boys and bury them in the chyme. G≠kao N!a'an tricks and kills the lions. |

After the document summary comes the translation into English, and this is followed by the same document showing commentary and annotation within boxes, then printing, half-pages at a time, directly from the screen. This display mode is presently being used for all levels of commentary and note, some quite informal, but will eventually be modified for more standardised annotation.

Finding files such as these by combinations of words and conducting multi-condition searches, as well as other operations like adding sub-documents to a master document, appending further text to an earlier file, editing two documents simultaneously with a split screen, alphabetising wordlists, substituting different spellings, and tagging specific files for specific kinds of list (such as literary, ethnological, etc.) are dealt with in an evolving 'Instruction Booklet' that I would be happy to discuss with interested colleagues.

## *NOTE ON ORTHOGRAPHY*

The orthography used in this paper is the Practical Ju/'hoan Orthography developed by the late Patrick Dickens under the auspices of the Nyae Nyae Development Foundation of Namibia. This orthography was published in 1991 in the *South African Journal of African Languages* 11:1. It has been given the endorsement of the Nyae Nyae Farmers' Co-operative, the community educational and political organisation which has as members the majority of the Ju/'hoan-speaking people of Namibia. It has also been officially recognised by the Government of the Republic of Namibia. The related educational programme of the NNDFN, which will use this orthography, has been made a recognised part of the Namibian Basic Educational Reform comprising child and adult literacy. A Ju/'hoan-English English-Ju/'hoan dictionary of over four thousand entries using this orthography was been completed by Patrick

Dickens. Four Ju/'hoan people were fully literate in their own language by 1991 through the use of this orthography, and many more will become so as educational plans, including self-generated curriculum materials, progress.

## ACKNOWLEDGEMENTS

Research support for this paper was provided partly by the United States National Endowment for the Humanities, Translation Grant #21441-89 entitled 'Ju/'hoansi Kokxuisi: Ju/'hoan Bushman Folklore and Other Texts'. The NEH is an independent federal agency of the United States. Further support was provided by the Nyae Nyae Development Foundation of Namibia, under whose curriculum-development project related textual and linguistic work was undertaken.

This paper could not have been written without the pioneering orthographic and dictionary work in the Ju/'hoan language of the late Patrick Dickens. Thanks go to his excellently schooled pupil, G≠kao /Kaece of /Aotcha, Namibia, who as one of the first few young Ju/'hoansi literate in his own language prepared the transcript of the folktale used in the methodological portion of the paper.

Finally, I thank /Kunta Boo of /Aotcha, for the story of Kha//'an and !Xuma, told in February, 1991. I also thank the many other storytellers, in Namibia and Botswana, from whom I have heard versions of this story since 1971. To me it is very moving that one hundred years before the first time I recorded this story, the Bleeks and Lucy Lloyd were painstakingly writing out stories with similar ideas about transcending human limitations through particular conceptualisations about magical potency.

# The Place of Lloyd's !Kuñ Texts in the Ju Dialects

Patrick Dickens

## *INTRODUCTION*

The purpose in examining Lloyd's !Kun texts was to fit her informants' linguistic data more exactly into what is known today about the JU group of languages. The term 'JU' was coined by Westphal (1971:380) to refer to some of the San-speaking people living in north-western Botswana, north-eastern Namibia and southern Angola. It is derived from the fact that the word meaning 'person' in these languages is always something like 'JU', for example [z ù] in Tjum!kui, [zù] in eastern Ovamboland, and 'zhu' or 'dzhu' in Lloyd's manuscript. The term '!Kung' (or variants thereof, including the phonetically more correct '!Xũ') has been used previously to refer to this group, but from a linguistic point of view it is perhaps not quite satisfactory since it could refer both to the group as a whole as well as to the north-western sub-group who speak a dialect quite distinct from their south-eastern neighbours. The former group refer to themselves as '!Xũ' whereas further south, people refer to themselves as 'Ju/'hoansi' (older spelling 'Ju/wasi').

Snyman (1980:2) gives a rough pre-war distribution of the JU groups as follows:

!Xũ – north (and west) of the Omatako Omuramba
Ju/'hoan – between the Omatako and Epukiro Omurambas
≠Au//ẽi – south of the Epukiro Omuramba.

This distribution accords approximately with Köhler (1981:462) except that he divides the !Xũ sub-group here further into northern and western subgroups.

# COMMENTARY

The vocabulary of 'The Moon and the Hare' (previously published by D.F. Bleek in 1935) was compared with that of the JU dialect spoken in the Tjum!kui area (Ju/'hoan), and that spoken to the north-west of Tjum!kui in eastern Ovamboland, western Kavango and southern Angola (!Xũ). Both W. Bleek and L. Lloyd (1911:xii) and D. Bleek (1935b:261) are vague regarding the provenance of Lloyd's informants, so although one cannot be certain of their precise place of origin, some phonological and lexical aspects of her data confirm that her informants spoke !Xũ rather than Ju/'hoan.

The most obvious phonological features common between her data and that of !Xũ (from Heikkinen 1986, 1987 and Snyman 1980) are the following:

1. The lateral click [//] instead of the palatal [!] in words such as *//gu* 'water', *//go̰* (cf. !Xũ *g//ú*, *g//o̰* but Ju/'hoan *g!ú*, *g!o̰*).
2. The bilabial stop [b] instead of the nasal [m] in words such as *daba* 'child', *//gaba* 'enter' (cf. !Xũ *dàbà*, *g//aba* but Ju/'hoan *da'àmà*, *g!à'ámá*).
3. The diphthong [oe] instead of the vowel [o] in *kue* 'say'/particle (cf. !Xũ *koè*, but Ju/'hoan *kò*).
4. A vowel followed by the velar nasal [˜] instead of a nasalised sequence of vowels, for example in *!kaṅ* 'tree', *≠ga-aṅ* 'long' (cf. !Xũ *!à˜*, *g≠à'à˜* but Ju/'hoan *!ãìh*, *g≠ã'í*).
5. The presence of a nasal or vowel-nasalisation as opposed to its absence, for example in *ssiṅ* 'drink'/plural suffix, *!kõa* 'tell' (cf. !Xũ *sà˜*, *!õá*, but Ju/'hoan *sì*, *!óa*).

There are many examples of lexical items common between Lloyd's data and !Xũ, but not found in Ju/'hoan. Some of those found in 'The Moon and the Hare' are:

| | |
|---|---|
| *ara* | 'completely' |
| *debbi*, *dibbi* | 'return' |
| *taṅ* | 'body' |
| *//horu*, *n//o̰ru* | 'blood' |
| *//kau* | 'arrow' (cf. Ju/'hoan 'wooden-tipped toy arrow') |
| *ta* | 'and, but'. |

It is more difficult to pin-point Lloyd's data by syntactic means because !Xũ and Ju/'hoan are quite similar in this respect. It is also the case, however, that the discourse of 'The Moon and the Hare' is extremely simple and it seems possible that the informants Tamme and !Nanni could have simplified their language in the interest of clear understanding and explanation. In particular there is a distinct lack of what Heikkinen (1987:55) terms 'adverbial sentence links' such as 'if, when, because, and although'. It will be seen that only two conjunctions of this kind occur in the story, namely *ta* 'and/but' and *ka* 'while'. In her translation Lloyd inserted other conjunctions in order to make the narrative hang together, for example in *Ma ti !!ke, ta ti /kua //ku /kx'ao* (p.9628) '*When* thou diest, thou dost not smell badly' in which 'when' or 'if' is not explicit, and ... *ma ti /kua u a ba !nuerre, ta na ti !kuṅ a* (p.9640) '... thou shalt not go away to thy father's country; *for* I will kill thee' in which 'for' (meaning 'because') is absent.

Below is presented a list of the vocabulary found in the story which is compared to the Ju/'hoan and !Xũ equivalents where these could be found. Because Lloyd was sometimes inconsistent in the use of diacritics, these have been omitted with the exception of (i) a superscript tilde to show vowel nasalisation; (ii) a subscript tilde to show vowel pharyngealisation (replacing Lloyd's loop), and (iii) a dot above *n* for a velar nasal. In addition, to simplify the typography, the following replacements have been made: / for ǀk, *kx'* for ɣ, and *x* for ‘X̣

| LLOYD | JU/'HOAN | !XŨ | GLOSSARY |
|---|---|---|---|
| a, ma | à | à, bà | you (sg) |
| ara | (tõà) | árá | completely |
| ba | bá | bá | father |
| daa | dà'á | dà'á | fire |
| daba | da'àmà | dàbà, dà'àbà | child |
| de | dí | dé | female |
| debbi, dibbi | (ʃè) | dábbí | return |
| duri | dóré | dóré | other |
| e | hè | è | this, these |
| e | ó | òá | be |
| e | è | è | we (excl.) |
| gu | gù | gù | take |
| ha | ha | hà | he, she |
| hn | hè | ạ́˜ | and (emphatic) |
| já, kãi | zã | kãi | good |
| ka | ká | ká | it, they |
| ko̰a | koa̰ | ko̰a | fear |

| LLOYD | JU/'HOAN | !XŨ | GLOSSARY |
|---|---|---|---|
| kue | kò | kòe | say |
| kwi | khúi | khúi | hot, ill |
| kx'a | kxà | kxà | ground |
| m | m̀ | ṃ̀m | we (incl.) |
| ma see 'a' | | | |
| me, mi | mí | mí | me, my |
| msa | m̀tsá | ṃ̀mtsá | we (dual incl.) |
| n'n | ã'ã | – | no |
| na | (mí) | nà | I |
| na | nà | nà | give me! |
| o kx'wi | òkxúi | òòkxúi | speak |
| ra | – | ra | away |
| sa | tsa̰, -tsá | tsá | two |
| saa | tsà'á | tsà'á | hear |
| sha, tcha | tʃa̰ | tsa̰ | pour |
| shu(wa) | ʃú(a) | sú(wa) | lie (in) |
| ssin | sé | sá˜, há˜ | see, look at |
| ssi, si | sì, tshì | sì | laugh |
| ta | tè | tà | and, but |
| taba | (kúrú, n≠òm) | (kúrú) | make |
| tai | ta̰è | ta̰é | mother |
| tamm | ta̰m | ta̰m | throw (down) |
| tan | ámá | thá˜, thànà | body, – self |
| tanki | (n/úi) | (n/úi) | other |
| tcha | – | tsá | approach |
| tchana | – | – | a fruit (Bleek 1935b:278) |
| tchin | tʃ'˜ | ds'á˜ | cry |
| tchin | tʃhì | tshà˜, sà˜ | drink |
| tchi, tchissin | tʃí, tʃísì | tsí, tsísà˜ | thing, things |
| tchu | tʃ'ù | ts'ù | house |
| tenne | tànì | tànnì | bring |
| ti | (kú) | (kí) | verb part. |
| tsau | tsáu | tsáo | rise |
| tsema | ts'èmà | ts'ema | small |
| tsin | tsh˜, s˜ | tshà˜ | younger sibling |
| txa | txá | txá | shoot |

| LLOYD | JU/'HOAN | !XŨ | GLOSSARY |
|---|---|---|---|
| u | ú | ú | go |
| umm | ḿ | 'ḿ | eat |
| Uwe | – | Huwe | (name of early Bushman) |
| zau, dzau | dshàú | dsháo | woman |
| zhu(a), dzhu | zù | zù | person |
| /gaa-ssin | g/à'ásì | g/à'ásà˜ | eyes |
| /ge(ya) | g/àe(a) | g/è(ya) | come |
| /gi | g/ái | g/í | come out |
| /kaa | /'ã | /à'á | give |
| /kam | /ám | /ám | day |
| /kua, /kui | /óa | /óa | not |
| /kx'ao | /kx'áu | /x'áo | bad |
| /na | n/á | n/á | imp.part. |
| /ne | n/ái | n/é | head |
| /ne e | n/è'é | n/e'e | one |
| /ne //a | (n!ã'à) | (g!axru-n/a'a) | big |
| /u(wa) | /'ú(a) | /'ú | put in |
| /xu | /xú | /xú | divining charm |
| /Xue | – | – | (name) |
| ≠ã | ≠'ãá | – | odour |
| ≠ga-an | g≠ã'í | g≠à'à˜ | long, deep |
| ≠gumm | g≠òm | g≠òm | be silent |
| ≠khi | ≠hái | ≠hí | many |
| ≠nau | n≠haò | n≠ạ̀ò | fall |
| ≠ne-amm | n≠à'm | n≠à'm | beat |
| ≠xã | ≠xã | ≠xã | far |
| ≠xo ≠xo | – | ≠o ≠oo | knife |
| !gauru | (g//omm) | – | knobkerrie |
| !hun, (n)!kun | !hũ | !hṹ | kill |
| !ka | !aah | !àà | run |
| !kan | !ãìh | !à˜ | tree |
| !kan (-a) | !ãih | – | rattle, bang |
| !kao | !aoh | – | spouse |
| !kõa | !óa | !õá | tell |
| !korro | !oroh | – | (big) hole |
| !kou | !'áu | !'áu | scream, call |

| LLOYD | JU/'HOAN | !XŨ | GLOSSARY |
|---|---|---|---|
| !kun | !xũ | !xũũ | Bushman |
| !nu | n!ún | n!ũ | stand |
| !nua | n!õ'à | n!õ'a | throw |
| !nṵe | n!oè | n!òè | bag |
| !nuerre | n!óré | n!óré | country |
| !!hã, //hã | !'hã | //'hã | son |
| !!hi | !'hái | – | hare |
| !!ke | !ái | //áe | die |
| //go̰ | g!o̰ | g//o̰ | male, man |
| //gu | g!ú | g//ú | water |
| //horu | (/'ang) | n//o̰ru | blood |
| //kau | tʃhì | //áu | arrow |
| //ke//ke(ya) | (khũia, khòè) | – | resemble |
| //ku | //kx'ù | //x'ù | smell |
| //kuonna | //'óana | //'òana | carry |
| //na | n//á | n//ã | say, refuse, object |
| //na | n//ah | n//à | leave, let be |
| //nuai | n!úi | n//úi | moon |
| //zke | (!xóana) | – | reside |

What follows is an annotated reproduction of 'The Moon and the Hare' as it appears in Lloyd's original manuscript. A morpheme-by-morpheme translation is also given for those interested in the language itself. A modern, easy-to-read (and therefore slightly loose) translation of the story concludes the paper.

## *Lucy Lloyd Manuscript* 9627-9672, 10027-10030.

### *The Moon and the Hare*[1]

9627

*Uwe*[2] *ti taba tchissiǹ*[3] *e.*
Uwe make things these.

*Ta !!hi e /kua*[4] *o kx'ui*[5] *ja.*
And Hare this not speak good.

*Ta !!nuai ti*[6] *o kx'wi ja;*
And Moon speak good;

*ta !!nuai ti o kx'ui,*
and Moon speak,

*!kun //ke//ke ha dibbi,*
Bushman resemble him return,

*/kua !!ke ara.*
not die outright.

*Ta !!hi //na*
And Hare object

Uwe made these things. And the Hare did not speak nicely. For the Moon spoke nicely; for the Moon said that the Bushmen should like himself return again; (that they) should not die outright. But the Hare objected

Author's footnotes and other comments

1. Tamme from his grandfather Nakka.
2. *Uwe e !kuǹ*. Uwe was a Bushman. (Editor's translation).
3. *Uwe ti taba umm tchissiǹ*. Uwe made food things (i.e. animals which are eaten).
   (!Nanni says that the Moon's two houses were respected by the Hare, and that the Hare was bound by the Moon in one of them so that his tail is short.)

Editor's footnotes

4. The symbol lk standing for the dental click has been replaced by [/].
5. The symbol ) standing for an ejected velar affricate has been replaced by [kx'].
6. *ti* is a verb particle corresponding approximately to Ju/'hoan *ku*, and !Xũ *ki* or *ke*.

9628

*'ṅ-ṅ; !kuṅ !!ke ≠ā*
'No; Bushman dead odour

*//ku /kx'ao.' Ta //nuai !kōa*
smell bad.' And Moon tell

*!!hi, ta kue, '!Kuṅ*
Hare, and say, 'Bushman

*//ke-//ke*[1] *hṅ debbi,*
dead and return,

*hṅ /kua !!ke ara.'*
and not die outright.'

*Ta !!hi !kōa //nuai, ta kue,*
And Hare tell Moon, and say,

*'Ma ti !!ke, ta ti /kua //ku /kx'ao.'*
'Thou die, and not smell bad.'

*Ta !!hi //na; ta kue*
And Hare object[2]; and say

(saying) 'No, the odour of the dead Bushmen smells badly.' And the Moon spoke to the Hare and said, 'The dead Bushmen they (are to) return; they (are) not to die outright.' And the Hare spoke to the Moon and said, 'When thou diest, thou doest not smell badly,' and the Hare objected and said

Editor's footnote

1. Possibly there is a confusion here between *//ke* or *!!ke* 'die' and *//ke//ke* 'resemble'.
2. *//na* is usually translated by Lloyd as 'object' or 'refuse' in the context of an argument. It would seem from comparison with !Xũ and Ju/'hoan that strictly speaking it simply means 'say'. However, verbs of 'saying', 'telling' and so on generally require *ta kue* 'and say' immediately preceding direct speech and this could have led Lloyd to translate *//na* in this way.

9629

*'Na*[1] */kui saa a, ṅ-ṅ,*
'I not hear thee, no,

*!kun ≠ã /kao.' Ta gu*
Bushman odour bad.' And take

*!kun !!ke !nue*[2]*, ta !nua*
Bushmen dead bag, and throw

*ta !nua ara; ka*
and throw completely; they

*≠nau !kun !nuerre*
fall Bushman country

*!!ke !nue ≠nauwa !kuṅ*
dead bag fall Bushman

*!nuerre. Ta !!hi gu kwi*
country. And Hare take illness

*!nueya, kwi tsema.*
bag, illness small.

'I do not listen to thee, no, the odour of the Bushmen smells badly.' And took the bags of the dead Bushmen and threw them away, and threw them quite away; until they fell into the country of the Bushmen; the dead people's bags fell into the country of the Bushmen. And the Hare took illnesses in a bag, small illnesses.

Editor's footnote

1. Lloyd usually transcribes this pronoun 'I' by two words, i.e. *n a*. The single word *na*, however, corresponds well both with !Xũ *nà* 'I, for me' and Ju/'hoan *nà* 'for me', and we have re-transcribed it as one word throughout.

Author's footnote

2. *!!hi !nue, !!hi ti gu !!hi !nue ta ti /uwa !kuṅ kwi, kwi e !kuṅ ti !!ke, ta ti !nua.* The Hare's bags, the Hare took the Hare's bags and put into (them) the Bushman's illness; the illnesses which the Bushman , when ill, die of and throw them (i.e. the bags) away.

9630

*ta /nin-a, ta ti tamm ha /xu*
and sit-on, and throw his charms[1]

*ta o kx'ui ha /xu, '!Kuṅ*
and speak his charms, 'Bushman

*kwi tsema, /na tsau.' Ta ha*
ill small, may arise.' And his

*/xu !kōa ha, ta kue*
charms tell him, and say

*'!Kuṅ kwi tsema, /na*
'Bushman ill small, may

*tsau.' Ta !!hi ssin ha /xu,*
arise.' And Hare see his charms,

*ta /ni, ta*
and sit, and

and sat upon it, and threw his pieces of divining wood, and spoke to his pieces of divining wood, 'When the Bushmen are a little ill, they shall (?) arise.' And his pieces of divining wood spoke to him, and said, 'When the Bushmen are a little ill, they shall(?) arise.' And the Hare saw his pieces of divining wood and sat, and

Editor's footnote
1. Charms, i.e. 'pieces of divining wood'.

9631

*ti si ha /xu. Ta //nuai*
laugh his charms. And Moon

*o kx'ui !!hi, ta kue, 'A !!hã*
spoke Hare, and say, 'Your son

*!!ke, n/a debbi, hṅ /kua*
die, may return and not

*!!ke ara.' Ta !!hi !kōa //nuai*
die outright.' And Hare tell Moon

*ta kue, 'Me !!hã ≠a //ku /kx'ao.'*
and say, 'My son odour smell bad.'

*Ta tsau ta gu ha !!hã, ta /u*
And rise and take his son, and insert

*ha*[1] *!nue, ta gu, ta !nua*
him bag, and take, and throw

laughed at his pieces of divining wood. And the Moon spoke to the Hare, and said 'Thy dead child shall return, it (?) shall not die outright.' And the Hare spoke to the Moon and said, 'The odour of my son smells badly.' And arose and took his son and put him into his (the Hare's) bag; and took it up, and threw (it) away

Editor's footnote

1. */u ha* is more likely */uwa* (!Xũ /'*úwa*) 'put (him) into'. However the translation is not affected.

9632

*!nu arra*[1] *!nuerre*
throw completely country

*tanki. Ta /Xue /ni, ta ti ssi*
other. And /Xue sat, and laugh

*!!hí. Ta !!hi /ge shu,*
Hare. And Hare come lie down,

*te tchiṅ ha !!hā. Ta /Xue gu*
and cry his son. And /Xue take

*!kaṅ*[2]*, ta /ge ≠neamm !kaṅ-a*[3] *!!hi*
stick, and go hit stick Hare

*/ne; ta //horu ti sha, ta !!hi*
head; and blood flow, and Hare

*shu, ta ti tchiṅ.*
lie down, and cry.

threw (it) quite away into another country (place). And /Xue sat, and was laughing at the Hare. And the Hare went to lie down, (and) was crying for his son. And /Xue took a stick[2], and came to beat the Hare; beat, wounding the Hare's head; and the blood flowed; and the Hare lay down, and was crying.

Editor's footnote

1. *!nu arra* is probably more likely *!nua* 'throw' *ra* 'away', i.e. a confusion between *ara* 'completely, outright' and *ra* 'away'.
3. Lloyd's translation suggests that *!kaṅ-a* is 'stick'. From the suffix *-a* it would seem more likely that *!kaṅ* here is a verb, meaning 'rattle, bang' in series with the preceding verb *≠neamm* 'beat'. A better translation might thus be 'beat the Hare, banging him on the head' (cf. Ju/'hoan *!āih* 'bang, rattle, clank').

Author's footnote

2. *Ngoba !gauru, ka !gu e // ´i; ha /ne ti /ne //a.* A Makoba knobkerrie, the name of which is *// ´i*; its head is large. (The word *!kaṅ* is a general term for 'tree, wood, stick'. Ed.)

9633

*Ta //nuai //na, ta kue,*
And Moon object, and say,

*'//Na !!hi.' Ta /Xue /kua saa,*
'Leave Hare.' And /Xue not listen,

*ta n≠eamm !!hi, ka !kōa //nuai*
and beat Hare, while tell Moon

*te kue, '!!Hi ti //na; ta /kua*
and say, 'Hare object; and not .

*//ke-//keya msa*[1] *//ke, /na debbi*
resemble us two, then return

*ta ti tchiṅ-a zhua //ke*
and cries for person who die

*ara. Ta !!hi ti //na,*
outright. And Hare objected,

*ti /kua //ke//ke*
not resemble

And the Moon objected, and said, 'Let the Hare alone!' And /Xue did not listen, (and) was beating the Hare, while speaking to the Moon; and said, 'The Hare was objecting; (he) does not, resembling us[1.] die and (?) return, for he cries for (one who) dies altogether. For the Hare objected and does not resemble

Author's footnote
1 *sa /Xue, sa //nuai* /Xue and the Moon.

9634

*msa, /na debbi.' Ta !!hi de*
us, return.' And Hare-female

*//na, ta kue, 'E ti //ke, e ti //ke*
object, and say, 'We die, we die

*ara ta e ≠a ti //ku*
outright and our odour smell

*/kx'ao, /Xue. Ma ti ≠neamma me !kao*
bad, /Xue. Thou beat my spouse

*/ne kue !gauru; ta me !kao*
head with knobkerrie; and my spouse

*/kua //ke//keya a, ta e dzhu*
not resemble thee, and be person

*duri; ta a tai ti e Ku-//na-*
other; and thy mother be Ku//na

*/gaa-ssin*[1]*; ta a ba e*
eyes; and thy father be

us, who (?) return.' And the Hare's wife objected, and said, 'When we die, we die outright, for our odour smells badly, /Xue. Thou beatest my husband's head with a knobkerrie; and my husband does not resemble thee, and is a different (kind of) person; for thy mother is Ku//na-/gaa-ssin[1]; and thy father is

Editor's footnote

1. *Ku-//na-/gaa-ssin* or *Ku//na /gaassin*, i.e. Ku//na's Eyes.

9635

*Xe-//n'u; ta m ti /kua // 'ke !nuerre*
/Xe-//n'u; and we not live(?) country

*/ne e. Ta e !nuerre tanki, ta*
one. And our country other, and

*e tai tanki ta e tai e*
our mother other and our mother be

*!!hi. Ta a tai tanki; ta a*
are. And thy mother other; and thy

*nuerre tanki. Ta /Xue saa, ta ko̰a,*
country other. And /Xue hear and fear,

*ta shu, ta ti tchiṅ, 'ṅ-ṅ, zau*
and lie down, and cry, 'No, woman

*tāi o kx'ui mi; na ti ko̰a zau*
desist speak me; I fear woman

*o kx'ui.' Ta tchiṅ, tchiṅ, ta //ke;*
speak.' And cry, cry, and die[1],

*ta shuwa kx'a. Ta !!hi-di*
and lay on ground. And Hare-female

*gu !kaṅ[2] ta /ge !nu, ta ti*
take stick and go stand, and

*≠neamm /Xue*
beat /Xue

/Xe-//n'u; and we(?) do not live in one country. For our country is different, and our mother is different; for our mother is the Hare. For thy mother (is) different; and thy country is different.' And /Xue heard; and was afraid; and lay down crying. And /Xue lay down and was crying, 'No; the woman must not speak to me; I am afraid of women's speaking', and cried and became insensible, and lay on the ground. And the Hare's wife took a stick[2], and came to beat /Xue

Editor's footnote

1. *//ke* 'die' or 'become insensible'.

Author's footnote

2. *!kaṅ e !ke*. The stick was a (pointed) digging-stick. (She poked /Xue with it, his [illegible] and eyes.)

9636

*//ke, ≠ne-amm ≠ne-amm /Xue*
die, beat beat /Xue

*//ke, ti u, ti tsaa ha tchu;*
dead, go, reach her house;

*/ge /ni. Ti taba //gu kwi, ta /ge*
go sit. Make water hot, and go

*tcha /Xue kue //gu kwi. Ta /Xue*
pour /Xue with water hot. And /Xue

*tchiṅ, tchiṅ ko̰a //gu kwi. Ta*
cry, cry fear water hot. And

*!!hi zau o kx'ui /Xue, '/Xue ≠gumm*
Hare woman speak /Xue, /Xue be silent

insensible, was beating /Xue (while) insensible, went away and reached her house; came to sit down; made water hot, and came to pour hot water upon /Xue. And /Xue cried, cried being afraid of the hot water. And the she-Hare told /Xue that /Xue must be silent

9637

*'/Xue, na ti !kun a, n/a ≠gumm.'*
'/Xue, I kill thee, be silent.'

*Ta /Xue ti tchiṅ, '//Na mi yai!*
And /Xue cry, 'Leave me oh!

*Tãi n!kuṅ mi, yai!' Ta !!hi*
Desist kill me, oh!' And Hare

*zau o kx'ui /Xue: '/Xue, na ti*
woman speak /Xue: '/Xue, I

*!hun a, /na ≠gumm.' Ta /Xue ti*
kill thee, be silent.' And /Xue

'/Xue! I shall kill thee. Be silent.' But /Xue was crying 'Leave me alone! Oh dear! Desist from killing me! Oh dear!' But the she-Hare said to /Xue, 'I shall kill thee! Be silent!' And /Xue was crying and exclaimed, 'Desist from killing me! Oh dear!' But the she-Hare

*tchiṅ ta kue: 'Tãi !kuṅ mi yai!'*
cry and say: 'Desist kill me oh!'

*Ta !!hi-de*
And Hare-female

9638

*kue: '/Kam e, na ti !kuṅ /Xue.'*
say: 'Day this, I kill /Xue.'

*Ta //nuai o kx'ui !!hi-de,*
And Moon speak Hare-female,

*ta kue: '//Na /Xue.' Ta !!hi-de*
and say: 'Leave /Xue.' And Hare-female

*//na: 'Ta /Xue ti ≠ne-amm me !kao,*
object: 'And /Xue beat my spouse,

*ta na ti !kuṅ /Xue.' Ta //nuai*
and I kill /Xue.' And Moon

*//na, ta kue: '//Na /Xue.'*
object and say: 'Leave /Xue.'

*Ta /Xue saa, ta shu,*
And /Xue hear, and lie down,

exclaimed, 'Today I will kill /Xue.' And the Moon spoke to the she-Hare and said, 'Let /Xue alone.' And the she-Hare objected (saying), 'But /Xue beat my husband and I will kill /Xue.' But the Moon objected; and said: 'Let /Xue alone.' And /Xue heard and lay

9639

*ti tchiṅ, ta kue: '!!Hi tãi*
cry, and say: 'Hare desist

*!kuṅ mi yai!' Ta //hi kue: 'Na ti*
kill me oh!' And Hare say: 'I

crying. And (he) said, 'Hare! Desist from killing me! Oh dear!' And the Hare said, 'I will kill thee.' And /Xue

*!kuṅ a.'* *Ta* */Xue saa;* *ha ti tchiṅ,*
kill thee.' And /Xue hear; he cry,

*'Na ti !!ke, yai! Ná ti !!ke, yai!'*
'I die, oh! I die, oh!

*Ta* *!!hi-de:* *'/Xue, ≠gumm, na*
And Hare-female: '/Xue, be silent, I

*!kuṅ a,* */Xue tãi* *tchiṅ.'*
kill thee, /Xue desist cry.'

heard; he was crying, 'I shall die! Oh dear! I shall die! Oh dear! And the she-Hare (said) '/Xue! Be silent! I am the one(?) who kills thee! /Xue leave off crying.'

9640

*Ta* */Xue //na:* *'//Na* *mi, na u m*
And /Xue object: 'Leave me, I go my

*ba* *!nuerre.'* *!!Hi-de !* *!kõa*
father country.' Hare-female tell

*/Xue, '/Kamma e,* *ma ti /kua u*
/Xue, 'Day this, thou not go

*a* *ba* *!nuerre,* *ta* *na ti !kuṅ*
thy father country, and I kill

*a.'* *Ta* */Xue //na,* *'//Na* *mi,*
thee.' And /Xue object, 'Leave me,

*na u, yai! //Na* *mi, na u* *m* *ba*
I go oh! Leave me, I go my father

*!nuerre,* *yai!*
country, oh!

And /Xue objected (saying), 'Let me alone, that (?) I may go to my father's country.' The she-Hare told (?) /Xue, 'Today, thou shalt not go away to thy father's country; for I will kill thee.' And /Xue objected (saying), 'Let me alone that I may go away! Oh dear! Let me alone that I may go away to my father's country, oh dear!'

9641

*//Na mi, na u m ba*
Leave me, I go my father

*!nuerre, yai! //Na mi, na u m*
country, oh! Leave me, I go my

*ba !nuerre, yai, tãi n!kuṅ*
father country, oh, desist kill

*mi, yai! //Na mi, na u, ssiṅ m*
me, oh! Leave me, I go, see my

*tai, yai, tãi !kuṅ me, yai!'*
mother, oh, desist kill me, oh!'

*!!Hi-de //na: '/Kam e, na /kua*
Hare-female reply: 'Day this, I not

*saa //nuai, na /kua ko̰a //nuai,*
hear Moon, I not fear Moon,

*ta ti !kuṅ a.'*
and kill thee.'

Let me alone that I may go away to my father's country! Oh dear! desist from killing me! Oh dear! Let me alone that I may go away, to see my mother! Oh dear! Desist from killing me. Oh dear!' The she-Hare replied (saying), 'For today, I do not listen to the Moon, I am not afraid of the Moon, but (?) will kill thee.'

9642

*Ta !!hi //go shu shu ta tsau,*
And Hare male lie lie and rise,

*ti !kuṅ /Xue; ta /Xue /kua //ke*
kill /Xue; and /Xue not die

*ara, ta //ke tsema, ta tsau;*
outright, and die small, and rise;

*ta ti si, ta kue: 'Eehe,*
and laugh, and say: 'Yes,

*Ku //na /gaa-ssiṅ //hã,*
Ku//na Eyes son,

*/Xe-//n'u //hã /kui //ke ara,*
/Xe-//n'u son not die outright,

*/Xue !gu[1] /ne[1].' Ta*
/Xue name be one(?)'. And

And the male Hare was
lying down, and arose,
killing /Xue; but
/Xue did not die
outright, but was a
little dead, and
arose, and was
laughing, and
exclaimed, 'Ha! Ha!
The son (?) of Ku//na-
/gaa-ssin, the son(?)
of /Xe-//n'u does not
die outright,
..............[1]

Editor's footnote

1. Left untranslated by Lloyd. Suggested translation: '.../Xue's name (stands) alone.'

9643

*//nuai /ge ≠ne-amm /Xue,*
Moon go beat /Xue,

*ka ha tchiṅ; ≠ne-amm /Xue,*
while he cry; beat /Xue,

*≠ne-amm /Xue, ≠ne-amm !kuṅ*
beat /Xue, beat kill

*/Xue. Ta /Xue shu shu, ta*
/Xue. And /Xue lie lie, and

*/kua //ke ara, ta ssi,*
not die outright, and laugh,

*ta ti si, si ka*
and laugh, laugh while

*o kx'wi. Ta /kam /gi*
speak. And sun come out

*ta /Xue*
and /Xue

Moon came to beat
/Xue, until he cried;
beat /Xue, beat /Xue,
beating killed /Xue.
And /Xue lay; and /Xue
was lying; and did not
die altogether; but
sat up, and was
laughing, laughing and
talking. And the sun
rose, and /Xue

9644

*//ga //nuai*[1]*, ta /u*[2] *//nuai tchu,*
go Moon, and put in Moon house,

*ta /ni. Ta //nuai o kx'ui ha, ta kue:*
and sit. And Moon speak him, and say:

*'/Xue, na ti !kuṅ a, /na u a*
'/Xue, I kill thee, so go thy

*tai !nuerre.' Ta /Xue shuwa*
mother country.' And /Xue lie on

*kx'a, ti tchiṅ, tchiṅ, tchiṅ, ta*
ground, cry, cry, cry, and

*//ke. Ta //nuai gu*
die. And Moon take

went to the Moon, and entered[2] the Moon's house, and sat down; and the Moon spoke to him, and said, '/Xue, I shall kill thee; do (?) go away; go to thy mother's country.' And /Xue lay on the ground crying, continuing to cry, and died. And the Moon took

Author's Footnote

1. */Kam /gi, ta ha /u //nuai tchu.* The sun rose and he (/Xue) entered the Moon's house.

Editor's footnote

2. The use here of the transitive verb */u* 'put in, insert' instead of *//gabba* (see manuscript p.9116) 'enter' seems to be a mistake. (cf. !Xũ */'ú* 'put in' versus *g//àbá* 'enter' and Ju/'hoan */'ú* and *g!à'ámá.*) This usage suggests that the informant may have been helping Lloyd by using a semantically closely related and more familiar word, despite its being ungrammatical.

9645

*!kaṅ, ta /ge ≠ne-amm /Xue //ke.*
stick, and come beat /Xue dead.

*Ta /Xue shu, shuwa kx'a, ta ti*
And /Xue lie, lie on ground, and

*tchiṅ, tchiṅ-a //gu. Ta //nuai*
cry, cry for water. And Moon

*o kx'wi /Xue: '/Xue u a !nuerre,*
speak /Xue: '/Xue go thy country,

*/ne tchiṅ*[1] *//gu kue a !nuerre.'*
drink water thy country.'

*Ta /Xue //na: 'M tai yai hei,*
And /Xue object: 'My mother alas,

*me !nuerre*
my country

a stick and came to beat the dead /Xue. And /Xue lay, lay on the ground, and was crying, crying for water. And the Moon said to /Xue, '/Xue go to thy country; cry for water in thy country.' And /Xue objected (crying out) 'Alas, my mother, My country is

Editor's footnote

1. Lloyd translates *tchiṅ* here as 'cry', but in the context 'drink' seems more likely. (cf. !Xũ *tshà~* 'cry' and Ju/'hoan *tʃhi* and *tʃ'ĩ* respectively.) It is likely that these words were confused, so the translation should read '… and drink water in thy country ….'

9646

*≠xã, yai hei, //nuai tãi*
far, alas, Moon desist

*n!kuṅ mi, yai, //nuai tãi*
kill me, alas, Moon desist

*n!kuṅ me yai.' Ta //nuai //na,*
kill me alas.' And Moon say,

*ta kue /Xue u ha*[1] *!nuerre. Ta /Xue*
and say /Xue go his country. And /Xue

*//na, ta kue, 'Me !nuerre ≠xã.'*
object, and say, 'My country far.'

*Ta /ni ti tchiṅ ha*[1] *!nuerre:*
And sit cry country:

*'/Kam*
'Sun

far off! Alas!
Moon! Desist from
killing me! Alas!
Moon! Do not kill me!
Alas!' And the Moon
repeated, and said
/Xue must go to this
country. But /Xue
objected. And (he)
said, 'My country is
far off.' And (he)
sat down, crying for
his country, (and
saying), 'When the
sun

Editor's footnote

1. *u ha* 'go to his' and *tchiṅ ha* 'cry for his' should more likely be *uwa ha* and *tchiṅ-a ha* respectively since these verbs are used transitively here. Probably the *-a* suffix of the verb was not pronounced distinctly, being run together with the following *ha*.

9647

*/gi, na u me !nuerre, yai he.'*
rise, I go my country, alas.'

*Ta //nuai tsau, ta gu ≠xo≠xo, ti*
And Moon rise, and take knife,

*tcha /Xue. /Xue /ni, ti ssiṅ ha,*
come /Xue. /Xue sit, look at him,

*ka si ta kue: 'Ehe, ehe.' Ta*
while laugh and say: 'Ha ha, ha ha.' And

*//nuai /geya ha, ti kx'ui ha:*
Moon come to him, speak him:

*/Xue, u a*[1] *!nuerre.'*
/Xue, go thy country.'

rises, I will(?) go to my country. Oh dear!' And the Moon arose, and took a knife(?), coming towards /Xue. And /Xue sat, looking at him, meanwhile laughing, and said(?), 'Ha ha, ha ha.' And the Moon came to him, saying to him, '/Xue, go away to thy country.'

Editor's footnote
1. This should be *uwa a* instead of *u a*. (See Editor's footnote, p.27).

9648

*Ta /Xue //na, ta kue: 'ṅ-ṅ, na*
And /Xue object, and say: 'No, I

*/kui u me !nuerre; ta ti ko̰a me*
not go my country; and fear my

*!nuerre, ta me !nuerre ≠xã.'*
country, and my country far.'

*Ta //nuai gu /Xue; ta /Xue ti*
And Moon take /Xue; and /Xue

*si, ta kue: 'E he. Kue*[1]*,*
laugh, and say: 'Ha ha! Mind,

*na shu, //nuai !kuṅ mi.'*
I lie, Moon kill me.'

*Ta shu, ta //nuai*
And lie, and Moon

But /Xue objected; and said 'No, I will not go away to my country; but am afraid of my country, for my country is far off.' And the Moon took hold of /Xue; and /Xue was laughing, and exclaimed, 'Ha ha! ....[1] I will lie down, so that the Moon may kill me.' And he lay down, and the Moon

Editor's footnote

1. *kue* left untranslated by Lloyd. Suggested translation 'Mind!, Get out of the way!' (cf. !Xũ *kòe* or *kxòe*, and Ju/'hoan *kxòe*.)

9649

*ti !kuṅ ha ka ha si, ta kue,*
kill him while he laugh, and say,

*'Ehe.' Ta //nuai o kx'ui ha: '/Xue,*
'Ha ha!' And Moon speak him: '/Xue,

*≠gumm; na !kuṅ a.' Ta /Xue saa,*
be silent; I kill thee.' And /Xue hear,

*ta //na, ta kue: 'Na /kui*
and reply, and say: 'I not

*≠gumm, ta ti o kx'ui.' Ta //nuai*
be silent, and speak.' And Moon

*o kx'ui /Xue: '/Xue, na ti !kuṅ a,*
speak /Xue: '/Xue, I kill thee,

was killing him while he was laughing, and exclaimed 'Ha ha!' And the Moon said to him, '/Xue! Be silent! I am the one who is killing (will kill?) thee!' And /Xue listened, and replied, and said, 'I will not be silent; but will speak.' And the Moon said to /Xue, '/Xue! I will kill thee,

9650

*/na ≠gumm.' /Xue o kx'ui //nuai:*
so be silent.' /Xue speak Moon:

*'Na /kui ko̰a a, na ti o kx'wi*
'I not fear thee, I speak

*m a*[1] *!kuṅ mi.' Ta*
although thou kill me.' And

*//nuai saa, ti !kuṅ /Xue, ka /Xue*
Moon hear, kill /Xue, while /Xue

*tchiṅ: 'Yai, yai, yai.' Ta !kuṅ /Xue,*
cry: 'Ah, ah, ah.' And kill /Xue,

*ta tsau, ta /ge /ni,*
and rise, and come sit,

'Be silent!' And 'Xue said to the Moon, 'I am not afraid of thee, I will speak although thou (if thou?)[1] dost kill me.' And the Moon heard, killing /Xue, while /Xue cried out, 'Ah! Ah! Ah!' And (he, i.e. the Moon) killed /Xue, and arose, and came to sit down,

Editor's footnote

1. In the manuscript it appears as though *ma* was at first written as a single word (which suggests the translation is simply 'thou') but later separated into two by means of a slash, with *m* translated as 'although' or 'if' and *a* as 'thou', even though *a* appears nowhere else in the text as a subject pronoun. No conjunction corresponding to this *m* could be found either in !Xũ or Ju/'hoan and it appears that Lloyd divided this word and translated it in this way to make her translation more coherent. 'Although' would ordinarily occur as *xáú ká* in !Xũ and as *xábé ká* in Ju/'hoan.

9651

*ti si, ti si /Xue. Ta /Xue !!ke,*
laugh, laugh /Xue. And /Xue die,

*ta shuwa kx'a, /kua !!ke ara,*
and lie on ground, not die outright,

*ta !!ke tsema, ta shu, ta shu, ta shu,*
and die small, and lie, and lie, and lie,

*ta /kua !!ke ara, ta tsau; tsau,*
and not die outright, and rise; rise,

*/ni, ta si, ta o kx'wi //nuai, '//Nuai,*
sit, and laugh, and speak Moon, 'Moon,

*!kuṅ mi.' Ta //nuai //na,*
kill me.' And Moon refuse,

laughing, laughing at /Xue! And /Xue died, and lay on the ground, did not die altogether, but died a little and lay, and lay, and lay, and did not die altogether, but arose, sat, and laughed. And said to the Moon: 'Moon, kill me.' But the Moon refused,

9652

*ta kue, 'Na ti ko̰a a, ta na ti*
and say, I fear thee, and I

*!kuṅ a, ma ti /kua !!ke ara,*
kill thee, thou not die outright,

*ta na ti ko̰a a.' Ta /Xue saa,*
and I fear thee.' And /Xue hear,

*ti shuwa kw'a, ti tchiṅ. Ta //nuai*
lie on ground, cry. And Moon

*/kaa /Xue kue //gu, ta /Xue tchiṅ*[1].
give /Xue water, and /Xue drink.

*/Xue tchiṅ*[1] *//gu, /ni, ta ti si //nuai.*
/Xue drink water, sit, and laugh Moon.

*Ta //nuai /kaa ha kue*
And Moon give him

and said: 'I fear thee, and I kill thee, but thou dost not die altogether, and I fear thee.' And /Xue heard, and lay on the ground and cried. And the Moon presented /Xue with water, and /Xue cried out[1]. /Xue cried[1] about the water, sat, and laughed. And the Moon presented him with

Editor's footnote

1. Lloyd translates *tchiṅ* here as 'cry', but in the context 'drink' seems more likely, thus '... and /Xue drank the water ...' (See Editor's footnote 1, p.26).

9653

*umm, ha ti umm. Ha umm ta /ni,*
eat, he eat. He eat and sit,

*ta o kx'ui //nuai: '/Kam ti /gi,*
and speak Moon: 'Sun rise,

*na ti u m tai !nuerre, /na na*
I go my mother country, so give me

*tchana, na /uwa me !nue, /uwa !nue*
? I put in my bag, put in bag

*sa, /na //kuonna, /na tenne m tai*
two, carry, bring my mother

*!nuerre.'*
country.'

food, he ate. He ate and sat, and said to the Moon: 'The sun rises, I go to my mother's country, let me (have) .... that I may put it into my bag, into two bags, let me carry it, let me take it to my mother's country.'

9654

*Ta //nuai //na; ta kue, 'Na /kui*
And Moon refuse; and say, 'I not

*/kaa a kue tchana.' Ta /Xue saa, ti*
give thee ?.' And /Xue hear,

*tchiṅ, ti tchiṅ-a tchana. Ta //nuai*[1]
cry, cry for ?. And Moon

*gu !kaṅ /ge ≠ne-amm /Xue*
take stick come beat /Xue

*ka /Xue tchiṅ, ≠ne-amm !kaṅ-a*
while /Xue cry, beat bang

*/Xue, ta /Xue shu,*
/Xue, and /Xue lie,

And the Moon refused and said: 'I will not present thee with ...' And /Xue heard, cried, cried for ... The Moon took a stick, came to beat /Xue, when /Xue cried, beat the stick on /Xue's head, and /Xue lay

Author's footnote

1. !Nanni: *//Nuai tshi ti //ke//keya /Xue tshi; ti ≠gaan; //nuai ≠gaan; /nu /ne //a; n//uai tshi /kua e tshi tsema, ta e tshi /nu /ne //a. //Nuai sa /Xue, ti taba tshi ≠khi, /kui taba tshi /ne e, taba tshi ≠khi*. The Moon's thing was like /Xue's thing; it is tall, the Moon is tall, it is big. The Moon's thing is not a little thing, for it is a big thing. The Moon hears /Xue, makes many things, does not make one thing, makes many things.

9655

*ti tchiṅ. Ta //nuai gu //kau,*
cry. And Moon take arrow,

*txa /Xue. Ta /Xue shuwa kx'a,*
shoot /Xue. And /Xue lie on ground,

*ti tchiṅ. Ta /Xue tsau, ti e daba*
cry. And /Xue rise, be child

*tsema, ti shu ti tchiṅ. //Nuai !nu*
small, lie cry. Moon stand

*ti ≠ne-amm /Xue, /Xue tchiṅ. /Xue*
beat /Xue, /Xue cry. /Xue

*tsema, ta /kua e dzhu /ne //a,*
small, and not be person big,

lay and cried. And the Moon took an arrow, shot /Xue. And /Xue lay on the ground and cried. And /Xue arose and was a little child, lay and cried. The Moon stood, and beat /Xue. /Xue cried. /Xue was little, and was not a big person,

9656

*ta e daba tsema ta shu,*
but be child small and lie,

*ti tchiṅ. Ta ti tchiṅ, ta //na*
cry. And cry, and refused

*ta kue, '//Nuai, //na me, na e daba*
and say, 'Moon, leave me, I be child

*tsema, //nuai tãi ≠ne-amm !kuṅ*
small, Moon desist beat kill

but was a little child and lay and cried. And cried, 'Moon let me be, for I am a little child, Moon leave off beating, killing me.' And the Moon refused. 'Thou art not a little child, but art a grown up person, and I will kill thee. And shot

*mi.' Ta ||nuai ||na, 'Ma /kua e*
me.' And Moon refuse, 'Thou not be

*daba tsema, ta e dzhu /nu /ne ||a,*
child small, and be person big,

*ta na ti !kuṅ a.' Ta txa /Xue;*
and I kill thee.' And shoot /Xue;

*ta /Xue shu, ti tchiṅ. '||Nuai ||na*
and /Xue lie, cry. 'Moon leave

*mi, yai he. ||Nuai ||na mi yai he.'*
me, alas. Moon leave me alas.'

/Xue and /Xue lay and cried: 'Moon, leave me be, oh dear, Moon let me be, oh dear.'

9657

*Ta ||nuai /kua saa, ta ||na,*
And Moon not hear, and refuse,

*ta kue, '/Kamma e, na ti !kuṅ*
and say, 'Day this, I kill

*a, /na ≠gumm, na !kuṅ a.' Ta ti*
thee, be silent, I kill thee.' And

*≠ne-amm /Xue, ka /Xue tchiṅ,*
beat /Xue, while /Xue cry,

*≠ne-amm !kuṅ /Xue, /Xue shu,*
beat kill /Xue, /Xue lie,

*ti tchiṅ, 'Tãi n!kuṅ daba tsema,*
cry, 'Desist kill child small,

*yai.' Ta ||nuai !kõa /Xue, '/Kamma*
alas.' And Moon tell /Xue, 'Day

the Moon did not listen, and refused. And said: 'Today I will kill thee, do be silent, I will kill thee.' And beat /Xue, as /Xue was crying, beat killing /Xue. /Xue lay and cried, 'Leave off killing a little child, oh dear!' And the Moon spoke to /Xue: 'Today, I kill a little child, I do not fear a little child.' And said to his wife: 'Give me hot water,

*e, na ti !kuṅ daba tsema, ti /kua*
this, I kill child small, not

*ko̰a daba tsema.' Ta o kx'wi ha dzau,*
fear child small.' And speak his woman,

*'Na //gu kwi,*
'Give me water hot,

9658

*na tcha /Xue.' Ta ha dzau //na;*
I pour /Xue.' And his wife refuse;

*ta ha /ge ≠ne-amm ha dzau ka*
and he come beat his wife while

*ha dzau tchiṅ. Ta ha dzau gu !kaṅ*
his wife cry. And his wife take stick

*ti ≠ne-amm ha ka ha !kou.*
beat him while he scream.

*Ha kue, 'Hai hai, me dzau, tāi*
He say, 'Hi hi, my woman, desist

*≠ne-amm me.' Ta ha //na*[1] *ha dzau,*
beat me.' And he leave his woman,

*ta ha dzau gu !kaṅ*
and his woman take stick,

that I may pour it on /Xue.' And his wife refused, and he went to beat his wife, while his wife cried. And his wife took a stick, beat him while he screamed. And he let alone?/refused[1] his wife, and his wife took a stick,

Editor's footnote
1. *//na* is sometimes translated as 'let be/let alone' and sometimes as 'refuse/object'. (cf. !Xũ *n//ā* 'say' and *n//à* 'leave', and Ju/'hoan *n//á* and *n//ah* respectively.)

9659

*ti ≠ne-amm ha, ka ha !ka.*
beat him, while he run.

*Ha dzau ≠ne-amm !kan-a ha /ne;*
His woman beat bang his head;

*ta ha ti tchiṅ. Ta ha dzau*
and he cry. And his woman

*//na ha; ta /ge /ni ta ti si.*
leave him; and come sit and laugh.

*Ta ha /ge !nu, ti tchiṅ,*
And he come stand, cry,

*'!!He he, !!he he.' Ta ha dzau*
Alas, alas.' And his woman

and beat him, while he ran. His wife beat with the stick upon his head; and he cried. His wife let him alone; and came to sit, and laughed. And he came to stand, and cried, 'Oh dear, oh dear,' and his wife

9660

*!kõa ha, '/Kam tanki, na ti !kuṅ*
tell him, 'Day other, I kill

*a.' Ta ha !!na, 'Tãi n!kuṅ*
thee.' And he object, 'Desist kill

*mi.' Ta ha dzau //na, 'Na*
me.' And his woman refuse, 'I

*/kui saa a, /na a tãi*
not hear thee, thou desist

*o kx'wi, /na ≠gumm.' Ta ha*
speak, so be silent.' And he

*o kx'wi ha dzau, 'Na /kui*
speak his woman, 'I not

said to him, 'Another day, I will kill thee.' And he objected: 'Leave off killing me.' And his wife refused: 'I will not listen to thee, but will kill thee, do leave off talking, be silent.' And he said to his wife: 'I do not

9661

*ko̰a a.' Ta ha dzau !kõa ha,*
fear thee.' And his woman tell him,

*'Ta /kam tanki na ti !kuṅ a, ti*
'And day other I kill thee,

*/kua ko̰a a, /na ≠gumm.' Ta ti*
not fear thee, be silent.' And

*!kõa ha dzau, 'Na ti e //go̰ ta ti*
tell his woman, I be man and

*/kua ko̰a a; /kam tanki na ti*
not fear thee; day other I

*!kuṅ a, na ti /kua ko̰a a ba,*
kill thee, I not fear thy father,

*ta ti /kua*
and not

fear thee.' And his wife said to him: 'Another day I kill thee, I will not respect thee, do be silent.' And (he) said to his wife: 'I am a man, and do not fear thee; another day I will kill thee, and not fear thy father, and not

9662

*ko̰a a dzhu-essiṅ, ta ti !kuṅ a,*
fear thy people, and kill thee,

*a dzhu-ssiṅ ti !kuṅ mi. Na ti /kui*
thy people kill me. I not

*saa a o kx'wi. Ta ti !kuṅ a.'*
hear thy speak. And kill thee.'

*Ta ha dzau !kõa ha, 'Na /kui*
And his woman tell him, 'I not

fear thy people, and will kill you, thy people will kill me. I will not listen to thy talk, but will kill thee.' And his wife said to him: 'I do not fear thee, kill me.' And the man said to the woman,

*ko̰a a; !kuṅ mi.' Ta //go̰ o kx'wi*
fear thee, kill me.' And man speak

*dzau,*
woman,

9663

*'Na ti /kui !kuṅ a, na ti !kõa*
'I not kill thee, I tell

*a, ta a dzhu ≠khi, ta ti*
thee, and thy people many, and

*!kuṅ mi, ta na ti ko̰a a dzhu; na*
kill me, and I fear thy people; I

*ti /kua !kuṅ a, ti !kõa a.'*
not kill thee, tell thee.'

*Ta ha o kx'wi dzau, 'Na ti /kua*
And he speak woman, 'I not

*!kuṅ a, na ti !kõa a;*
kill thee, I tell thee;

*/na tãi n!kuṅ mi; /na //na mi.'*
desist kill me; leave me.'

'I will not kill thee, I will talk to thee for thy people are many, they will kill me, and I fear thy people. I do not kill thee, I will talk to (scold?) thee.' And he said to the woman: 'I will not kill thee, I say to thee, do leave off killing me, do leave me alone.'

9664

*Ta dzau //na: 'Na ti /kua !kuṅ*
And woman refuse: 'I not kill

*a, ta ti e dzau; ta ma ti e*
thee, and be woman; and thou be

And the woman refused, 'I will not kill thee, for (I) am a woman, but although thou art a man thou killest

*//go̰, ti !kuṅ mi; ta na ti /kua !kuṅ a,*
man, kill me; and I not kill thee

*ta e dzau.' Ta dzau //na,*
and be woman.' And woman refused,

*ta kue, '/Xue ti !kuṅ a, ta na /kui*
and say, '/Xue kill thee, and I not

*!kuṅ a, ta na dzau.*
kill thee, and I woman.

me; and I do not kill thee, being a woman.' And the woman refused and said, '/Xue will kill thee, for I do not kill thee, for I am a woman.

9665

*/Xue e //go̰, ti !kuṅ a, /Xue ti txa*
/Xue be man, kill thee, /Xue shoot

*a, ma ti !!ke. //Na !kuṅ /Xue.'*
thee, thou die. Leave kill /Xue.'

*Ta o kx'wi ha dzau, '/Kam tanki na*
And speak his woman, 'Day other I

*ti !kuṅ /Xue; ha /kua !!ke ara,*
kill /Xue; he not die outright,

*ta e dzhu tanki, ta na ti ko̰a.*
and be person other, and I fear.

*Na ti ko̰a /Xue,*
I fear /Xue,

/Xue is a man, and will kill thee, /Xue will shoot thee, that thou art dead. Leave killing /Xue.' And said to his wife: 'Another day I will kill /Xue; he does not really die, but is another person, and I fear him. I fear /Xue,

9666

*ta /Xue ti e dzhu tanki. Na ti*
and /Xue be person other. I

*/kua ssiṅ /Xue !nuerre. Ta /Xue*
not see /Xue country. And /Xue

*ti ssiṅ me !nuerre. 'Ta dzau*
see my country. 'And woman

*o kx'wi ha, '/Xue ti /kua ssiṅ a*
speak him, '/Xue not see thy

*!nuerre //ne //a, ta ti ssiṅ a !nuerre*
country big, and see thy country

*tsema; /na !kuṅ /Xue; /ne u a*
small; so kill /Xue; and go thy

and /Xue is another
person. I have not
seen /Xue's country.
And /Xue has seen my
country.' And the
woman said to him:
'/Xue has not seen
thy great country,
but has seen thy
little country, do
kill /Xue and go to
thy

9667

*!nuerre.' Ta ha //na: 'Na ti ko̰a*
country.' And he object: 'I fear

*/Xue; /Xue ti tabe //gu, //gu ti !kuṅ*
/Xue; /Xue make water, water kill

*mi; ta na ti ko̰a /Xue; /Xue e dzhu*
me; and I fear /Xue; /Xue be person

*tanki; ta na ti ko̰a /Xue; /kui !kuṅ*
other; and I fear /Xue; not kill

*/Xue.' Ta ha dzau o kx'wi ha,*
/Xue.' And his woman speak him,

country.' But he
objected: 'I fear
/Xue, /Xue makes the
rain, the rain kills
me, so I fear /Xue;
/Xue is another
person, and I fear
/Xue, do not kill
/Xue.' And his wife
said to him,

9668

*'!Kuṅ /Xue.' Ta ha //na, 'Na ti ko̰a*
'Kill /Xue.' And he refuse, 'I fear

*/Xue; ta /Xue tai e*
/Xue; and /Xue mother be

*N //na /gaa-ssiṅ*[1], *ta /Xue ba e*
Ku//na eyes, and /Xue father be

*/Xe-//n'u; ta na ti ko̰a /Xue, ta /kui*
/Xe-//n'u; and I fear /Xue, and not

*!kuṅ /Xue; ti ko̰a /Xue; ta /Xue ti*
kill /Xue; fear /Xue; and /Xue

*taba tchi ≠khi; ta na ti ko̰a /Xue,*
make thing many; and I fear /Xue,

'Kill /Xue.' And he refused: 'I fear /Xue, for /Xue's mother is 'I let drop the eyes'[1], and /Xue's father is …, and I fear /Xue, and do not kill /Xue, I fear /Xue, for /Xue works many things, and I fear /Xue,

Editor's footnote

1. Earlier /Xue's mother is *Kun//a-/gaa-ssin*, i.e. Kun//a's Eyes. The female name *Kun//a* is also found in Ju/'hoan.

9669

*ti /kui !kuṅ /Xue; ta, na ti !kuṅ*
not kill /Xue; and I kill

*/Xue, /Xue ti taba tchi tanki, ha ti*
/Xue, /Xue make thing many, he

*!kuṅ mi, ta na ti ko̰a /Xue. Ta*
kill me, and I fear /Xue. And

*/Xue tsiṅ*[1] *e Me-she-dza*[2]*, ta na ti*
/Xue brother be Me-she-dza, and I

*ko̰a /Xue tsiṅ; na ti ko̰a /Xue ba,*
fear /Xue brother; I fear /Xue father,

*na ti ko̰a /Xue tai; ta ti ko̰a /Xue*
I fear /Xue mother; and fear /Xue

*taṅ-a.' Ta ha dzau //na; ta kue,*
body.' And his woman object; and say,

*'!Kuṅ /Xue.' Ta ha //na, ta kue,*
'Kill /Xue.' And he refuse, and say,

*'n-ṅ, na ti ko̰a /Xue; /kui !kuṅ /Xue;*
'No, I fear /Xue; not kill /Xue;

*ta /Xue ti taba tchi tanki ta*
and /Xue make thing other and

*!kuṅ mi.'*
kill me.'

and do not kill /Xue. If I killed /Xue, /Xue would work other things, he would kill me, so I fear /Xue.' For /Xue's brother[1] is ...[2] and I fear /Xue's brother; I fear /Xue's father, I fear /Xue's mother; and I fear /Xue himself.' But the woman objected and said, 'Kill /Xue.' And he refused and said, 'No, I fear /Xue, do not kill /Xue; for /Xue would work other things and kill me.'.

Editor's footnote

1. *tsiṅ* 'brother' more exactly 'younger sibling'. (cf. Ju/'hoan *tshĩ*.)
2. *Me-she-dza* is very likely 'I-return-again'.

9670

*Ta dzau o kx'wi ha, '!Kuṅ /Xue.'*<br>
And woman speak him, 'Kill /Xue.'

*Ta ha //na; 'n-ṅ, /Xue ti taba tchi*<br>
And he refuse; 'No, /Xue make thing

*tanki; ha ti !kuṅ mi; ta na ti ko̰a*<br>
other; he kill me; and I fear

*/Xue.' Ta dzau o kx'wi ha, '*[1]*Ma ti*<br>
/Xue.' And woman speak him, 'Thou

*ko̰a /Xue, /kam tanki, na ti !kuṅ a.'*<br>
fear /Xue, day other, I kill thee.'

*Ta ha saa; ta shuwa !korro ≠ga-aṅ,*<br>
And he hear; and lie in hole deep,

*ti tchiṅ.*<br>
cry.

And the woman said to him: 'Kill /Xue.' And he refused: 'No, /Xue would work other things, he would kill me, for I fear /Xue.' And the woman said to him: 'Because[1] thou dost fear /Xue, another day, I will kill thee.' And he heard, and lay down in a deep hole, cried.

Editor's footnote

1. Observe that there is no word corresponding to Lloyd's 'because'.

10027

*The Moon and the Hare*[1] (continued)

*//Nuai ti //na, 'Na /kui saa a.*
Moon object, 'I not hear thee.

*Ta e-ssiṅ*[2] *dzhu /kui saa a, ta ti*
And our people not hear thee, and

*//ke tsema, ta ti debbi, ti /kui saa*
die small, and return, not hear

*a, ti //ke tsema.' Ta !!hi saa, ta*
thee, die small.' And Hare hear, and

*//na, ta shu shuwa ha tchu. Ta ti*
object, and lie lie in his house. And

*//na, 'n-ṅ, na /kui saa a, ta*
object, 'No, I not hear thee, and

*e //ku /kx'ao;*
we smell bad;

The Moon objected (saying) 'I do not listen to thee. For our[2] people do not hear (listen to) thee, but die a little, and return, do not hear thee, die a little.' And the Hare heard and objected, and lay down, lay down in its house. And it objected, 'No, I do not listen to thee, but we smell badly;

Author's footnote
1. !Nanni, from his paternal grandfather Karu.

Editor's footnote
2. This corresponds to !Xũ *èha˜* 'our (and nobody else's)', i.e. emphatic 'our'. (cf. Heikkinen 1986:10)

10028

*e ≠a ≠gaaṅ, ta //ku /kx'ao;*
our smell long, and smell bad;

*ta e ti //ke ara, ta /kui saa*
and we die outright, and not hear

*a, ta ma /kui //ku, ta a //ku*
thee, and thou not smell, and thy smell

*tsema.' Ta //nuai saa, ta kue,*
small.' And Moon hear, and say,

*'n-ṅ, e ti //ke tsema.' Ta !!hi saa,*
'No, we die small.' And Hare hear,

*ta kue, 'n-ṅ, e ti //ke ara, ta /kui*
and say, 'No, we die outright, and not

*saa a.' Ta shuwa ha tchu, ti tchiṅ,*
hear thee.' And lie in his house, cry,

*'!!Naaa, !!naaa, !!naaa.' Ta ha zau*
Alas, alas, alas!' And his woman

*o kx'wi ha, 'n-ṅ, tẽ ntchiṅ, ta*
speak him, 'No, desist cry. And

our smell is long, and smells badly; for we die outright, and do not listen to thee, for thou dost not smell; for thou smellest a little.' And the Moon heard, and said, 'No; we die a little.' And the Hare heard and said, 'No, we die altogether and do not hear thee.' And (it) lay in its house, crying (with tears) 'Alas! Alas! Alas!' And his wife said to him, 'No; leave off crying; for

10029

*ma /kui e daba, ta e dzhu*
thou not be child, and be person

*/nu /ne //a; te ntchiṅ.' Ta //nuai*
big; desist cry.' And Moon

*si, 'Ha-ha, ha-ha, ha-ha,'*
laugh, 'Ha ha, ha ha, ha ha,'

*ta /niṅ-a ha daa, ti si. Ti si*
and sat at his fire, laugh. Laugh

*!!hi; ta !!hi saa, ta //na; 'n-ṅ,*
Hare; and Hare hear, and object; 'No,

*tẽ nsi !!hi; ta !!hi ti tchiṅ-a //ke*
desist laugh Hare; and Hare cry for die

*ara. //Nuai te si !!hi.*
outright. Moon desist laugh Hare.

thou art not a child, but art a grown up person; leave off crying.' And the Moon laughed, 'Ha, ha, ha, ha, ha, ha!' and sat at his fire, laughing. And laughed at the Hare; and the Hare heard and objected, 'No, leave off laughing at the Hare; for the Hare is crying (for one who) dies outright. Moon stop laughing at the Hare.

10030

*Ta !!hi //ku /kx'ao, ta ti tchiṅ-a*
And Hare smell bad, and cry for

*//ke ara; //nuai tẽ*
die outright; Moon desist

*si-si !!hi.'*
laugh laugh Hare.'

For the Hare smells bad, and is crying (for one who) dies outright; Moon stop laughing at the Hare.'

## *MODERN TRANSLATION*
## *'THE MOON AND THE HARE'*

Uwe made these things. The Hare did not speak nicely, but the Moon spoke nicely. The Moon said that the Bushmen should, like himself, return again, and that they should not die outright.

But the Hare objected, 'No, dead Bushmen smell bad.'

And the Moon said to the Hare, 'Dead Bushmen will return – they do not die outright.'

The Hare said to the Moon, 'When you die, you do not smell bad. I am not listening to you. No, a Bushman smells bad.'

And he took the bags of dead Bushmen and threw them far away, and the bags of death fell into the Bushmen's country. Then the Hare took a bag of small illnesses, and sat on it, and threw his divining charms and spoke to them, 'A Bushman who is slightly ill, may he arise.' And his charms told him, 'A Bushman who is slightly ill, may he arise.' Then the Hare looked and his charms, and sat and laughed at them.

Then the Moon spoke to the Hare, 'May your dead arise, and indeed not die outright.'

But the Hare said to the Moon, 'My son smells bad.' And he got up and took his son and put him into his bag and threw it far away into another country.

And /Xue was sitting and laughing at the Hare. The Hare went to lie down, crying for his son. Then /Xue took a stick, and came and hit the Hare, banging his head. Blood flowed and the Hare lay crying.

Then the Moon said, 'Leave the Hare alone.' But /Xue would not listen, and beat the Hare, while the Moon was saying, 'The Hare was arguing, but he does not resemble us who die and then come back, and he is crying for someone who died outright. The Hare was saying that he does not come back after death like us.'

Then the she-Hare said, 'We die outright, and we smell bad, /Xue. You are beating my spouse's head with a knobkerrie, but my spouse is not like you; he's another kind of person, for your mother is Kun//a's Eyes and your father is /Xe//n'u, and we do not live in the same country. Our country is different, and our mother is different – our mother is a hare. And your mother is different, and so is your country.'

/Xue listened and was afraid, and lay down and cried, 'No woman, don't speak to me. I am afraid of the woman's speech.' Then he cried and cried and lay insensible on the ground.

The she-Hare took a stick and came and stood there, and beat and beat /Xue while he was unconscious, and then left and went to her house and sat down. The she boiled water and came and threw it on /Xue. /Xue cried and cried in fear of the hot water. Then the Hare-woman spoke to /Xue, '/Xue, be quiet! I will kill you, so be quiet!'

But /Xue cried out, 'Leave me alone! Oh! Stop killing me!'

And the Hare Woman said to /Xue, 'I am going to kill you. Be quiet!'

And /Xue wept and replied, 'Don't kill me. Oh!'

The she-Hare said, 'Today, I am going to kill you, /Xue.'

Then the Moon spoke to the she-Hare, 'Leave /Xue alone!'

But the she-Hare argued and said, '/Xue beat my spouse and I will kill him.'

But the Moon said, 'Leave /Xue.'

But the Hare said, 'I will kill you.'

/Xue heard, and cried out, 'Oh, I'm dying! I'm dying!'

The she-Hare said, '/Xue, be silent! I will kill you. /Xue, stop crying!'

But /Xue said, 'Leave me alone so that I can go to my father's country.'

The she-Hare told /Xue, 'Today you will not go to your father's country, for I will kill you.'

/Xue argued, 'Leave me alone, oh! Leave me alone so that I can go to my father's country! Leave me alone, stop killing me, so I can go to my father's country, and see my mother!'

But the she-Hare replied, 'Today I will not listen to the Moon, but will kill you.'

Then the he-Hare who was lying down, got up and killed /Xue, but /Xue was not completely dead, just slightly dead, and he got up and laughed and said, 'Yes, Kun//a's Eyes and /Xe//n'u's son does not die completely. /Xue's name stands alone.'

Then the Moon came and beat /Xue making him cry, beat him and beat him and killed him. But /Xue lay for a bit, and did not die outright, and laughed as he spoke.

Then the sun rose and /Xue went into the Moon's house and sat down. The Moon spoke to /Xue, '/Xue, I will kill you, so go to your mother's country.' /Xue lay on the ground, crying and crying and crying, and was insensible. Then the Moon took a stick and came and beat the insensible /Xue. /Xue lay on the ground, and cried for water.

The Moon said, '/Xue, go to your country and drink water in your country.'

/Xue replied, 'My mother, alas! My country is far. Moon, stop killing me, oh!' And /Xue argued, 'My country is far.' And he sat crying for his country,

'Oh! When the sun rises I will go to my country.' Then the Moon got up and took a knife and approached /Xue. /Xue sat and watched him laughing, 'Ha ha!'

Then the Moon came to him and said, '/Xue, go to your country.'

But /Xue objected, 'No. I won't go to my country. I'm afraid of my country, for my country is far.'

The Moon took hold of /Xue, and /Xue laughed, 'Ha ha! Hey, let me lie down so that the Moon can kill me.' So he lay down and the Moon killed him while he was laughing, 'Ha ha!'

Then the Moon said, '/Xue, be silent, I am killing you.'

/Xue heard him and replied, 'I will not be silent, but will speak.'

But the Moon said, '/Xue, I will kill you, so be quiet!'

/Xue replied, 'I am not afraid of you, and I will speak even though you are killing me.'

The Moon heard this and killed /Xue while /Xue was crying, 'Oh! Oh! Oh!'

So the Moon killed /Xue, then stood up and sat down, laughing at him. /Xue died and lay on the ground, but he was not completely dead, only slightly dead, and he lay and lay and lay but he wasn't completely dead.

Then he sat up and laughed and said to the Moon, 'Moon, kill me!'

But the Moon refused, 'I am afraid of you. You do not die outright, and I fear you.' Then /Xue lay on the ground and cried.

The Moon gave /Xue water, and /Xue drank it, and sat and laughed at the Moon. Then the Moon gave him food and he ate it and sat and said to the Moon, 'When the sun rises I will go to my mother's country, so give me the *tchana*, for me to put in my two bags, and carry them to my mother's country.'

But the Moon refused and said, 'No, I will not give you the *tchana*.' /Xue heard this and cried and cried for the *tchana*.

And the Moon took a stick and came and beat /Xue while he cried, beat him banging his head, and /Xue lay and cried. The Moon took an arrow and shot /Xue, and /Xue lay on the ground crying.

Then /Xue got up and became a small child, and he lay there crying. The Moon stood there beating him while he cried. /Xue was small; he was not a grown-up person, but a small child and he lay crying and crying, 'Moon, leave me alone, for I am a small child! Moon, stop beating me to death!'

But the Moon said, 'You are not a small child, but an adult and I will kill you.'

Then he shot /Xue while he lay there crying, 'Moon, leave me, oh! Moon, leave me!'

But the Moon would not listen, 'Today, I will kill you, so be quiet so I can kill you.'

And he beat /Xue while he cried, he beat him to death as /Xue lay crying, 'Stop killing a small child!'

The Moon replied, 'Today, I will kill a small child, and not fear a small child.' Then he spoke to his wife, 'Give me hot water, so that I can pour it over /Xue.'

But his wife refused, so he came to beat his wife while she cried. Then his wife took a stick and beat him while he screamed, and said, 'Hey wife! Stop beating me!' and he went away from his wife and his wife took the stick and beat him as he ran away. His wife beat him on the head, and he cried. Then his wife left him alone and came and sat down laughing. And he came and stood weeping, 'Alas! Alas!'

His wife told him, 'One day, I will kill you.'

He said, 'Don't kill me!'

But his wife replied, 'I am not listening to you, so stop talking and shut up!'

He said to his wife, 'I'm not afraid of you.'

And she said, 'One day I will kill you, so be quiet.'

Then he told his wife, 'I am a man, and I am not afraid of you. One day I'll kill you – I am not afraid of your father, and I am not afraid of your relatives, and I will kill you and your relatives will kill me. I am not listening to you, and I will kill you.'

His wife replied, 'I am not afraid of you. Kill me!'

But the man said to the woman, 'I will not kill you. I am afraid of you, and you have many relatives and they will kill me, and I fear your people, so I will not kill you, I am telling you.' And he said to her, 'I will not kill you, I tell you, so stop killing me, please leave me alone.'

The woman replied, 'I will not kill you, for I am a woman and you are a man. Even if you kill me, I will not kill you, because I am a woman.' And she added, '/Xue will kill you, not I, because I am a woman. But /Xue is a man and he will kill you. He will shoot you dead, so stop killing /Xue.'

He replied to his wife, 'One day I will kill /Xue. He does not die completely but becomes another person, and I am afraid. I am afraid of /Xue, for he becomes another person. I have not seen /Xue's country, but /Xue has seen mine.'

The woman said to him, '/Xue has not seen your big country, but has seen your small country. Kill /Xue and go to your country.'

But he said, 'I am afraid of /Xue. /Xue makes rain and rain kills me. I am afraid of /Xue – he is another kind of person, and I fear him and will not kill him.'

But his wife said, 'Kill /Xue.'

He refused, 'I fear /Xue, /Xue's mother is Ku//na's Eyes and his father is /Xe//n'u, and I fear /Xue and will not kill him. /Xue can make many things, and I am fearful of him and will not kill him. He can make many things and will kill me. And /Xue's younger brother is I-Return-Again, and I am afraid of his brother, and his father and his mother and /Xue himself.'

But his wife said, 'Kill /Xue!'

But he said, 'No, I'm afraid of him, and will not kill him, because /Xue can do strange things and may kill me.'

'Kill him,' said his wife.

'No,' he said, '/Xue can do strange things and kill me. I am scared of him.'

'You are scared of /Xue,' said his wife, 'And one day I will kill you.'

He heard this, and lay in a big deep hole and cried, 'I will not listen to you. And our people will not listen to you. For we die slightly, and then return. We do not listen to you, for we die slightly.'

But the Hare heard, and said, lying in his house, 'No, I will not listen to you, for we smell bad, and our odour lasts long and smells bad, and we die outright. I will not listen to you, for you do not smell – you have only a slight smell.'

The Moon heard this and said, 'No, we die slightly.'

The Hare argued, 'Oh no, we die outright, and we will not listen to you.' He lay in his house and wept, 'Alas! Alas! Alas!'

His wife said to him, 'Stop crying. You are not a child, but a grown-up person, so stop crying.'

Then the Moon laughed, 'Ha ha ha ha ha!' He sat by his fire laughing, laughing at the Hare.

The Hare heard him and said, 'No, stop laughing at me. The Hare is weeping for the fact that death is final. Moon, stop laughing at me. For the Hare smells bad, and weeps because death is final. Moon, stop laughing at me!'

# Reading San Images

John Parkington, Tony Manhire and Royden Yates

## *PAINTINGS AS DOMESTIC ARTEFACTS*

Paintings on the walls of rock shelters and caves in the Western Cape are immovable and relatively permanent images. The paintings are located in direct association with domestic debris such as bedding materials, food refuse and artefacts, although the correlation between the amount of debris and the number of paintings is not simple. There are, for example, sites with many paintings and scant evidence of occupation, but it would be extremely unusual to find no paintings in a site with a deep occupation deposit. The normal pattern would be to find lots of rocky overhangs, some with and some without paintings, scattered along the krantzes of the landscape. Many of the paintings are visible from some distance and few appear to be placed in inaccessible locations. Our impression is that, in the past, hunters sheltering from the sun or gatherers resting during the day may well have used a painted cave in the painted landscape. Certainly people would almost always have slept within metres of painted images, which would have danced in the flickering firelight. The rubbing and repainting of previously painted images (Yates and Manhire 1991) illustrates clearly that people continued to interact with paintings for some time after their original execution.

For some twelve years now the Spatial Archaeology Research Unit of the University of Cape Town has been recording the location and content of rock painting sites as well as other sites in the Western Cape. The integrated map, photographic and descriptive record stands at over 2 500 sites, most of them located in systematically searched segments of the landscape. The objective of such field recording is to understand the meaning of the painted assemblages in the context of the later pre-colonial history of the area. Because there are absolutely no written or oral records that refer directly to the Western Cape paintings, the context is provided by the archaeological history of the region derived from our excavation programme. Distanced somewhat from these paintings in both space and time are recent observations on Kalahari San people, genetically close to the now extinct painters but who do not paint, and observations derived from residual nineteenth-century San people (/Xam) in the Karoo and Drakensberg regions. These latter informants may have been contemporary with the latest paintings or engravings in those areas.

Our programme recognises two parallel avenues of enquiry. On the one hand we need to investigate San patterns of expression, visual and verbal, material and symbolic. On the other hand we need to assemble and study the painted imagery that is the primary target of understanding. 'Truth' in this kind of enquiry will always be an inferential statement supported as unambiguously as possible by patterning in and between these two sets of observations. The importance of following both avenues is to ensure, on the one hand, that interpretations are well grounded in the anthropology of San people and, on the other, that cross referencing to the paintings is well grounded in the empirical record.

Our perspective is thus evidently empirical but not empiricist. Like Hodder (1986) we believe that 'our reconstructions of historical meanings are based on arguments of coherence and correspondence in relation to the data as perceived'. We import ideas and test their usefulness against the patterning of the archaeological record, in this case the painted record. The position we take is that, regardless of the source of inspiration, the process of interpretation is incomplete until ideas are operationalised and tested against the image record. The problem of competing interpretations is resolved in Popperian fashion by repeated attempts at refutation. The archaeological remains and not the source of the hypothesis is the ultimate arbiter. We argue that the theoretical origin of any hypothesis determines only the kind of insight sought, not the reliability of the knowledge gained.

Of particular concern to us is the recognition that painted images were chosen from an almost infinite set of possibilities and assembled as compositions in specific and observable patterns. We accept that compositions may be difficult to define, but submit that the images we refer to later are well associated both spatially and formally. Regardless of how many authors were involved or how much time it took, the assemblage of images retained a coherence that reflected, or made material, the prevalent group notions of meaning. We suggest that these acts of painting in themselves can be studied as durable residues of past intentions.

One issue, of course, is that of the correct identification of subject matter. Is this a bag? Is this an eland? Is this bleeding from the nose? Patently, we feel, no theory and no amount of reference to anthropological observation will allow us to identify a bag unless it looks like one. Knowing what kinds of bag the San people make helps us to build an expectation, but the form of the painted image is critical. Thus all interpretations in rock art studies depend on the empirical identification of what is depicted. Meanings flow from such identifications either because of painted conventional references or from ethnographically recorded associations. By convention we mean a device repeatedly used for depicting some element in an image or composition: hook-heads or sets of parallel lines, for example.

Like others, we have set ourselves the tasks of identifying recurrent image choice, of understanding the conventions of composition, and of relating this to social and historical events in the lives of Western Cape hunter gatherers. In the long term we would like to know who painted, how paintings functioned as highly visible artefacts, and how this may have changed through time. This paper is part of our programme.

The making of a painting can be seen, in one sense, as a series of decisions about content and composition. Whether to depict male or female or a particular species of animal, the choice of size, colour, orientation and association, are decisions that define the final expression of paint on the shelter wall. The issue raised here is that of the meaning of the painted images for the viewer, specifically one contemporary with the painting or one who shared the reference system of the painter. In this way we privilege the informed viewer and ask, 'What references are made in the painting, what conventions are used, and what can be read into the images?' The challenge for us as outsiders is to 'know what it was like to have been a San'.

How might we achieve this? Collingwood (1946) has argued that re-enactment is a valid, perhaps the only, way to know the past, given that we cannot have been there nor can we take contemporary accounts as unproblematic documents. Although experimental archaeology is the most explicit field of re-enactment, the use of ethnographic analogies and resort to the most appropriate documents, such as the Bleek and Lloyd material, also constitute an attempt to assume the identity of past actors. In our view all rock art researchers use a form of re-enactment by choosing literature that most closely approximates in space and time to the context of the society of now extinct painters. Here we will consider the paintings as special kinds of artefacts, try to re-enact their manufacture and, thus, read their meaning.

Lewis-Williams (1981,1983) and others (Lewis-Williams and Dowson 1989, Lewis-Williams and Loubser 1986) have already isolated many references to trance and altered states of consciousness in paintings. They have shown, also by a combination of empirical image recognition and ethnography, that flecks or lines of paint coming from the face or nose, lines of paint on the face and several recurrent body positions are best interpreted as references to the shaman entering trance. Many geometric designs such as spirals, chevrons and zigzags, as well as more complex compositions are analogous to the entoptic visions of modern shamans. From these observations they conclude that the art is essentially shamanistic.

Solomon (1988) has offered a complementary, but somewhat different, and occasionally competitive, interpretation of the meanings intended by the painters. She believes that the images, when read in conjunction with the Bleek and Lloyd material (Bleek 1924, 1931, 1932a,b,c, 1933, a,b, 1935a, Bleek & Lloyd 1911), reflect a preoccupation with gender, expressed through metaphors of rain and fertility. She makes a strong case for recognising the genderisation of time, space and form in San expression. From this she suggests that the paintings are a material remnant of gender struggle in hunter gatherer society, not satisfactorily recognised previously by either archaeologists or ethnographers.

Whilst recording our support for both these programmes, we feel they do not exhaust the concerns of San painters. Nor, in our view, has the question of composition been adequately addressed. Here we add to the comments on the depiction of time and space, and suggest that at least in some paintings a concern to differentiate between initiated and uninitiated men is shown. We offer interpretations of conventions such as hanging bags and karosses, and make the connection between the eland and the conventionalised depiction of initiated men.

## *REFERENCES TO TIME*

In rock shelters scattered through the Cape Fold Belt mountains we have recorded some fifteen examples of what we take to be net-hunting scenes (Figures 1-4). Although variable, these paintings make use of depictions of vertically arranged cross-hatched nets, wooden net supports, small antelope either singly or in groups, and human figures. In all cases (Manhire, Parkington and Yates 1985, Parkington 1989) the images are folded out so as to express the identity of and relationships between elements rather than to view them, perhaps ambiguously or less informatively from a single point perspective. There seems here to be a deliberate distortion of spatial relationships to create a conventionalised spatial composition. Thus, the net is painted as a vertical impediment to the direction implied by the orientation of the antelope. A more surprising pattern is that almost without exception the antelope face right toward a net or nets that form the right-hand edge of the scene. We have to set this in its regional context. Manhire's (1981) study of 285 painted sites in

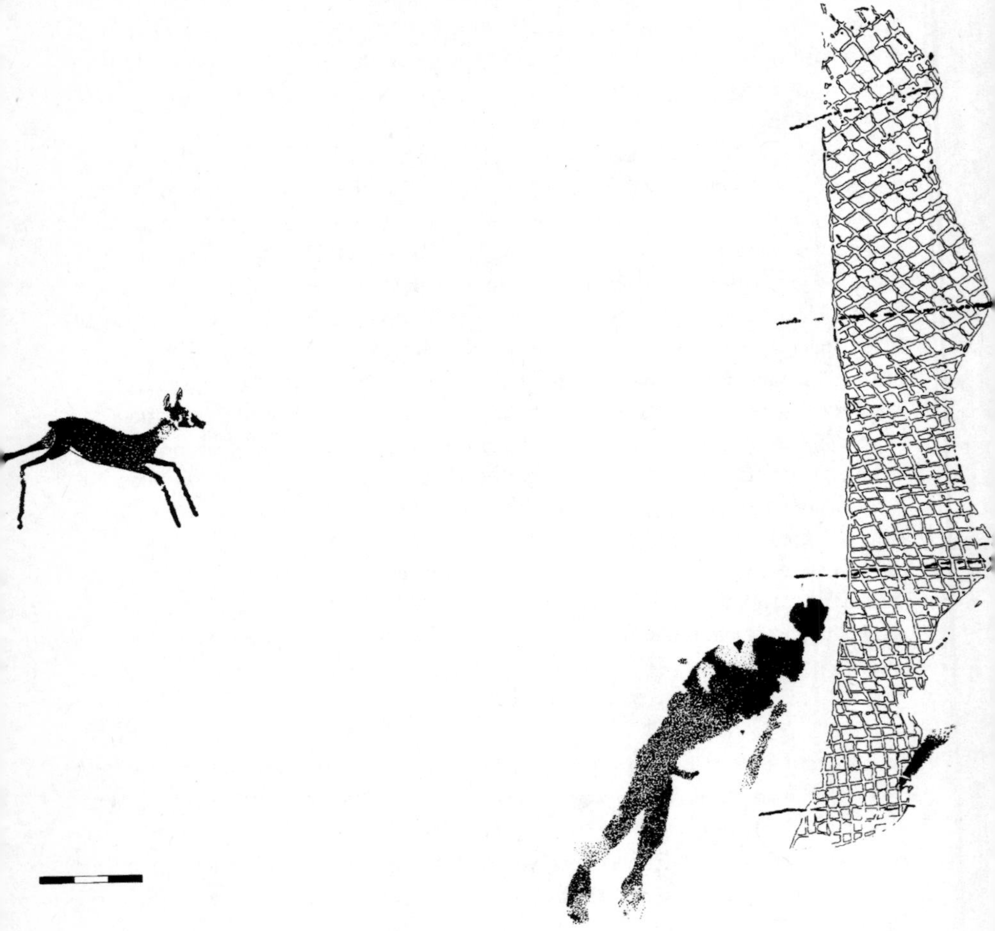

**Figure 1.** *Net hunting: A white cross-hatched net with red supports, a small antelope and human figure (male). Scale in this and subsequent figures in centimetres.*

the Sandveld plains, immediately west of these net scenes, generated a ratio of 2,7:1 for right to left facing animals, 2,1:1 for small antelope and 1,5:1 for human figures. Although it is clearly the preferred orientation in general, the tendency to face right is significantly emphasised in the net scenes where we have observed a ratio of 14:1.

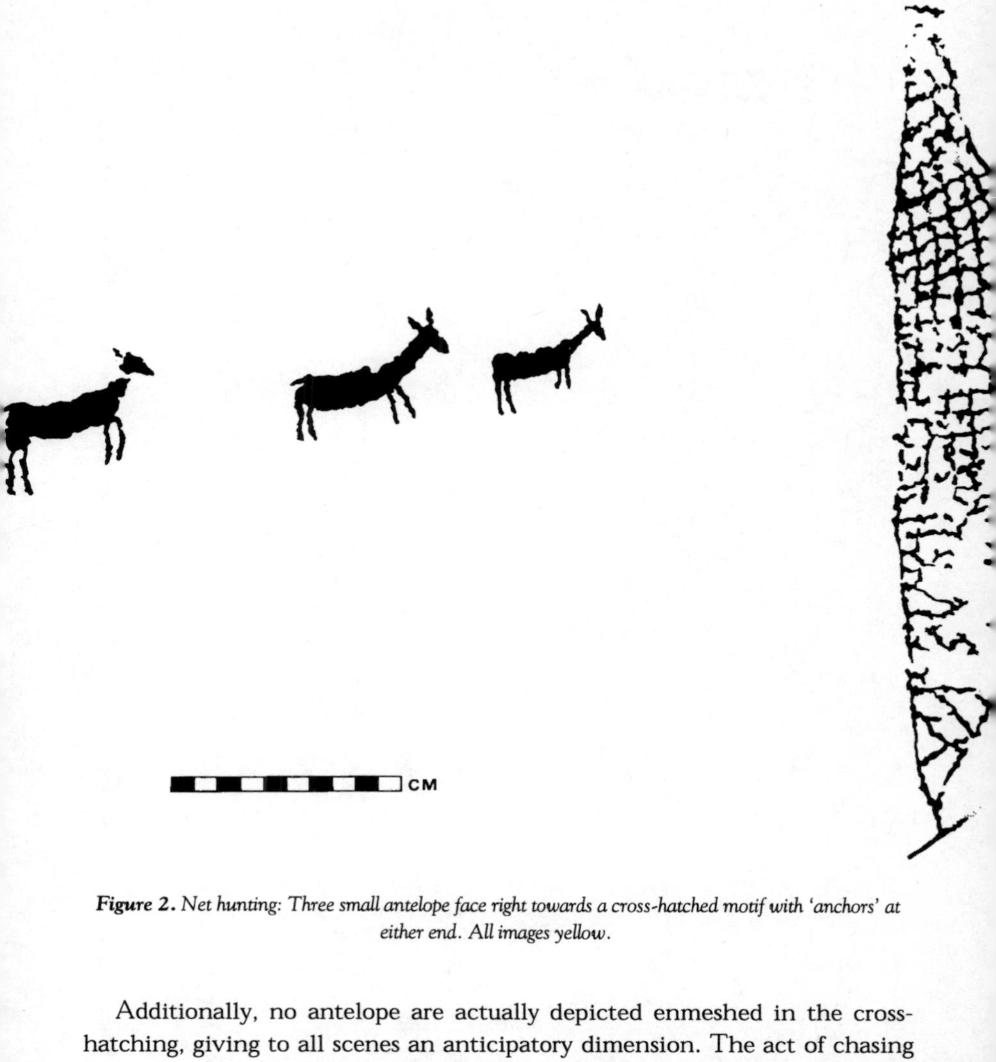

**Figure 2.** *Net hunting: Three small antelope face right towards a cross-hatched motif with 'anchors' at either end. All images yellow.*

Additionally, no antelope are actually depicted enmeshed in the cross-hatching, giving to all scenes an anticipatory dimension. The act of chasing small antelope into a net strung across a narrow kloof clearly includes an element of time. It is also inherently and necessarily directional, giving great significance to the orientation of the compositions. The destination, both temporally and spatially, centres on the net. If the painting of such an event

***Figure 3.** Net hunting: Nine small antelope face towards an elongated motif, seven human figures carrying items of unrecognizable nature are depicted behind the antelope and at either end of the 'net'. All images red.*

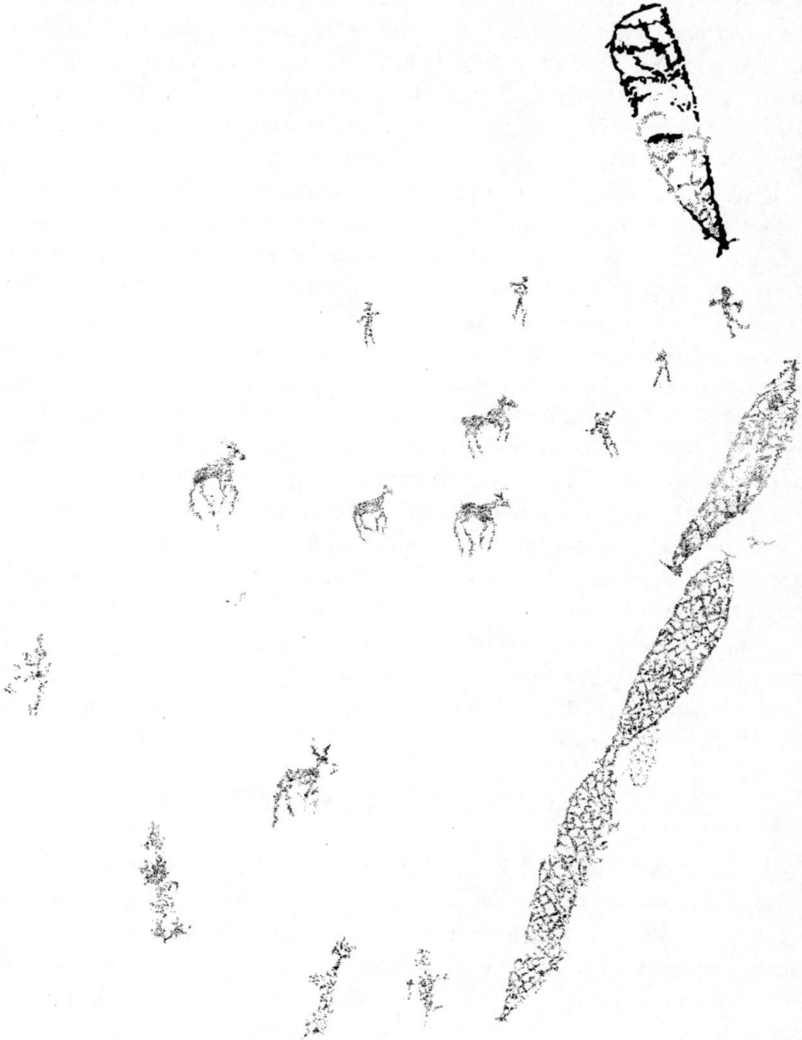

**Figure 4.** *Net hunting: Five or more small antelope face right towards a line of cross-hatched motifs. Several human figures are visible. All images red. Stippled areas represent less well preserved parts of the composition.*

were to attempt to capture the time-span involved, to incorporate sequence, then some conventional reference to before and after needs to be made in the compositional arrangement. In the case of the nets the convention seems to be that the temporal dimension is reflected in, or included in, the spatial dimension of left to right. Destination, outcome or objective is depicted at right. Solomon (1988) has referred to the spatialisation of time. The net scenes considerably strengthen her argument.

Other paintings, whilst referring to different kinds of occasion may also use the same convention. Figure 5, for example, is a painting of exclusively male images, and may also include two large animal shapes. Here the figures are all naked and appear to be repetitively, almost stereotypically, painted. Like a series of frames in a time sequence portraying a cartoon character, they appear to reflect the progress, again from left to right, of a single individual male through time. Here again we note the use of space to depict time. The orderly progress of the left half dissolves into the disorderly frenzy of the right half in much the same way as a dancer is seized by boiling evergy when he enters the trance state (Katz 1982). As if to confirm this, lines of paint emerge from many of the faces, a convention Lewis-Williams (1981, 1983) has clearly identified as signalling trance. The parallel red lines that 'drip' from the upper bodies may be sweat, the parallel lines along which men walk may be the dancing groove, worn into the sand, both of which have the same kind of potency as is associated with the nasal haemorrhage. The intention here may have been to capture the experiences associated with entry into trance depicted using the left-right convention for before and after, the occasion generic rather than specific.

## *REFERENCES TO CATEGORIES OF PERSON*

In Figure 6 there is another clear left to right directionality, with approximately fifty human figures, apparently all male, and an eland torso all facing right. The humans are organised into two processional lines, a decision that surely emphasises the directionality, reinforces the impression of movement and refers, presumably, to the nature of the occasion depicted. At the right-hand end of the longer, upper line of human figures are eight naked black figures without the set of clothing and equipment that characterises all those behind them. Above the naked men, at the destination implied by the orientation of the line, are nine or so bags and a bow. The elongated shape of these bags recalls the 'long bag' that Bleek (1928b) described the Naron using to

**Figure 5.** *Entering trance: Male human figures face right on a set of parallel lines; to the right the linearity is replaced by a variety of orientations and postures. All images red.*

**Figure 6.** *Initiation: Two processions of human figures face right along with an eland (torso only); five 'palettes' reproduce the colours of the human figures; hunting bags are located at top right. The colours of the three 'palettes' on the extreme left are red, white and black (from right to left).*

hold arrows, poison, quiver and bow, and which she clearly distinguished from round collecting bags. Because in the paintings, too, the long, slightly tapering shape is usually associated with arrows, we take the shapes in Figure 6 to be hunting bags and, thus, associated with men.

The cloaked or clothed figures are upright and variable in size and detail, whereas the naked figures are somewhat stereotyped and bend at the knee and waist, below the hunting bags. In the lower line are figures with eared caps, dancing sticks and small flecks of paint which may depict the nasal haemorrhage often associated with a trance occasion. Whereas all in the lower line are naked, there is a clear attempt to contrast naked and clothed figures in the upper line, even though this too might be a line of dancers. Two sets of contrasts are implied here by the organisation of image choice. One is that between naked and clothed, the other is that between dancing sticks and bows, arrows and quivers.

This painting is so structured in terms of content and composition that identification of the occasion depicted seems possible. We interpret the occasion as an initiation event and regret that there are no ethnographic accounts of such from the Western Cape. Schapera, in his generalisations about San (for him Bushman) boys' puberty ceremonies (1930:122-26), noted that among Kalahari hunter gatherers groups of boys who have become proficient at hunting large game are taken by older men to secluded places from which women are excluded. 'Magicians' are in charge of the rites which include learning the mens' */gi* dance and the enduring of tough living conditions. The boys 'may have no fire and eat no meat, but live only on a little water and on raw roots and berries' (Schapera 1930:123). This is a ritual re-creation of primordial circumstances. During the extended dances a supernatural being approaches the dancers, reminding us of the juxtaposition of eland torso and human figures.

Fourie, writing of the Auen male initiation, specified that 'during the day their bodies are blackened from head to foot with powdered roasted *//noun* (a staple vegetable food)' (quoted in Schapera 1930:124). They are cicatrised by the magicians by receiving cuts (*/gi* cuts) between the eyebrows, marks which 'are supposed to make them "see well", i.e. to bring them good luck in hunting' (Schapera 1930:125). Over a four- or five-day period the boys are re-introduced to plant foods, honey and meat, in that order, are given back their bows and arrows, are tested in the stalking and killing of game, and returned to their homes. They have made the transition to hunter, symbolically reflected in the plant, honey and meat sequence. After the ceremony 'they are now regarded as men, they can marry, and they take part in the councils of men and associate with them' (Schapera 1930:125). Bleek's (1928b:23-25) description of boys' initiation ceremonies among the Naron is almost identical. Note here the creation of husbands and hunters in seclusion, the passing on of license to marry and kill.

The correspondence between painted and written imagery is remarkably close. Figure 6 seems thus to reflect an initiation event wherein young men are guided by older, already initiated men in ceremonies that included the experiences of trance and acceptance into the company of hunters. The extent to which initiated men felt themselves to be a distinct interest group in the precolonial Western Cape is still open to analysis, but the possibility for conflict is clearly there, given the proscription on marriage for the uninitiated. We look now at the specific references implied by elements in Figure 6, beginning with the bags and proceeding to karosses and eland.

In the crevices along the walls on many shelters we have found the remains of wooden pegs, from which bags, bows, quivers and other items of equipment were hung. The meaning of the hanging bags, shown in some paintings with supporting peg, is thus explained as a reference to a cave or rock shelter as the location for the initiation event. The bags, all of the same kind and seemingly (male) hunting rather than (female) collecting bags, metaphorically stand for the new status of initiated hunter to which the young men aspire and towards which they are shown to move in procession. Significantly, the bags are associated with the upper line of figures, including the cloaked men, whereas all obvious references to trance, such as eared caps, fly whisks and dancing sticks are in the lower line with naked men. By this device the hunting and trancing aspects, although related, are separately presented.

Cloaked or kaross-clad images have long interested us, at least in part because they do not resemble in any close way the photographic images of recent Kalahari hunter-gatherers wearing karosses. Because of this we suggest that they are not literal garments but conventional depictions of clothing from which some significance could be derived by the informed viewer. For the moment we continue to refer to them as cloaks or karosses. We have noted the very significant association of karosses with bows, arrows and quivers, and the virtual absence of kaross-clad women. This we believe is not explained in terms of our inability to detect breasts on figures with karosses but as an intended male reference in the mind of painter and viewer. We suggest here that the reference is even more specific, serving to identify men who have undergone initiation. In describing the dress codes of the Naron, Bleek noted (1928b:9) that 'the boys now wear an apron like those of the men, but no cloak of any sort till they are in their teens and are taken out to learn hunting'.

The conventionalised depiction of what we call karosses reminds us, as it did Lewis-Williams (1983:56-57), of the similarly conventionalised depiction of the eland torso, an example of which is aligned with the men in Figure 6. In both conventions the head and legs, usually in a different colour, emerge from a shape that is almost never colonised by other elements. Moreover, like eland, cloaked figures feature prominently in processions where they repeat in a limited range of rather static postures. Did the similarity serve to remind the contemporary viewer of a relationship between initiated men and eland? Does the eland, perhaps especially the one orientated with the men in Figure 6, reflect the cohesive force that united initiated men into a recognisable interest group? We offer the following preliminary observation in support of this idea.

Figures 7 and 8 have been traced from paintings in the same Western Cape rock shelter and illustrate some formal similarity between a group of cloaked human figures and an eland. The men, if so they are, have been merged so that the shape of the merged cloaks resembles the widespread eland torso form.

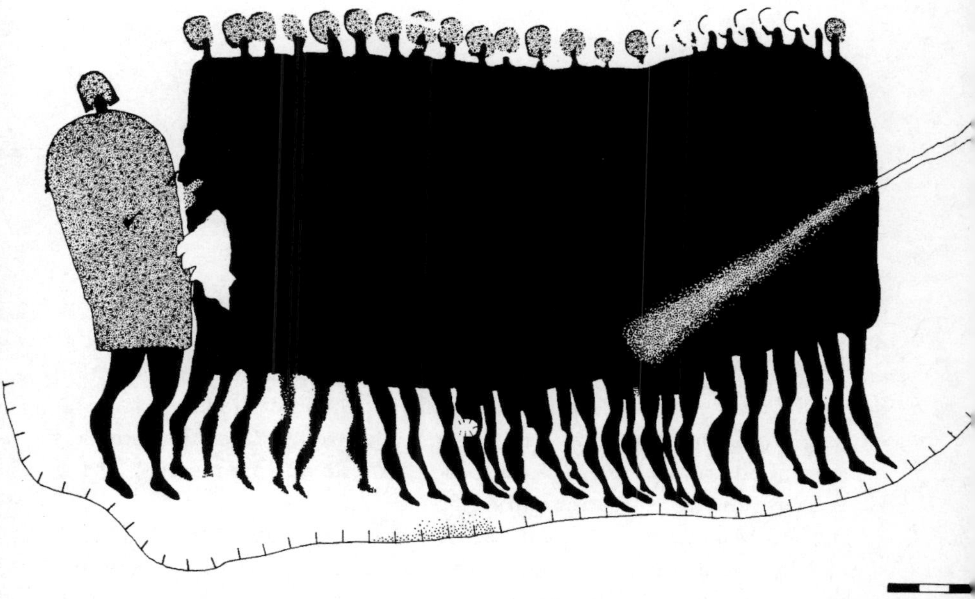

**Figure 7.** *Cloaked figures; A group of (probably male) human cloaked figures merged and facing right. A 'classic' cloaked figure stands to the the left of the group. Solid areas are red, stippled areas yellow. The line at the base of the composition represents a step in the rock surface.*

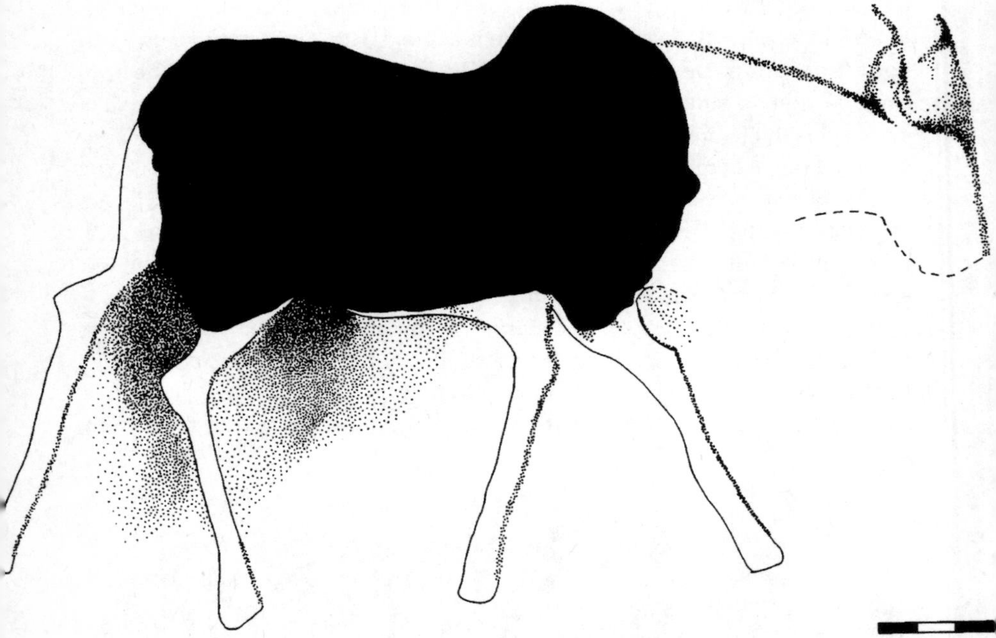

**Figure 8.** *Eland: Facing right. The solid area is red, the areas enclosed by lines are weathered white and the stippled areas represent either lighter or dispersed red pigment.*

The effect of rendering the cloaks as one solid shape is to underline the solidarity of the group of initiated men. It may be that the kaross or cloak in this and other images is specifically an eland-skin garment and its depiction designed to reflect the intimate relationship between initiated men and this animal. The Bleek and Lloyd informants made it quite clear that artefacts made from an animal never ceased to be that animal. The meaning of the kaross may thus be the 'wearing of the eland'.

The suggestion that eland paintings might symbolise the 'councils of men' specifically initiated hunters, requires us to assess the role of the eland in the Bleek and Lloyd material and in other accounts. In Orpen's (1874) report on the stories he heard from the young, perhaps uninitiated, guide Qing, for example, the eland is most prominent in a creation tale involving Cagn, who 'made all things', his sons Cogaz and Gewi and the first eland. Stripped of detail, this tells of Cagn's making of an eland, his seclusion of it in a secret place, the killing of the eland by the sons whilst Cagn was elsewhere, the re-creation of elands by Cagn and the resultant relationship between eland and hunters. Of the killing Cagn said, 'You have spoilt the elands when I was making them fit for use' (Orpen 1874:4). When the re-created elands turned hostile, Cagn said, 'You see how you have spoilt the elands' (Orpen 1874:4), and he drove these elands away. Then he 'told Gcwi, Go and hunt them and try to kill one, that is now your work, for it was you who spoilt them' (Orpen 1874:4). This proved difficult until Cagn gave his blessing. Finishing the story, Orpen wrote, apparently in Qing's terms, 'That day game were given to men to eat, and this is the way they were spoilt and became wild' (1874:5).

Eland are surprisingly infrequently mentioned in the published Bleek and Lloyd documents (Bleek 1924, 1931, 1932a,b,c, 1935a, 1936a; Bleek & Lloyd 1911). Whereas shamans, whom Bleek calls sorcerers, may assume the guise of springbok, jackal and bird, no transformation into eland is recorded. Once again, however, eland feature prominently in a creation context (Bleek 1924: 1-9), and one remarkably similar to that recounted by Orpen (Lewis-Williams 1981). /Kaggen creates an eland bull which he refers to as a person, rubs down with honey and visits at a secluded waterhole as it grows to adulthood. In his absence his son-in-law Kwammang-a kills the eland and butchers the carcass, which is hereafter referred to as meat. As with the Orpen version, a key element here is the question of permission. /Kaggen is as upset about the lack of his sanction of the kill as he is about the death of the eland, and his resolve to 'fight the eland's fight' may be more literal than Lewis-Williams (1983:46) allows. The killing of the eland shifts its reference from that of 'person' to that of 'meat', a parallel to the notion of 'spoiling' in Orpen's version.

The appropriate roles for eland and hunter are created in the same sequence of events, in which the question of permission is crucial. These stories explain the relationship between the hunter and his prey, quintessentially the largest and fattest of the large antelope, and provide a scenario for the creation of all subsequent hunters. It is surely no coincidence that ritual behaviour attaches to the killing of the first eland and much less so to that of any other game species. The hunter's job is to kill the eland even though it is the creator's favourite. The unease associated with this act may have been diminished by the rites of initiation, sanctioned, as it were, by the eland presence. The eland is the *animal de passage* because 'it is as though a person changes status through the eland' (Lewis-Williams 1981:72).

Under these circumstances it is highly appropriate to find the eland associated with the creation of young hunters at initiation ceremonies such as those of Figure 6. No doubt the eland was felt to be present as boys were symbolically and literally led out of society and through a process of re-introduction to hunting that recalled the original creation event. Given the parallel between game and women (Marshall 1959, McCall 1970, Solomon 1988), it is not surprising that the ceremony creates potential husbands, nor that this animal features prominently, too, in the menarcheal rites of young women (Lewis-Williams 1981). It is possible that the eland of Figure 6 is specifically a male, whereas that associated, or identified with the young girl is specifically female.

Among the potential meanings associated with eland depictions we wish here to draw attention to that related to initiated men. This reference is dominant in the few verbatim San accounts that have survived, as the previous paragraphs illustrate. By contrast, references to medicine people as 'eland's men' or otherwise taking on eland power through trance seem lacking. In the Western Cape, at least, therianthropic paintings of eland-headed people are unknown, unlike those involving elephants or other antelope. Our reading of the kaross as torso makes kaross-clad figures therianthropes of a kind, but not necessarily generated by trance-related conflation. We suggest that the evidence for reading eland as symbol of trancer is equivocal, whereas that as symbol of initiated men is stronger. The reference seems to be to transformation rather than to tranceformation. Some connection between initiation and trance is, in any event, implicit in Figure 6.

Both Vinnicombe (1976) and Lewis-Williams (1988) have commented on the phrase 'people of the eland', a reference made by a baPhuti man Mapote to How (1970) early in this century. He had said to her that he would paint an eland because the local people were 'of the eland'. Whereas Vinnicombe chose to fit the phrase to the whole of local San society, Lewis-Willliams has argued that it might refer only to the local shamans, who might well have been the painters as well. If Mapote was indeed thinking of only a segment of the local San community in using the phrase, he might just as well have implied initiated men as shamans.

This may also be the occasion to rethink the metaphor of the dying eland. The current consensus is to see the dying eland as a metaphor for the trancer entering trance, a state referred to as half-death by Kalahari San (Lewis-Williams 1981:91). If, as we argue here, the most prominent eland death in the verbatim accounts is that of the first eland, creating the first hunter, then another reading becomes possible. The death of the eland is the birth of the hunter, the metaphor related to initiation rather than to trance.

## *REFERENCE TO PLACE AND BELONGING*

Whereas the paintings discussed so far have an obvious directionality and an implied motion, others (Figures 9 and 10) convey a sense of closure and rest.

**Figure 9.** *Human group: Bags, bows and quivers hang above a group of seated human figures. All images red.*

**Figure 10.** *Human group: Both males and females involved. Note the standing (probably male) figure at right with lines emerging from armpits and one hand. An unusual feature is the presence of two diminutive male figures associated with the seated clapping females. Colour red.*

Paintings such as these have already been mapped and interpreted on several occasions (Maggs 1967, Manhire, Parkington and Yates 1985, Yates, Golson and Hall 1985, Parkington 1989). Again, although variable, they associate hanging bows, quivers and bags – this time very variable in shape and size, and including women's bags – with groups of men, women and, arguably, children in predominantly seated postures. The composure of the posture is reinforced in some, perhaps in all, by the depiction of the outermost figures as orientated inwards, drawing attention into the scene rather than out of it. The decision to paint both sexes conveys an impression of the wholeness of the band rather than the specificity of a particular subset or interest group. The compositions are circular in shape rather than linear, an aspect occasionally reinforced by encircling lines from which bags may hang or on which people may sit. In at least two instances such paintings are placed in rock recesses that act as caves within caves.

In constructing this set of images the painters have been careful not to imply movement, not to reflect time, and not to omit any member from the group. In some, and perhaps originally in most, examples there is a standing figure, probably a trancer, allowing us to add this occasion to the other references. Among these latter is again the use of hanging equipment as a device to represent, in this case, the domestic cave location. Taking the domestic reference further, we note the lack of disruption, the completeness and timelessness of the composition, and might argue that this genre of painting is a reference to social cohesion and to the sense of long-term ownership of the landscape and the homes within its rocks by hunter-gatherer groups. The trance occasion seems in other parts of southern Africa to epitomise the ritual core of hunter-gatherer feelings, to be their 'central religious occasion'. The social cohesion generated by this religious ritual is mirrored and given material expression in the compositional organisation of the paintings. During the last two millennia the hunter gatherers' relations with the land were successively challenged by the appearance of herding groups and later colonial settlers. Under pressure, they survived longest in the caves and rock shelters of remote areas. Figures 9 and 10 embody the group cohesion and domestic harmony necessary to withstand threat.

## *CONCLUSION*

We have shown here that aspects of composition – specifically orientation and organisation – exhibit a consistency that implies the use of conventions in the pre-colonial paintings of the Western Cape. The contrast between processional compositions (Figures 1 to 6) which depict sequence, movement or transformation, and rounded compositions (Figures 9 and 10) which avoid such connotations, is striking. We intend to expand the sample of processional and non-processional paintings to establish whether this is a regional or sub-continental convention. It may turn out to be a promising but spurious idea to be abandoned after repeated empirical scrutiny.

More extensively treated here is the meaning implied and intended by the frequent depictions of eland, and in particular by its use in Figure 6. As Lewis-Williams has suggested (1981:55-65), the role of eland in San thought seems essentially to be that of an *animal de passage*, perhaps primarily involved in the initiation of the new male hunter. Our approach has been to try to cross-reference between a very explicit and detailed painting, the ethnographic accounts of San male initiation drawn from elsewhere in southern Africa and eland references in nineteenth-century San stories. Our contention is that the consistency is overwhelming. Further, we argue that the significance of the eland in San texts such as Figure 6 lies in the transition from boy to man rather in that of dancer to trancer. Thus we should read eland in terms of initiated male hunter rather than as tranceformed shaman in this painting. Significantly, perhaps, Figure 6 associates the eland with the distinction between naked and kaross-clad male figures. From this we make the suggestion that the conventionalised depictions of 'karosses' should read as meaning 'initiated'. We point also to the fact that references to trance are associated in Figure 6 with naked men in a segment of the composition deliberately separated from the naked/clothed contrast.

If we are correct in recognising a convention for distinguishing between boys and men, we may wonder whether other social distinctions are not also preserved in the painted images. That between men and women is currently under review (Solomon 1988). It has been noted that in the past archaeologists and ethnographers have portrayed San society as unrealistically seamless, devoid of internal struggles or interests. Ecological explanations follow from such a view of social homogeneity, because the siting of the impetus for action or change within social relations becomes difficult. Critiques of this portrayal stress the need to seek the origins of social and economic change within the divisions and tensions of San society (Mazel 1987, Solomon 1988, Wadley 1987). Recognition of the conventions used to depict different kinds of people may help in this search.

Examples of metaphorical treatments of marital and in-law problems in /Xam society abound in the Bleek and Lloyd collection of stories (Bleek 1924, 1931, 1932a,b,c, 1933,a,b, 1935a, 1936a, Bleek & Lloyd 1911), suggesting that the tensions were strongly felt. An obvious arena of tension would have been the variable access to meat experienced by men as they aged and became less effective hunters. What all San literature makes clear is that the reins of ritual power were firmly held by the aged, and predominantly but not exclusively by older men. In Marxian terms San relations of production consist not only of access to bows, arrows, and poison, but also of access to the knowledge of charms, tattoos and ritual practices that sanction and bring success in hunting, the most esteemed economic activity. Old men, by controlling these spheres and fulfilling these roles, empower themselves. Bleek has noticed that,

> Old men tattoo a successful hunter in return for an offering of game in order to give him good luck in finding the next buck. These cuts are optional. I have seen a noted hunter, an old man, who had only three; but as a rule the seniors manage to instil such a fear of a run of ill luck into the younger men that there is rarely a buck shot of which they do not get the tit-bits. (Bleek 1928b:11)

The challenge remains to find the conventions used to depict these older men.

## *ACKNOWLEDGEMENTS*

We thank particularly Yvonne Brink, Pippa Skotnes and Anne Solomon who have generously shared their thoughts about San expression, both visual and verbal. They may well not agree with what we have written here.

# The Thin Black Line

## Diversity and Transformation in the Bleek and Lloyd Collection and the Paintings of the Southern San

Pippa Skotnes

The field of San painting studies has become entrenched within the discipline of archaeology. Since it is often the business of archaeology to bleed knowledge from silent objects which do not easily yield their secrets, this is not as anomalous as it may seem. If left to art historians the highly productive marriage between San ethnography and San painting might well have taken place. It was, nevertheless, within the discipline of archaeology that this successful arrangement occurred.

The paintings will not, however, escape the critical attention of artists and art historians for ever, and if their contribution is to be productive, certain aspects of the paintings that are currently of little interest to archaeologists must be considered and explored. In this paper it is my intention to question the validity of the current trend to search for uniformity, generic similarities and common purpose in the paintings, and to suggest, by way of examples, that the ethnography, particularly the testimony of the Bleek and Lloyd informants, does not support this trend. Further, I would suggest that acknowledging the significance of formal and iconographic diversity in the paintings is central to ridding them of their status as mere ethnographic phenomena and appreciating them as art.

An artwork is an ontologically distinct reality. It is neither, on the one hand, something that merely represents or depicts, nor, on the other hand, a collection of signs and symbols. It is rather a manifestation of ideas, a reality in which the so-called sign and so-called signified are so interpenetrated that they become merged. Response to the artwork is predicated on this very conflation and it is in this conflation that its power resides.

The power of pictures is eternally manifest. Since the earliest records of response they have moved people in manifold ways. They have evoked feelings of peace, happiness or sadness; they have acted as intermediaries for worship, have inspired idolatry and iconoclasm. People have travelled great distances to see them, have cried before them, have vandalised them, have been aroused and titillated by them. They have been censored and venerated; and when Roland Barthes, for example, looking at a photograph of his dead mother, saw her transcended, he acknowledged their redemptive quality.

The culture of the people who painted in the shelters of southern Africa is dead, and in the sense that we have no single testimony from an artist or from a person intimately acquainted with the art as it was practised, it is doubly dead. This has been a source of pessimism for some who have tried to understand the iconography, meaning and function of the paintings. Art historians particularly, whose methodologies depend on an established chronology and the ability to compare and assess pictorial developments, have had difficulty in approaching the art and have largely shied away from it. But the paintings themselves are not dead. In Eliot's terms, they are part of an eternal present. They do not, like science, accumulate significance, they are not superseded, they do not pass out of date, are not superannuated and we must assume that, like all art, they share with the paintings of all other periods the power to affect the lives of their viewers.

Because of our ignorance of San culture as it was practised by San painters in the various southern African regions in which it occurs, the term 'southern San rock painting' or 'southern San rock art' has become widely applied. It implies a belief in the common purpose of all paintings made on rocks by the San during their long history in this region. This term is, as such, problematic, general and reductionist. It carries the same doubtful significance as the term 'African art' and similarly fails to recognise the rich formal, iconographic and stylistic diversity that exists.

San painting has been widely accepted as one of the longest and oldest tradition of painting in the world, pre-dating or at least contemporary with the paintings of the Upper Palaeolithic in Europe and extending through to the nineteenth century. The problems of analysis presented by this vast body of material, with no direct ethnography and no discernable chronology, have been dealt with in a variety of ways. One of the early attempts to understand the paintings rested on the appreciation of their beauty and the acknowledgement of the observational and imaginative skills of the artists (Battiss 1948). The paintings were approached as art in the Western sense, and something of their function was suggested. This approach never got very close to the meaning of the paintings, since the preoccupation with their form and aesthetic was never linked in any meaningful or consequential way to their content. As a reaction to this, more recent attempts to understand the paintings have been concerned with content, that is, the interpretation of the meaning of individual figures in the paintings, without necessarily taking into account the form which expresses it (the Rock Art Research Unit of the University of the Witwatersrand). This has been achieved largely through the analysis of nineteenth- and twentieth-century San ethnography[1] and proceeds from the assumption that there exists a pan-San cognitive system with the trance dance and the trancing shaman as the central and most significant feature of it. The perceived similarity in the paintings country-wide is seen as evidence.

This ethnographic approach has revolutionised research into rock art and invested it with a potential previously absent. But this revolution has incurred losses. The approach is partly a product of and strongly dependent upon its own method for recording the paintings – the simple technology of the acetate tracing. Tracing replaces the originals with linear, stylistically arbitrary, monochrome copies, and has absolved the researcher of the need to address the iconographic diversity and stylistic variety that exists in the paintings by effectively eliminating them. The pervasive thin black line has rendered all paintings equal, stylistically similar, visually bland. This translation of pictorial form into diagram has been applied to the illustration and recording of various other forms of African art by Westerners, more commonly in the anthropological literature, and is peculiar to the study of what was previously known as 'primitive art'. Indeed the depiction and recording of these arts has never been subject to the same standards of verisimilitude as has the study of Western art.

In any visual art there is an interdependence of form and content. The painting is itself the *only* evidence we have of the meaning it expresses. The visuality of the paintings is their *most important* feature, for it is this alone that distinguishes them from storytelling, narratives or ritual acts. In Danto's words, 'Before the work of art we are in the presence of something we can grasp only through it, much as only through the medium of bodily actions can we have access to the mind of another person' (1988:29). This interrelationship of form and content has been a feature of art historical investigation since the last century. Further, these investigations insisted that the analysis of content be linked to the religious, social or political concerns of the artist. Wolfflin's strongly formalist analysis of art was already being contested (as indeed was the supremacy of the study of 'high art' as opposed to the more popular arts) in the late nineteenth century by the Viennese school of art history, which emphasised that art was part of a cultural and social system and that its context was an important part of its meaning (Antal 1949). Later, in his seminal work of 1955, Panofsky insisted on the essential symbiotic relationship of what he termed 'archaeological research' and what he called 'aesthetic re-creation' particularly in cases where corroborative text was not available (Panofsky 1955:16). This aesthetic re-creation involved an analysis by an 'informed' and 'sensitive' viewer of the way in which the painting was formally arranged. Panofsky so valued the dependence of form and content that he used Leonardo's example of two weaknesses leaning together to make up one strength to compare their relationship. The halves of an arch cannot even stand upright: the whole arch supports a weight. 'Similarly, archaeological research is blind and empty without aesthetic re-creation and aesthetic re-creation is irrational and often misguided without archaeological research' (1955:19).

In his definition Daniel McCall stated, 'art history is analysis and criticism of art, the sociology of artistic creation and the position of the artist in society, as well as history of the development of styles' (McCall and Bay 1975). And in his discussions on art, Hegel insisted that 'the artwork is not an object for the understanding alone, but also for the senses and the imagination' (Mitias 1980:70). Hence he went on to suggest that 'the true end of art, is to reveal truth in the form of sensuous artistic configuration. Accordingly the artwork presents truth in a sensuous form' (Mitias 1980:71).

Thus when Lewis-Williams asserts, while comparing art from as afar afield as Tanzania with southern African San art, that the considerable differences in style as well as 'Head-types, compositions, amount of detail, use of polychrome techniques and other features' (1987a) are superficial and that to pay heed to them is to obscure their common meaning, he fails to recognise the essential interdependence of form and content and robs the paintings of their peculiar and exclusive (perhaps their only) ability to reveal this truth.

This pervasive tendency throughout the history of the study of San painting to separate the content of a painting from the form which expresses it is, to the art historian at least, a significant problem. This is particularly true when within the current ethnographic approach the perceived content of the paintings is linked to the re-creations of the paintings in the form of the thin black line drawings, the style and form of which bear little resemblance to the originals. Often too, even today, details in the paintings are not recorded in the tracings, further distorting their content. This method patronises their aesthetic and they are treated with little of the respect accorded Western painting. Deprived of their aesthetic significance, they are viewed as ethnographic specimens or productions of the 'primitive' mind however full of religious feeling it may be acknowledged to be, mere illustrations of San belief or illustrations of theories of San belief. In short, the very paintings under discussion are virtually ignored.

As I have suggested earlier, it is this reduction of the paintings into stylistically uniform line drawings that has enabled the researcher to find such widespread similarities in the paintings and posit a pan-San cognitive system. In addition, in the study of ethnographic texts only similarities amongst geographically separated groups of San are invoked and this further focuses attention away from the diversity and contradictions that do exist.

My contention is that the paintings of southern Africa are stylistically, formally and iconographically diverse, displaying marked inter-regional and even intra-regional differences and that these differences are in themselves indications of cognitive and cultural diversity. In defence of this, I would like to use as an example one feature of the paintings, that of transformation as it is reflected in the therianthrope and the zoomorph, and relate this feature to analogical expressions of it in one of our richest sources of ethnography, the Bleek and Lloyd Collection. This figure, which previously presented researchers inclined towards the narrative, descriptive interpretation of the art with considerable problems, has now assumed some centrality in explaining the art within the trance hypothesis. However, far from originating in only one area of San life, the trance state of the shaman, the transformed or liminal being is generated in many areas of San belief and as such interpretations of paintings which include this feature may and reasonably should differ widely.

Despite the many stories of shamans and medicine people, the thousands of pages of the Bleek and Lloyd Collection taken from /Xam informants make no mention of the trance dance we know so well from the ethnographies of the !Kung. Indeed, Lucy Lloyd does refer to healing dances in her interviews with !Kung informants, but, apart from the //Ken dance which initiated shamans, we have no evidence from these records that the /Xam practised trance dances at all. There also appear to be differences in the way the !Kung and the /Xam viewed trance performance and the activities of the shaman. Based on the work of Lorna Marshall, Katz and Lee, Lewis-Williams describes the world of trance as 'not remote from daily life, an arcane experience reserved for initiates only, but ... an integral part of the camp's life' (1986:250), and yet Dia!kwain, one of Lloyd's /Xam informants, insisted that 'we who are not sorcerers do not know what they are doing [in another place], but those who are sorcerers know their mates and what they are doing' (Bleek 1935a:14). Indeed much of the shamanistic activities described by Dia!kwain appear to have taken place at night when all but the shaman were asleep.

Shamanistic activity accounts for one category in the Bleek and Lloyd Collection where transformations occur. Shamans were able to assume many different forms. These forms could be used for good as well as malicious intent. In //Kabbo's place, 'sorcerers' would turn themselves into birds, or, if they wanted to kill people, jackals (L V-9 4701r). Jackals could, however, also become the assumed form of the shaman who wanted to know whether friends or relatives who are away from home were well. He would locate the person and bark, and having been given a bone which he would chew like a dog, he would make sure that they got home safely, then leave (Bleek 1935a:15-19). Similarly the shaman could become a lion or a bird and encountering such a creature, the people would realise its true identity and treat it well.

Lions were also a favourite guise of both the benevolent and the evil shaman. 'The lion and the man's story', told by Dia!kwain, tells of how a hunter, while out in the hot noon, becomes sleepy and is taken by a lion who traps him in the fork of a tree. (L V-7 4457-4525). The man tries to escape when the lion goes to get a drink, but the lion again presses him into the tree. '... and the lion licked the man's tears on account of it and the man wept on account of it; thence he (the lion) licked the man's eyes.' Eventually, the man manages to escape and runs home. The lion follows his tracks and the people, seeing it coming, shoot at it but it will not die. An old woman offers a child to the lion, but having tasted the tears of the man, it is the man alone that the lion desires. Soon, the realisation dawns on the people that the lion is in fact a 'sorcerer', and that he will not be killed until the man whose tears he tasted has been handed over. This being done, the lion kills the man and the people are able to kill the lion.

Lions, often interpreted within the framework of the trance hypothesis as transformed malevolent shamans, when depicted in the paintings may thus quite reasonably be interpreted as lions behaving as lions, as benevolent or as malevolent transformed shamans, as wild cats wreaking vengeance on hunters who kill them (L VIII-23 8080-8083), or as the following story suggests, lions behaving as men. Rachel, one of Lloyd's informants, tells how her sister, /A khumm is called by a lion but does not answer (L VI-2 4026-4033). 'He put his tail upon his tongue, while he questioned [her], seeking the place at which /A khumm appeared to be' (4026/7). /A khumm felt that the lion had become a man, but that he sounded like a man only because his tail was in his mouth. She did not answer him because she nevertheless knew he was a lion and did not want him to find her and kill her.

Another important feature of the trance hypothesis is the identification of the shaman with the eland during trance states. As with painted depictions of eland in some regions, stories of eland are relatively rare in the published Bleek and Lloyd records (given their centrality in other ethnographies), and transformations into eland are not identified. But the close relationship of man with eland is discussed in relation to hunting rituals and even paintings such as the one at Game Pass shelter, so pivotal to the trance hypothesis, can be interpreted in this context.

The strong sympathetic relationship of the hunter to the hunted eland is well described in !Kung as well as /Xam ethnography. Indeed, the sensations of identification the hunter feels with his prey verges on transformation itself. Quite apart from dress and costume, where hunters wore masks, caps, horns or feathers to disguise and identify themselves with their prey (Skotnes 1990:19), they experienced sensations which linked them more closely. These are described in relation to the eland, but are also discussed with regard to other bovids. When hunting springbok, for example, //Kabbo felt the black stripe on the face of the springbok, the blood running in the veins of the springbok and the rustling of their feet. These all produced physical sensations in the hunter that //Kabbo called 'the springbok sensation' (Bleek & Lloyd 1911:333).

Other categories of /Xam belief where transformations occur include the activities of /Kaggen, the people of the early times, !Kwa (the rain), young women at menarche, and an amorphous category of *ad hoc* transformations.

In one of his first acts of creation, /Kaggen transformed a piece of shoe into an eland, and /Kaggen said:

> 'What does my brother think he has seen yonder?' And the young Ichneumon said: 'A person is yonder, standing yonder.' And the Mantis [/Kaggen] said: 'You think it is magic; but it is a very small thing, it is a bit of a father's shoe, which he dropped. Magic it is not.' And they went home. (Bleek 1924)

And once the eland had been killed by the Meercat, and /Kaggen lamented the death of the eland which he had loved and had nurtured on honey, he created the moon, once from his shoe (//Kabbo's version) and once from a feather (/Han≠kass'o's version). And in his anger at the death of the eland, /Kaggen created hunters.

/Kaggen is much more than the archetypal trancing shaman. He was not only capable of transforming himself, he could facilitate transformation. He could restore life or change the world by dreaming. He could conjure wings in fire, he could take the form of lice or a puffadder to startle the hunter of a dying eland. He could become invisible or transform into a lion. /Kaggen is mercurial, a super-trickster, creative and destructive simultaneously, violent though unwittingly benevolent, old but child-like, male but effeminate, active not only in the past but influencing the present, and while he symbolises much of the contradictions occurring in the trancing shaman, he was as Hewitt (1986a) points out, a supernatural being believed to participate actively in (the people's) lives. He thus existed independently of /Xam thought. This quality of independent action applies to many of the stories of shamans on out-of-body travel. There appeared to be little in the way of socially constructed ritual to control their activities.

But /Kaggen and the shamans were not the only agents of transformation in the /Xam world. Stories from the formative period when members of the early race – those that preceded the /Xam in their country – were all people (though bearing animal names and often animal traits), are rooted in the expectation of transformation. These people all became the animals whose names they bore. (This was a result of the Anteater's laws which insisted that each animal marry its own kind and behave in accordance with its own animal nature.) Conversely, according to one informant, the people of today were all once springbok until their transformation into human beings (facilitated by /Kaggen). These transformations include the transformation of the wind. 'The wind was formerly a man, he became a bird. Therefore, he is tied up in cloth. His skin is that which we call cloth' (L V111-8 6694rev). These narratives, though ostensibly concerned with a distant past are not distinguished from historical stories and indeed, are often interpenetrated.

Young women at menarche were considered particularly dangerous and susceptible to the unwelcome interference of !Khwa, the rain, if strict rules of confinement were not adhered to. The results of the transgression of these rules were mostly the unhappy transformation of men into trees, or people into frogs. Thus in many of these stories an educational function is present.

//Kabbo tells the story, titled by Lucy Lloyd, 'Men enchanted by a girl and changed into trees' (L 11-2, 295-305), of a man, playing his goura who is transfixed by the stare of a menarcheal girl, or a 'new maiden', and undergoes a transmogrification. Later he is joined by another man carrying a quiver who experiences a similar fate. But the story has another significance. Through ten pages, //Kabbo struggles to articulate the nature of this transformation. And in so doing he stresses an essential dialectic in one phrase '... he is a tree, he is a man ...'. The man still has all the features that characterise him as a man, yet he *is* a tree.

> ... he still has his nails,
> he still has his eyes,
> he still has his nose,
> his eyes remain, he is a tree,
> he has his head,
> he has his head hair,
> he talks, he is a tree ...

As with the characters who participated in the stories of the early times who were indeed people, yet often behaved in a manner characteristic of the perceived natures of the animals whose names they bore, this transformed man retains much of his human morphology while at the same time strongly resembling the tree he had become. His liminal condition can be directly ascribed to the transgressions of cultural rules and the power of the woman at first menarche, herself in a liminal state.

In another story of a young menarcheal woman, !Khwa is angered by her persistent killing of the water children. A whirlwind carries the girl to a spring where she becomes a frog. Later the whirlwind carries her parents into the spring, along with their mats and belongings. The parents become frogs, the father's arrows become reeds, and today all the things which grow around a spring are the belongings of these early people. Not only were the people transformed by the girl's transgressions, but each cultural artefact reverted to its original state.

The existence of stars is often attributed to similar acts of transgression on the part of confined women. Staring at a man by one such woman resulted in his transformation into the Lion Star (L 11-1 237-40). Similarly, the existence and configuration of the Corona Australis or *≠nabbe ta !nu*, is ascribed to a young maiden transfixing with her gaze the dassie who was feeding his people, and their conversion into stars (L 11-37 3333-43).

But these young women were also capable of acts of creation with beneficial consequences. All these acts also involved transformation. 'The girl who made the milky way by throwing ashes into the sky' describes the transformation of wood ashes into stars:

> The Milky Way gently glows; while it feels that it is wood ashes. Therefore it gently glows. While it feels that the girl was the one who said that the Milky Way should give a little light for the people that they might return home by night. For the earth would not have been a little light, had not the Milky Way been there. It and the stars. (L 11-28 2505-24)

*Ad hoc* transformations are overtly or obliquely referred to in many of the /Xam narratives. One man's transformation into a lion, for example, is achieved by his friends squashing him into a fat mouse's skin. Once so altered, he catches his sister-in-law who had been mocking him and bites her head, carrying her off (L V111-17 7527-49).

The therianthrope or the zoomorph in the paintings is thus an indication of a change from one state or form to another, attributes of both being reflected in its morphology. Yet this liminal state, this process of becoming, is never witnessed in the ethnography. The shaman may feel him or herself to have undergone a change – //Kabbo's description of the man turned tree has a certain experiential ring to it – others may perceive the change once it has taken place, but the depiction of the therianthrope or zoomorph is a particularly visual, painterly creation. In combining human features with elements depicting or symbolic of human experiences, it embodies various contrasts; the physical with the experiential, the perceived with the conceived. And in these formal, visual terms it is evidence of that process which Max Beckmann called 'magical', the translation of three-dimensional matter and of ideas into two dimensional form (Chip 1969:190). It is the painterly solution to what has been experienced or to what is known but has not been experienced, it is the reification of belief.

The trance hypothesis interprets the therianthrope and the zoomorph as being descriptive of or symbolic of the trancing shaman during the trance dance. This interpretation, in the light of the many accounts of transformations in the Bleek and Lloyd Collection fails to recognise that these were a part of the range of experiences described by the /Xam as a normal part of their existence. Sometimes they were imbued with symbolic significance, sometimes as a banal part of everyday life with an occasional educative role. In their own terms, there was no need to explain these phenomena as only emanating from some supernatural power, or as an epiphenomenon of a socially constructed ritual (and, indeed, they did not). These transformations that occupied the /Xam world were not lured to appear in it, nor were they conjured from the imagination of the individuals who described them. When Lloyd's informant Rachel described the water's children, she had not seen them herself but she *knew* them to be striped like zebra and beautiful, being the children of great things (VI-1 3942opp). These figures perceived as physically real thus existed independently of human thought, they were understood to take their own initiative.

In conclusion, the ethnography itself does not support the reductionist interpretation of every painting as an emanation of the trance dance or trance performance, even in paintings which include therianthropes or zoomorphs where the case for the implication of trance performance is the strongest. Since form and content are so inextricably linked, the formal diversity of the paintings is undoubtedly linked to the ethnographic diversity. The 'thin black line' is more than just a convenient method for recording the paintings, it has influenced and restricted interpretation, ignoring diversity. The attempt to reduce this diversity to a purely causal relationship with the trance dance (which we do not even know to have been universally performed), therefore, proceeds only at the expense of the paintings themselves, the richness of San art and the veracity of our understanding.

## *ACKNOWLEDGEMENTS*

I am very grateful to Duncan Miller and Malcolm Payne for discussing the ideas contained in this paper with me and for making useful suggestions when I wrote it in 1990. I thank John Parkington and Bruce Arnott for reading and commenting on an earlier version of this paper. My research has been generously supported by the University of Cape Town.

## *NOTE*

1. Three separate sources of ethnography (Orpen's nineteenth-century reports of interviews with Qing, the Bleek and Lloyd Collection and ethnographies of extant San from Botswana and Namibia) provide the range of ethnography available to the San painting researcher. While none of these provides direct reference to the communities who made the paintings, sufficient common ground in San thought appears to exist to suggest their cautious use in interpreting the content of the paintings. Indeed, interpretation could not proceed without them.

# Archaeology of the Flat and Grass Bushmen

Janette Deacon

Narratives and beliefs of the /Xam, taken verbatim from six major informants by WHI Bleek from 1870 to 1875, and by his sister-in-law Lucy Lloyd from 1870 to 1884, have been used extensively in the interpretation of rock paintings and engravings in southern Africa (Vinnicombe 1976; Lewis-Williams 1981). By contrast, until very recently (Wadley 1987; Deacon 1992), the records have not been used as a major source of analogues for interpreting Later Stone Age cultural remains other than rock art. Most hypotheses and models used in Later Stone Age studies have been based instead on more recent ethno-archaeological work conducted in the Kalahari in the 1950s, 1960s and 1970s. The purpose of this paper is to show that there is potential for using the /Xam testimony to interpret the distribution of certain kinds of occupation debris on very recent San sites, but that detailed models cannot be tested because erosion and the disintegration of most organic remains has meant that only durable materials have survived.

The informants who stayed longest with Bleek and Lloyd belonged to two neighbouring dialectal groups. The Flat Bushmen (//Kabbo, /Han≠kass'o and /A!kunta) lived at the Bitterpits and other water sources between Kenhardt and Vanwyksvlei, and the Grass Bushmen (Dia!kwain, ≠Kasin and !Kweiten ta //ken) lived around the Katkop hills between Kenhardt and Brandvlei (Figure 1). All the men who were interviewed had served sentences at the Breakwater Prison in Cape Town. The only woman, !Kweiten ta //ken, was the sister of Dia!kwain and the wife of ≠Kasin. The Hardast or Hartebeest River Bushmen and the Mountain or Berg Bushmen lived to the north and south respectively but were not interviewed for any length of time and we do not know whether their dialects were also distinctive.

Two of the three Flat Bushman men, //Kabbo and /Han≠kass'o, gave quite detailed descriptions of the area where they lived around the Bitterpits, about fifty kilometres south of present-day Kenhardt. Neither Bleek nor Lloyd ever visited the area the informants came from, however, and all the interviews

*Most of the informants came from an area south of Kenhardt. Compare with places marked on //Kabbo's map on p. 26.*

were conducted in Cape Town, mostly at the Bleeks' home in Mowbray. The opportunity for mapping the precise location of the Flat Bushman living sites with the informants on hand therefore never arose, but fieldwork conducted from 1985, using a sketch map drawn by Bleek on information from //Kabbo (see pp. 26-27), descriptions from //Kabbo and /Han≠kass'o, and information from present-day farmers, has led to the finding of several places that were very probably occupied by Flat Bushmen in the nineteenth century (Deacon 1986, 1988; Deacon 1989). One of these, near the Bitterputs on the farm Arbeidsvreugd, was excavated in June/July 1988.

## *LIFE-STYLE OF THE FLAT AND GRASS BUSHMEN IN THE NINETEENTH CENTURY*

The Flat and Grass Bushmen were no longer pristine Stone Age hunter-gatherers at the time of their arrest and removal to the Breakwater Prison in Cape Town. They had been in contact with Khoikhoi pastoralists for a millennium or more and had learned to make pottery and to use iron. They had metal-tipped arrows; Dia!kwain, moreover, owned a gun at the time of his arrest (Cape Archives CO 3163, Jackson to Colonial Secretary 25 Feb. 1869) and //Kabbo hoped that Dr Bleek would give him one (Bleek & Lloyd 1911: 317). Apart from the fact that they were arrested by British Northern Border Police for crimes against white colonists ranging from stock theft to culpable homicide, several of the informants had worked for white farmers for short periods and all of them could converse to some extent in Dutch. Some of the narratives include mention of sheep, cattle and horses.

The nature of the relationship between the /Xam and their neighbours in the northern Cape is not at all clear but the /Xam were certainly not the only people living in Bushmanland in the nineteenth century. Travellers' accounts from the late eighteenth century onwards mention the presence of /Xam, Nama and Korana (Khoikhoi), Basters and white Trekboers (stock farmers) south of the Orange River, and of all these groups and Tswana north of the river. A group of Xhosa had also come into the region in the wake of clashes in the Eastern Cape and were settled around present-day Carnarvon early in the nineteenth century (Kallaway 1982). The /Xam appear to have been least well-off. Both large (several hundred) and small (single family) groups of /Xam south of the Orange encountered hardship during times of drought (Lichtenstein 1930; Burchell 1967; Thompson 1968). Contact with Tswana who supplied metal artefacts was evident as early as 1805 when the /Xam were using metal for arrowheads (Lichtenstein 1930). They had probably been trading such items for some time. The fact that the /Xam artefacts changed while the people kept their language and beliefs and intermarried with Korana and others simply reinforces the observation that changes in material culture do not necessarily mirror changes in other aspects of society. Beliefs are more enduring than technology. What changes in material culture may signal, however, are new contacts with people with a different technology.

From the latter half of the eighteenth century when the first recorded journeys to the north-western Cape were undertaken by Gordon in 1777 and Wikar in 1779, and later by Lichtenstein in 1805, Campbell in 1806, Burchell in 1811 and Thompson in 1824, there was already tension between the /Xam hunter-gatherers and their stock-keeping neighbours the Korana (Engelbrecht 1935:228). The close relationship between them is illustrated by the fact that Gordon used the terms 'Bushman' and 'Hottentot' almost interchangeably for people along the Orange River near Kenhardt, calling a member of a group described as 'real Hottentots', a 'wild Bushman' and noting that one of the 'chiefs' of the 'real Hottentots' was the brother of a Bushman he had met the previous day and who was said to be an 'Einiqua' or San (Raper & Boucher 1988:324-26). This emphasises the similarity between the San and the Khoikhoi in the region, the main difference probably being in their language and the degree to which they were reliant on domesticated stock.

The 'real Hottentots' whom Gordon saw camped on an island in the Orange River one day's journey west of the Hartebeest River confluence were described as follows: 'This tribe had ten mat huts among the trees; I estimate five or six persons in each hut, and [with] little gardens like the Kaffirs, but there was nothing except dagga or hemp in them. This they got from the Namaquas, and they from us ... These Hottentots have cattle, sheep and goats (though not many), and are great hunters. The sheep are smooth-haired like goats and have long, thin tails. N.B. They milk their sheep' (Raper & Boucher 1988:326).

Apart from historical records, archaeological evidence shows the presence of herders with sheep and pottery between 500 and 1500 BP, and possibly even prior to 2000 BP (Beaumont & Vogel 1989) at several sites in this area and to the east of the Orange River (Humphreys & Thackeray 1983; Beaumont *et al.* 1985; Morris 1988; Beaumont & Vogel 1989). The /Xam were therefore in contact with stock farmers at least 1 500 or more years ago and would have been familiar with pottery, sheep and possibly goats and cattle – but not with horses or wheeled vehicles – for more than a millennium before the whites met them along the Orange River.

It was illegal for white farmers, mostly Dutch-speaking Trekboers, to settle north of the Sak River before the region was annexed in 1847, although some did so, and many more made a living out of hunting for ivory, skins and meat. In the early nineteenth century the Cape Colony north of the Sak River was an 'open' frontier with a rough balance of power between the Korana and the Trekboers (Giliomee 1981; Penn 1986:62), but after 1870 it closed as the Korana were defeated and white colonists settled there permanently.

Contemporary accounts cited above, and records collated by Dunn (1931), Engelbrecht (1936), Ross (1975) and Strauss (1979), concur with Stow (1905: 275) that the 'only occupations [of the Korana] were those of making war upon the aboriginal inhabitants, following the chase, or making forays upon one another's kraals for the purpose of cattle lifting'. Thompson (1968:46) was more specific:

> They are ... inclined to cultivate peace with all the tribes around them, except the Bushmen, – towards whom they bear inveterate animosity, on account of their continual depredations on their flocks and herds. Their wars with the Bushmen are said to be prosecuted with such rancour, that quarter is seldom given on either side.

One of the reasons for this animosity was that stock raiding was an integral part of the Korana relations of production. Stock, particularly cattle which were highly valued by the Korana, was kept for wealth rather than for food, and if stolen by a rival Korana group one day there was a reasonable chance it could be recovered the next. The /Xam, however, raided for food. Resources in the north-western Cape were scarce and frequent periods of drought were a serious hindrance to hunter-gatherers who were denied access to water-holes and the Orange River. The Korana, and later the Basters and Trekboers, not only took possession of land and water, but their sheep and cattle reduced the availability of grazing for game. The farmers themselves were shooting game on a daily basis for many more people than the relatively small /Xam bands, and the availability of food dwindled (Cape Archives CO 4414, Anthing to Colonial Secretary 8 May 1862). By this inexorable process, the /Xam were increasingly divorced from their traditional means of production and they were obliged to resort to stealing.

Thompson's account of the difficulty he and his party experienced when they ran out of food and water in the vicinity of Kenhardt in 1824 is testimony to the low productivity of the region when drought-stricken, even when such aids as horses and guns were available (Thompson 1968:23-28). Consequently, when /Xam stole stock, they ate it as quickly as possible and this was something neither the Korana nor the Trekboers could countenance because the stock was effectively removed from the raiding merry-go-round. The /Xam complained that even if they were employed by Basters or Trekboers, they received too little food and were therefore compelled to steal. When Anthing, who had been instructed by the Colonial Government to investigate the situation of the northern Cape San in 1862, asked one man how they dared to steal when they knew they would themselves be killed, 'The answer was that it is a fight with death either way' (Cape Archives, op. cit.).

After the British Government annexed the area between the Sak and the Orange Rivers in 1847, there were many clashes between settlers and the /Xam and Korana. The situation came to a head in the Korana War of 1868/69 when the British Northern Border Police broke the power of the Korana leaders (Strauss 1979). In the aftermath, the people whom Bleek and Lloyd eventually interviewed were arrested under various charges and sent to the Breakwater Prison in Cape Town after their convictions. To deal with other landless /Xam and Korana still in the area, a government notice of 13 May 1869 (Cape Archives CO 3163), and an accompanying letter from MJ Jackson to the Colonial Secretary dated 6 April 1869, made it known that applications could be sent to Kenhardt for servants from amongst 'destitute women and children who are continually coming into Camp to beg for food, and in some circumstances men, so impoverished and lean as to be scarcely able to walk.' Subsequent correspondence shows that applications were received from as far afield as Mossel Bay. This organised withdrawal of personal freedom from both Korana and /Xam and the establishment of a labouring class was a pattern repeated throughout the eighteenth and nineteenth centuries as white colonists consolidated their position along the frontier zone in the Cape Colony (Penn 1986:67). In 1870 (Government Notice No. 467, 22 November 1870, *Cape of Good Hope Government Gazette*), the Government offered for lease a large number of farms from the Orange River to south of Kenhardt and it was part of Jackson's duty to see that 'marauding Bushmen' were no longer a threat. Dorothea Bleek notes that when a Mr van der Westhuizen bought the farm around the Bitterpits about fifty kilometres south of Kenhardt in 1874, there were forty-two Bushmen there who subsisted on ants' eggs, uintjes, tortoises, porcupines and game, chiefly springbok, ostrich and springhare (Bleek 1936c:202). By 1911 these /Xam had either died or moved to nearby towns.

The hunting and gathering life-style of the /Xam had thus become an anachronism, and they were essentially without land and livelihood by the early 1870s. The /Xam were aware of the damage that stealing of stock could inflict on stock farmers, and that by stealing sheep they could get even with their neighbours who refused to share food with them. Just as the Christian ethic led the white farmers to punish the /Xam for stock theft so the San sharing ethic, that was so ideologically important to them (Marshall 1976), led the /Xam to continue helping themselves to stock when they were hungry, regardless of the consequences.

With so much interaction between /Xam and neighbouring groups, we could expect that a mid-nineteenth century /Xam living site would be distinguishable from earlier ones by the presence of European trade items as well as goods and materials traded from metal-working people like the Tswana. It was this criterion as well as descriptions in the Bleek and Lloyd records that helped to identify sites for archaeological investigation.

## *LOCATION OF A FLAT BUSHMAN LIVING SITE*

Bleek was particularly interested in finding out where //Kabbo lived and must have quizzed him specifically on this point. //Kabbo, too, was anxious to impress on Bleek and Lloyd that he was a landowner as he wanted to return home. In an account to Bleek in June 1871, //Kabbo recounted a conversation he had had with a man in a train from Mowbray to Cape Town and back. When asked where he came from he said he had told the man that 'My place is the Bitterpits'. The name of the place appears in the /Xam text as //xara-//kam (Bleek & Lloyd 1911:298-99). Although he patiently related tales and personal history, //Kabbo longed to return home:

> I must remain at my (own) place, the name of which I have told my Master; he knows it; he knows, (having) put it down. And thus my name is plain (beside) it. (Bleek & Lloyd 1911:315-17)

He referred here to the fact that Bleek had drawn a map on information from //Kabbo giving the names of places in /Xam and English or Dutch and the names of the people who lived there (see pp. 26-27). On this occasion (3 Sept. 1871) he told Bleek 'My (Oud Jantje's place) is Bitterpits' (BII:370). On a part of the map that is difficult to decipher has been written 'Oud Bastard's pl [?place]' west of the Strandberg. It is written below the place name '//a Thain' (written in BII:371 as //a Tkhain) and to the left of a place name made illegible by ink blots, but which could be '//kaua //kun' or '//xarra//kam'. Below this is written '//hang /ass'o's pl' to the left of which is '//gubbo' and below this is written 'Jantje' (//Kabbo's Dutch name was Oud Jantje or Jantje Tooren and /Han≠kass'o was known as Klein Jantje) and 'Bitterputs a few hours'.

Later, in July 1878, /Han≠kass'o told Miss Lloyd that //Kabbo's place was //gubo or 'Blauwputs' (Bleek & Lloyd 1911:307n), a farm about fifteen kilometres south-east of the Bitterpits on the same drainage system. In another passage (LVIII:7751-52) /Han≠kass'o says his father-in-law's place is //gubbo and 'people call it Oud Bastard's Puts'. It may be that there is a difference between //gubo and //gubbo, but as /Han≠kass'o's description mentions several water points and other places as belonging to //Kabbo it is likely that //Kabbo owned quite a large piece of land and he and his extended family moved to camping places such as Bitterpits, Oud Bastards Puts and Blauwpits along the (usually) dry river course known today as the Lekkerlêleegte in the west and Basterspüt se Leegte in the east.

At the time of their capture, then, //Kabbo and /Han≠kass'o were living in the vicinity of the Bitterpits and Blaauwpits some fifty to sixty-five kilometres south of Kenhardt on the farms known today as Arbeidsvreugd and Blaauwputs. To narrow down the search for a place that would have been occupied by them or their immediate ancestors, descriptions of landmarks were sought. One of these was a white boulder described by /Han≠kass'o as being on or on the edge of the dry river bed or lichte (*leegte*) at his father-in-law's place (LVIII 20:7751-52). The only such boulder known to the local farmers is about three kilometres north of the Bitterpits. It is a white granite erratic about one metre high and a metre and a half long and is unusual in its size and colour. There are no obvious signs of a recent camp site, defined as one with potsherds and glass beads, nearby. About eight hundred metres south-east of the boulder, however, is a living site marked by hearths, stone artefacts, pottery and other cultural material scattered over an area more than a hundred metres square. It was found some years ago by the owner of the farm Arbeidsvreugd, Mr FJ Reichert Jnr. It is situated on flat stony ground that slopes very gently down to the *leegte* several hundred metres to the north and north-west, and southwards to the Bitterpits (not visible from the site). It appears to be very isolated with no obvious reasons for its location, but the records show that the Flat Bushmen did not stay close to water. Children were sent periodically to fill ostrich eggshells and skin bags from the nearest source. /Han≠kass'o said also that there was no food near the water and they preferred to camp close to a source of gambro or kambro (a fleshy root) (Bleek 1933a: 302). Mr Reichert showed us a number of gambro plants in the vicinity between the site and the Bitterpits.

Another reason for the placement of this site is that, although it does not rain often in that area, a heavy shower leaves much standing water unless the place is well drained. On one occasion, /Han≠kass'o recalled that he had had to dig a channel to lead water out of his hut, but the rain had continued to fall and the hut fell down (Bleek 1933b:389). The living site at Arbeidsvreugd is on soil less than fifty millimetres deep and is underlain by crumbly shale bedrock. These conditions presumably allowed run-off after heavy rain to flow down towards the *leegte* rather than to collect at the camp site. The surface of the ground is covered with a wide variety of small stones that have been thoroughly windblasted and include quartz, jasper, diorite and other hard rocks, as well as larger quartzite cobbles.

A combination of the descriptions of their home territory by //Kabbo and /Han≠kass'o and nineteenth-century artefacts at Arbeidsvreugd therefore led to identifying this site as one that had probably been occupied by them or their immediate ancestors and it was selected for archaeological investigation. Further information was then sought in the testimony of the Flat Bushmen to identify practices that may be traceable archaeologically.

## EXPECTATIONS FROM THE ETHNOGRAPHIC RECORD

Interpretation of the distribution of debris on a /Xam living site depends to a large extent on details in the Bleek and Lloyd records that describe /Xam lifestyle and artefacts. These details are brief and scattered through the more than 11 000 pages of testimony. The very scarcity of such information emphasises the degree to which the importance of beliefs and folklore to the interviewers overshadowed more mundane matters. In this section /Xam accounts of practices that may be visible through archaeological methods have been collated. They include accounts of huts, what they were used for and the way they were laid out on a living site, customs relating to the dispersal of bones, and descriptions of the kinds of artefact made and used around the home.

### *Huts and Site Layout*

The features of interest for ethno-archaeological investigation are what huts may have been used for, the way they were constructed, the way the huts were placed on a living site, and social reasons for this placement.

Although self-evident, it is nevertheless of interest to note that the /Xam informants thought it fit to comment from time to time that huts were places where people sought shelter from the wind, the sun and the cold, and where they slept (Bleek & Lloyd 1911:117, 229, 323, 337). Women pounded their pot clay next to the hut (ibid.:343). The Flat Bushmen would go to each other's huts to smoke there and to obtain stories (ibid.:301). The fire was made outside the hut and was used not only for cooking and warmth, but also for signalling the presence of people (ibid.:381), for preparing feather brushes used in springbok hunting (ibid.:359-361) and for making arrows, resin and poison (ibid.:363).

In addition to the family huts, special ones were built a little way away from the main encampment for a girl during her first menstruation (Bleek & Lloyd 1911;76-77; LV-20:5582) and for a hunter who had shot an eland and was resting overnight before his companions followed the spoor the next day (Bleek 1932b:235).

The form that huts took seems to have varied from a rough shelter made of bushes to a well-constructed 'beehive' in which a framework of branches was covered with reed mats. In the narrative 'The son of the wind', /Han≠kass'o makes it clear in accompanying notes that mat huts were commonly made and that bushes (asbos or *Mesembrianthemum* spp) were used to make a shelter to protect the mat hut from the wind (Bleek & Lloyd 1911: 103, 105, 109, 111), particularly the east wind (Bleek 1932c:337). Although mat-covered huts have usually been associated more with herders than with hunter-gatherers, /Han≠kass'o's descriptions and illustrations by Gordon in 1779 (Raper & Boucher 1988) and by Burchell in 1812 (Burchell 1967) show that even by the latter half of the eighteenth century the /Xam were making them.

An account of a /Xam encampment given by Dunn (1873:33), who travelled through the territory of the Flat and Grass Bushmen in 1871, is roughly contemporary with the interviews given by the /Xam informants to Bleek and Lloyd, but it gives little detail on the layout of a camp. While near Vanwyksvlei he saw an old Bushman man in 'a little shelter made of bushes' and near the Sak River to the west he passed a Bushman 'werf' consisting of a circle of bushes with a fireplace in the centre (ibid.:36). Such shelters made of bushes are still in evidence in the region today, often used by labourers and by farmers as a *braaiplek* (barbecue place). They are also found further west in Namaqualand (Webley 1984, 1986) where the Nama separate the *skerm* from the mat huts and use it only as a cooking shelter.

Amongst the Bleek and Lloyd records there are three illustrations of the arrangement of huts at a camp, two drawn by /Han≠kass'o. The first he drew in explanation of the narrative of 'Ddi-xerreten, the lioness and the children'. It is published on the same plate as a drawing by one of the !Kung boys, /Uma, who illustrates the placement of huts at his home (Bleek & Lloyd 1911: facing p.172).

Whereas /Uma's drawing is typical of the ring model observed amongst Kalahari !Kung in the 1960s (Yellen 1977), /Han≠kass'o's drawing shows a linear arrangement of huts on and near the crest of a hill. The third drawing is entitled '//nei-//nei. Huts (Bushman huts)'. It shows two rows of huts, the one with thirteen and the other with six (Bleek & Lloyd 1911: between pp.224 & 225). There does not appear to be any commentary directly on the drawing, but it is dated September 1878 which was about the time /Han≠kass'o told Lloyd of the treatment of bones at a camp and he talks of neighbours living in huts opposite each other. Mention of the placement of huts by //Kabbo when describing his intended return home is not explicit, but he says that his 'hut stood alone, in the middle; while they [his children] dwelt on either side' (Bleek & Lloyd 1911:307). In another narrative 'The young man of the Ancient Race, who was carried off by a lion, when asleep in the field', Dia!kwain explains in a note that there were several huts in a row on the werf or yard (Bleek & Lloyd 1911:187n).

One of the earliest European illustrations of a San rather than Khoi encampment is on a map of Colonel Gordon's journey along the Orange River drawn in 1779 at the junction of the Hartebeest River (which he mistakenly calls the Sak) about a hundred kilometres north of Kenhardt. It shows 'Saana or Saanaquas (formerly called Sonquas)' around a dead springbok shot by arrows, with some huts in the background. The huts are clustered together with the doorways all facing in the same direction in a row rather than in a circle (Raper & Boucher 1988, Vol. 2:p.356, Pl. 74,). A similar cluster or row can be seen in the illustration of a 'Strandloper' group (ibid.:Pl. 52) drawn in the same year on the west coast.

The difference between the ring and linear layouts may reflect a greater need in the northern Cape to orientate all the huts in the same direction to get protection from the prevailing wind. However, Yellen (1990) has reported that !Kung camps made more recently than the 1960s tend towards a linear rather than a ring model. This may suggest that contact with European-type village layouts may have influenced both the /Xam and the !Kung to place their huts linearly.

With so little information it is difficult to formulate test situations that may allow evidence of social activities to be gleaned from the archaeological investigation of a /Xam living site. Gender-related spatial distributions have been noted by Elizabeth Marshall Thomas who recorded that among certain Bushman groups in the Kalahari every fire has a man's side and a woman's side. As one faces the doorway of the shelter or hut, the man's side of the hut, and the fire alongside it, is on the right and the woman's side is on the left (Thomas 1988:49). This gender division of space was not noted by Yellen (1977) nor by the Bleek and Lloyd informants, however. Archaeologically it would be traceable only if the position of the fire in relation to the entrance to the hut could be identified, if men and women left gender-specific artefacts where they had sat or worked, and if there had been no erosion of the surface or post-occupation movement of artefacts.

## *Distribution of Bones*

Several remarks by //Kabbo and /Han≠kass'o indicate that the distribution of bones of animals eaten at a /Xam living site may carry information about the range of animals eaten, but cannot be related directly to the hunting prowess of individuals. Bones were discarded at the camp according to a pattern of 'nice' behaviour. Far from being thrown around – /Han≠kass'o told Lloyd in 1878 – the bones are put down opposite the entrance of the hut by the side of a little thorn bush. A person who lives opposite may gnaw the bones and put them in an ostrich breastbone used as a dish and then pour them on his own heap of bones, but another neighbour will put the bones on the heap of the person who killed the animal, or on to the heap of the person who lives opposite him (Bleek & Lloyd 1911:275-79). The result is that the heap of bones opposite each hut will not necessarily consist exclusively of the bones of animals hunted by the man of that hut.

Special practices were observed with regard to springbok remains. Springbok possessed 'magic arrows' and 'magic sticks' so all springbok bones were put 'nicely away'. Children were not allowed to play on springbok skins because people who played 'tricks' or showed disrespect towards springbok would become ill and could even die. Furthermore, a springbok would not be cut up by the person who shot it, so others would place the meat and pour the stomach contents and blood on the heap of bones opposite the entrance to the hut of the person who killed it (Bleek & Lloyd 1911:275-77). After the marrow had been eaten from the bones they, too, were placed on the heap of the man who killed the springbok.

Springbok shoulder-blades had special treatment. Women were not allowed to eat the meat from them because it would cause the hunters to miss their aim or become ill. /Han≠kass'o said that when the shoulder-blade bones had been gnawed, they were put out of reach of dogs in the sticks of the hut or else the hunter would miss his aim (Bleek & Lloyd 1911:281); he contradicted himself in a later passage, however, saying that he 'gave the shoulder blade bones to the dogs' because //Kabbo did so (Bleek & Lloyd 1911:285). The man who shot the springbok was given the upper bones of the forelegs and the back of the neck and his wife used the fat from the back and tail to soften the springbok skin to make bags that were traded for ochre and specularite or for arrows (Bleek & Lloyd 1911:281).

It is interesting to note that no ideological practices related to the distribution of sheep or cattle bones were mentioned, presumably because they were not thought of as 'hunted'.

## *Distribution of Artefacts*

In addition to the information on the disposal of bones at a living site, there is mention in the testimony of the informants that flaked and ground stone tools were still being made in the 1860s and 1870s. Dunn (1873:32, 36, 37) confirms this. Grindstones were used in the preparation of grass seeds, ant larvae or 'Bushman rice', clay for pot making, and ochre and specularite. Unretouched stones also had uses. For example, Dia!kwain said that when his mother was going out of the camp to look for Bushman rice, she would take a stone and plunge it into the ashes of the fire so that the evil things she had been dreaming of would remain in the fire instead of going out with her (Bleek & Lloyd 1911:365).

//Kabbo explained that stone knives were used to cut up game when metal ones were not available and were made by striking one stone against another (Bleek & Lloyd 1911:3, 11, 227). Whereas the Flat Bushmen made arrowheads of metal (BII:35), the Grass Bushmen made theirs of white stone that Lloyd thought was probably quartz crystal (Bleek & Lloyd 1911:227n).

The use of metal for arrowheads was noted by Lichtenstein who met San in the Karreeberge in May/June 1805. He wrote that the San acquired the metal by exchange with people to the east, or by plunder 'from the Hassagais of the Caffre tribes'. The San were 'ignorant, however, of the use of fire in working the iron: the triangular plates they use, are produced by beating the iron with stones, so that a whole day is sometimes occupied in making one' (Lichtenstein 1930:248). His informants told him that they used bone arrowheads when hunting game and reserved the iron-tipped arrows 'to be employed against mankind'. Consequently, when next he encountered a San hunter, Lichtenstein took the precaution of checking the arrows in his quiver, releasing him when he saw no iron-tipped ones (Lichtenstein 1930:273).

This practice of reserving iron tipped arrows for warfare was not universal, however. Arrows in the South African Museum collection said to have been used during the Korana War of 1868/69 on the Orange River north of Kenhardt are tipped with glass from soda bottles taken from Sir Walter Currie's wagon (SAM catalogue 2698). The method of construction of these glass-tipped arrows is essentially similar to several cruder examples made by /Xam at the Bleek's home in Cape Town in about 1874 and described by Goodwin (1945) and Clark (1977). Those described by Goodwin have glass inserts and are now in the South African Museum collection. Clark illustrates three more that were apparently made at the same time and were donated by Bleek to the University Museum at Oxford in 1875 and transferred to the Pitt Rivers Museum in 1886. Two of the latter are tipped with white chalcedony inserts, and at least one of the inserts has been backed or blunted along the side that is embedded in the mastic.

There is no record of who made the arrows, but the timing suggests they could have been made either by Flat or Grass Bushmen. Some years later, Lloyd asked /Han≠kass'o to comment on the arrows during an interview in 1878 and he gave further information on their manufacture, including details such as the inclusion of an ostrich quill barb, sinew binding, reed shafts, feathering and poison, but focusing on metal and bone rather than on stone-tipped arrows (Bleek & Lloyd 1911:360-63; Goodwin 1945). His remarks suggest he did not make them himself. In view of the fact that //Kabbo said the Flat Bushmen used metal whereas the Grass Bushmen used white stone, and that /Han≠kass'o's description of arrow-making is almost entirely devoted to the manufacture of an iron-tipped arrow, the examples made for Bleek in the early 1870s could have been made by one or more Grass Bushmen, possibly including Dia!kwain and/or his brother-in-law ≠Kasin. The white stone referred to by //Kabbo (Bleek & Lloyd 1911:227n) could therefore have been chalcedony as is used in the examples in the Pitt Rivers Museum.

The use of heat to straighten the reed shafts in a warmed split digging stone, to work with the iron, to melt the adhesive and to mix the poison, meant that arrows were made alongside a fire. In contrast to what Lichtenstein's informant said, /Han≠kass'o told Miss Lloyd that an iron-tipped arrow was used to shoot springbok and that neither poison nor quill barbs were applied to such arrows. The metal for the arrowheads was heated in the fire to facilitate insertion into the wooden foreshaft, and when cool the arrowheads were sharpened. 'We sharpen it so that it bites, and we polish it on a flat whetstone of soft stone, for we intend that it become white ... We take the whetstone and put it away in the earth under the sticks of the side of the hut, lest a child espy it and take it and break it' (Goodwin 1945:438-39).

Ground stone digging-stick weights were made and used by women (Dunn 1873:32; Bleek & Lloyd 1911:361). Women with weighted digging sticks were seen in the vicinity of Vanwyksvlei by Dunn in 1871 (Dunn 1873) and by Dorothea Bleek at Kenhardt in 1911 (Bleek 1936c:201). Dorothea Bleek's informant, already elderly in 1911, said she and her grandmother both used an iron tool to make the hole in the stone and smoothed the outer surface by rolling it on another flat stone.

Fragments of pottery are frequently found at /Xam living sites and the informants confirmed that clay pots were used for cooking (Bleek & Lloyd 1911:123-127, 155, 311, 375) and also as a drum (ibid.:351). /Han≠kass'o described the method of making clay pots using grass temper (ibid.:434-347), but curiously left out the all-important phase of firing.

Of particular ethno-archaeological significance is a remark made to Lloyd by /Han≠kass'o who said that the Flat Bushmen did not make ostrich eggshell beads, but traded them from the Berg Bushmen in the Kareeberge to the south (LVIII:7971r). If this was indeed the case, we would not expect to find bead-making debris on a Flat Bushman site.

From these various notes we could expect that artefacts on a nineteenth-century Flat Bushman living site would include upper and lower grindstones, hammerstones for fashioning iron tools, stone flakes suitable for knives (but not stone projectile points), whetstones for sharpening arrows, fragments of iron and pottery, possibly bored stones, and complete or broken ostrich eggshell beads but not partly manufactured ones.

## *EXCAVATIONS AT ARBEIDSVREUGD*

With these expectations, the site in the vicinity of the white boulder and the Bitterpits on the farm now known as Arbeidvreugd was investigated using archaeological methods to map the site, sample surface artefact scatters and excavate below the surface in selected areas. The primary aims of this work were to establish whether the placement of huts could be mapped and whether these were arranged in a circle or linearly; to see whether there was any consistent spatial patterning of artefacts and bones discernible on the site and whether this could be related to specific activities that may or may not be gender-related; and to obtain samples of charcoal for radiocarbon dating to establish whether the various parts of the site had been occupied over a relatively short period or whether there was much 'overprinting' of occupations at different times.

## *Placement of Huts*

A grid of one-metre squares was laid out over an area of 70 x 50 metres in which artefacts and pottery were clearly scattered. Hearths, alignments of larger stones, upper and lower grindstones and anvils were plotted on a plan of the site on the assumption that these immovable features and larger artefacts would not have moved far from their original positions and could therefore indicate the approximate positions of former huts.

Only one stone alignment convincingly suggested the possible position of a former hut. It is at the south end of the site and is composed of a double row of cobbles arranged in a semicircle. If stones were used to anchor brush screens and mat huts, the double row could represent the kind of hut and screen of bushes described by /Han≠kass'o. The entrance to the hut faces northwards with the hearth opposite the entrance and an upper and lower grindstone to the right of the hearth (looking southwards into the hut entrance). Most of the cultural material (pottery, stone artefacts, ostrich eggshell beads) was found to the left of the hut. Very few artefacts were found inside and to the right of the hut, but several rubbers (upper grindstones) were amongst the stones comprising the inner hut circle. A second grindstone was found at the rear of the outer hut circle.

On the rest of the site, where it is not possible to ascertain in which direction the hut entrances were facing, there is some correlation in the distribution of upper and lower grindstones, anvils and hearths. If we assume that these would not have moved far under natural conditions because of their size (in the case of grindstones) and because of their nature (in the case of hearths), their present positions may be a reasonable approximation of the position of huts, but not necessarily of the number of huts. There is no clear correlation between the number of huts and the number of hearths and charcoal patches on !Kung sites, although there is a tendency for a hearth to be placed near the entrance to each hut (see plots of camps in Yellen 1977).

The drawings of camps by the !Kung boy /Uma and by /Han≠kass'o (Bleek & Lloyd 1911: opp. p.172 & between pp.224 & 225) show four dwellings, two on either side of what /Uma describes as 'The Makoba's water' in the !Kung camp, and seven huts in one picture and nineteen in the other drawn by /Han≠kass'o. In the data gathered by Yellen (1977), not one of the sixteen camps analysed had more than seven huts. No scales are given in the drawings in *Specimens* (Bleek & Lloyd 1911), but it is perhaps relevant to note that the largest camp Yellen mapped (camp 14) covered an area 35 x 22 metres (about half the size of the one at Arbeidsvreugd) and had six huts and nineteen hearths and charcoal patches. At Arbeidsvreugd, over an area of 70 x 50 metres, there are thirty-three grindstones and eleven known hearths. Where clusters of grindstones and hearths occur, there are two hearths to nine grindstones at the northern end of the site and two hearths to seven grindstones in the central part of the site. If we assume that each of the recognisable hearths at Arbeidsvreugd represents a hut, then there could have been as many as eleven huts there.

Several factors may contribute to the low count of hearths relative to grindstones. The scarcity of firewood in the northern Cape landscape may have meant relatively ephemeral hearths at the entrance to each hut, with larger hearths being the only ones that have remained archaeologically visible. Alternatively, as /Han≠kass'o's drawings suggest more huts and people per camp than was customary amongst the !Kung, there may have been a consequent increase in the area occupied with dwellings spaced further apart. It is not possible to be certain whether the entire length of the site was occupied at one time, nor whether it represents repeated occupations. In either event the present placement of hearths and grindstones suggests a linear arrangement rather than a ring of huts and/or hearths.

## *Spatial Patterning of Artefacts*

Three parts of the site were selected for the detailed plotting of cultural material. Area 1 was at the south end, Area 2 was in the centre and Area 3 was at the northern end. These areas were selected because they showed a relatively high density of cultural material, but stone flakes, ostrich eggshell fragments and beads and pottery were present throughout the 70 x 50-metre grid and spilled over on to the surrounding area outside the grid as well.

Stone artefacts occurred in almost every square but only three squares had more than twenty and the highest score was thirty. In Areas 2 and 3 there were no formal tools apart from upper and lower grindstones. The majority of the unretouched flakes are relatively large (>50 millimetres long). Unretouched quartzite flakes are the most common, followed by smaller quartz flakes. The quartzite flakes came from blocks of quartzite on the site, but other materials such as pebbles of jasper and banded ironstone that occur in profusion were seldom used. It appears that the quartzite was selected for its size, availability and relative ease of working, reflecting an opportunistic strategy.

The ratio of untrimmed to utilised flakes in Area 3 is 61:1, and in Area 2 it is 90:1. There were no utilised flakes in Area 1.

In Area 1 there is a relatively high incidence of hornfels (15 per cent) in the unretouched flakes, and the same raw material was used for two backed bladelets that are the only formal tools found on the site. Both are slightly dulled (probably sandblasted) but are not patinated. Backed bladelets such as these are common on sites that date to about five hundred years ago in this region and Beaumont and Vogel (1989) have assigned them to the Swartkops Industry. A gunflint of the kind used in the nineteenth century was also found.

Lower grindstones scattered over the site are generally of the order of 200 x 250 millimetres in plan with a single ground surface smoothed through use. They were presumably used for grinding grass seeds and other plant foods, for preparing clay and gum for pot making (Bleek & Lloyd 1911:345) and for pounding ochre and specularite (Bleek & Lloyd 1911:375). Anvils, by contrast, are generally slightly smaller and have a pitted area on the upper surface as if they had been used for hammering metal or other hard materials. They may also have been used for breaking bones as /Han≠kass'o said that stones were used to break up bones into smaller pieces so they could be boiled in a pot (ibid.:347). Whereas grindstones tend to cluster together and are often associated with hearths, anvils tend to be more widespread and are often associated with stone flaking debris. Ostrich eggshell fragments are ubiquitous. In Area 1 no squares had more than eighteen fragments. In Area 2, however, there were two squares with more than a hundred fragments. In one it appeared that an ostrich eggshell water flask had been broken and partly buried because the pieces were fairly large, and included three fragments of the flask opening. By contrast, in Area 3 there were sixteen squares with more than a hundred fragments, mostly clustered around the large hearth but rarely burnt. Buried flasks are regularly found by farmers in the area today, but are only rarely decorated. One example, found on Droëgrond about twenty kilometres south of Arbeidsvreugd by Mr Reichert, has a series of ladder-like strips converging on the opening. No undoubtedly decorated fragments were found on the site at Arbeidsvreugd.

Whole and broken ostrich eggshell beads were found in all three areas but, apart fom thirty-three beads around the hearth in Area 3, they were not numerous. Of particular interest is the fact that there was no bead-making debris such as partly made beads and stone borers. This would substantiate /Han≠kass'o's statement that the Flat Bushmen did not make beads themselves, but obtained them from the Berg Bushmen to the south. The beads do not vary much in diameter (7-8 millimetres), with an aperture of about 2 millimetres which places them at the large end of the range in Later Stone Age assemblages (Jacobson 1987).

Bone, ostrich eggshell beads and water flasks and, to a lesser extent, pottery, tend either to be absent or in low frequency, or occur in relatively high quantity over the surface of the living area. This is particularly true of the bone. Tiny weathered fragments, each weighing less than 0,1 gram, were found in small numbers in most squares, but in several places whole or almost whole bones were found buried beneath the surface in soft patches of earth. The mass of unidentifiable bone fragments exceeded 30 grams in three squares surrounding the large hearth in Area 3, and in two squares near the hearth in Area 2. Identifiable bones, including springbok and sheep, were found both adjacent to and away from hearths in Areas 2 and 3, but the bone around Area 1 was rare and highly fragmented. Only two identifiable bones came from this area.

Potsherds are fairly thinly scattered with only eleven of the two hundred squares having ten or more sherds. The highest count for any one square is eighteen in Area 3. The sherds are of two basic kinds: those tempered with grass are relatively thick with a reddish surface and a black core; others have some grass and a high micaceous grit content and are reddish, soft, very small and weathered. In his description of pot making, /Han≠kass'o (Bleek & Lloyd 1911:343) says that the earth used for pots was red and included glittering particles; this would confirm the use of micaceous earth. There are no decorated sherds, but in the samples from the living site there are two plain rims, a few thickened base fragments and part of a round lug. There is no evidence for necks and pointed bases, nor is there any clear indication of the shallow open bowls with all-over decoration found in the Karoo to the south-east. However, several hundred metres to the north-west of the main site, sherds of a red burnished ware with quartz temper, decorated rim and a classic reinforced Khoi lug were found on the surface. One would expect to find pots of different manufacture on a site because pots were exchanged as gifts. /Han≠kass'o told Lloyd in September 1878 that his grandfather Tssatssi had bought dogs from /Gappem-ttu. His grandfather had trained the dogs to hunt jackals which he skinned, and /Han≠kass'o's grandmother dressed and sewed the skins into a kaross for /Gappem-ttu. When he presented the gift to /Gappem-ttu, /Gappem-ttu gave him a pot as a 'reward' (Bleek & Lloyd 1911:372-75).

Five glass beads were found during the excavations, and several more were picked up by Mr Reichert. Those recovered during excavation were described as follows, using the Kidd and Kidd system. From squares O70 and P78 came two IIa 12, circular translucent oyster white beads; from squares N76 and P77 came two IIa* circular transparent bright green beads; and from square K36 came a IVa 5/6 bead with an oblate/circular redwood outer layer and an apple green core. All were of a type manufactured in the second half of the eighteenth century and first half of the nineteenth century, probably in Venice (Karklins, personal communication 1 Nov. 1988). The photograph of /Han≠kass'o in the South African Museum collection and the painting of //Kabbo by WH Schroeder (Bleek & Lloyd 1911: frontispiece) show both men wearing earrings with beads.

Further evidence of trade came from six small pieces of metal (iron), one from Area 1 and five from Area 3. They were beaten flat and ranged in size from 15 x 30 millimetres to 10 x 11 millimetres. All seemed to be fragments of larger pieces rather than artefacts in themselves.

## *Dating the Hearths*

Five hearths were fully excavated. Three were shallow depressions about 0,7 metre in diameter and were filled with ash and small patches of charcoal. Most of the small bone and ostrich eggshell fragments that came from these hearths were not burnt and this suggests they were incorporated in the ash after the fire had gone out. The other two hearths, one in Area 2 and the other in Area 3, were larger (1,0 to 1,5 metres in diameter), and contained much larger quantities of charcoal and cultural material. Charcoaled branches still extended outwards from the ashy core in shallow depressions into which a quantity of cultural material had been incorporated.

Charcoal samples from three hearths, one each from Areas 1, 2 and 3, and ostrich eggshell fragments from the same hearth in Area 3, were submitted for radiocarbon dating. The results from Dr J C Vogel's laboratory at the Quaternary Dating Research Unit at the CSIR in Pretoria are as follows:

Charcoal from hearth in square L13 Pta-4857: 180 +/– 40 BP
(calibrated AD 1685, 1737, 1807 or 1931)
Charcoal from hearth in square P26 Pta-4863: 120 +/– 35 BP
(calibrated AD 1694, 1727, 1818 or 1922)
Charcoal from hearth in N/O 76/77 Pta-4851: 160 +/– 45 BP
(calibrated AD 1694, 1727, 1818 or 1922)

Ostrich eggshell from N/O 76/77 Pta-4905: 510 +/– 45 BP
(calibrated AD 1432)

Unfortunately all the charcoal values fall within a variable section of the calibration curve and the calibrated dates therefore range from the late seventeenth to the early twentieth century. However, since the glass beads were not manufactured before about 1750, and the twentieth-century dates are unlikely to date the /Xam occupation, the early nineteenth century dates (1807 and 1818) are preferred. The much earlier ostrich eggshell date reflects the fact that this material gives consistently older apparent dates than charcoal and is not reliable (Vogel, personal communication).

The results of the dating of these hearths give as clear confirmation of a nineteenth century dating for the site as can be expected from radiocarbon dating in this recent time period. While the fires from which the charcoal came may not have cooked the meat of animals hunted by //Kabbo and /Han≠kass'o, //Kabbo could well have sat around the fires as a child with his parents and grandparents.

## *GIFVLEI: A SITE OCCUPIED BY GRASS BUSHMEN*

As some of the information from the /Xam informants drew attention to the fact that the Flat and Grass Bushmen made certain artefacts differently, the second phase of archaeological investigation was aimed at excavating a Grass Bushman site to see how different it would be from the Flat Bushman camp at Arbeidsvreugd. Unfortunately, however, a shortage of funds curtailed this work and it was possible only to locate a nineteenth-century Grass Bushman site and to do a superficial assessement of the surface artefacts.

The three Grass Bushmen from the Katkop area to the west of the KBV triangle had a somewhat different history from their counterparts amongst the Flat Bushmen. Dia!kwain (David Hoesar) and his brother-in-law ≠Kasin (Klaas Katkop) were imprisoned for culpable homicide after shooting a white farmer, and !Kweiten-ta-//ken, Dia!kwain's sister, subsequently came to Cape Town with her children at the request of Bleek. At the time of their arrest, Dia!kwain and ≠Kasin could speak a little Dutch and ≠Kasin also spoke Korana. They had had at one time or another in their possession such items as guns, spoons, Western clothing and livestock but their hunting and gathering life-style had become an anachronism, and they were essentially destitute – without land or livelihood.

The archival records chronicle the events which led to their arrest (Cape Archives HA.80). Magistrate Jackson wrote from Kenhardt on 25 February 1869 that a farmer, Jacobus Casper Krieger (Jakob Kruger) had been murdered at a place called N'arries in the Division of Calvinia by 'Bushmen'. He wrote again on 16 March to report that three of the murderers had been apprehended – two of them were in prison in Calvinia – the third had been wounded and a fourth was still at large. 'The principal murderer however is named David Hoessar [*sic*] who boldly confesses that he fired the first and fatal shot at Kruger – Klaas Katkop having fired the second which hit the saddle.' David Hoesar's 'bold confession' that he had shot Kruger because he had threatened him seems to have impressed the judge who tried his case because, instead of being sentenced to death, he was given six years for culpable homicide and sent to the Breakwater Prison.

Unlike the site occupied by the Flat Bushmen at Arbeidsvreugd, which was located from descriptions given to Bleek and Lloyd in Cape Town, there were no similar descriptions of Grass Bushman camps given by Dia!kwain and ≠Kasin. They said they came from the Katkop hills and the farm Katkop does indeed have some scatters of artefacts marking living sites, but there was no assurance that they were the ones occupied by Dia!kwain and his family.

On the farm presently known as Gifvlei, some ten kilometres from Katkop, however, is a grave covered with stones (but without a gravestone) which local residents say is that of Jakob Kruger. Kruger is said to have ridden away on his horse after he was wounded by Dia!kwain and to have fallen off and died a few kilometres from Dia!kwain's camp. A search of the vicinity of the grave showed small scatters of artefacts at several places, but no pottery. A small spring, called a ghorra, is still active on the side of the hill known as Arries about three kilometres from the grave. On the slope above and alongside the spring there are more artefacts, potsherds and ostrich eggshell beads. It is possible that this was the site where Dia!kwain and his family camped. However, the spring was also a focus for other people, and the present owner, Mr Alwyn van Jaarsveld, says his father and grandfather camped there too. This is possibly substantiated by scatters of European porcelain.

The most rewarding result of this part of the investigation is that the artefacts found at Gifvlei could confirm the statements of //Kabbo and /Han≠kass'o who said that the Grass Bushmen used white stone for their arrowheads. Lucy Lloyd interpreted this as meaning quartz, but the white stone found at Gifvlei is a distinctive white chalcedony that probably occurs in that area as it has not been noted on other sites to the east excavated by

Beaumont (Beaumont & Vogel 1989). As at Arbeidsvreugd, the pottery at Gifvlei is grass tempered and has no decoration. It is therefore unlikely that pottery was used as a stylistic marker amongst the /Xam of the northern Cape, as may have been the case in the Zeekoei Valley (Sampson *et al.* 1989). The survey was too brief to establish whether ostrich eggshell beads had been made at the site or not.

## *MERGING ARCHAEOLOGY AND ETHNOLOGY*

The archaeological investigation of the Flat Bushman living site at Arbeidsvreugd has given some insight into the difficulties of interpreting the durable cultural remains at a place occupied by people who talked about their life-style but did not describe it in detail. Such insights are perhaps more useful for an archaeologist who has excavated sites without such information than for an ethnologist who has been able to observe the formation of such camps at first hand. Interpretation of spatial patterning is always thwarted by taphonomic processes that have contributed to the movement of some artefacts and the disintegration of organic materials. Knowing what has been lost makes it doubly frustrating, but at least the ethnography enriches the explanations for some of the observations.

Perhaps the most obvious co-relationship that has survived erosion at Arbeidsvreugd is that between grindstones and hearths. Here we can expect that hearths have not moved and that they are the clearest indication of where huts were situated. As we know that women tended to place their grindstones near the hearth, we can assume that where the two occur together we can reasonably suppose this marks the woman's working area close to her hut. Anvils, however, which were presumably used mostly by men for working metal for arrowheads and by both men and women for breaking up bones, grinding ochre and clay for pots, and for other tasks, are located both away from hearths as well as near to them. Their distribution provides some indication of the gender division of labour with women using them for some tasks near the hearth and men using them in areas away from the women and the hearth.

The distribution of ostrich eggshell fragments, potsherds, glass beads, stone tools, metal fragments and bone is patchy, but there are so many chance factors that govern where small items may accumulate that it does not seem justified to draw many conclusions. All that one can say is that there is often, but not invariably, a higher density of these items near hearths. Regrettably, the preservation of bone is not consistent enough to test the statements by //Kabbo and /Han≠kass'o about the disposal of particular bones.

Although one would expect to be able to find all or most of the pieces of a single pot from sherds in a limited area, this is not the case and it is not clear whether this is because some potsherds have disintegrated, or because broken pots continued to be used, or because some sherds were recycled. There is, however, an unexpectedly wide range of pot tempers, but no decorated sherds in the area investigated. This lack of decoration suggests that, at least in this region, group identity may have been based on the kind of temper used in pot-making rather than on decoration.

Factors governed by the superstructure of Flat Bushman society are embodied in the location of the Arbeidsvreugd site. It was one of a number frequented by the /Xam and possibly by //Kabbo and his family. It was deliberately situated away from their water source and away from the nearest Bruinkop where rock engravings occur. This was not a place from which one watched for the springbok and there are no permanent structures to which people would wish to return. Its very remoteness and its nineteenth century dating suggest in fact that it was inhabited at a time when the family wished to remain anonymous and to keep out of the way of farmers, yet be close enough to the Bruinkop to observe the movements of others. It was a last outpost in more ways than one.

From the site layout and small number of identifiable sheep bones, it is more than likely that the Arbeidsvreugd site was occupied by people with only a passing interest in livestock. If they kept any animals, they were not numerous. There is no indication of a kraal and the bones indicate only sheep and no cattle. The other identifiable bones show that springbok, hare and tortoise were also eaten.

The presence or absence of artefacts mentioned (and not mentioned) by the informants has been checked archaeologically. Coupled with the general absence of microlithic stone tools at Arbeidsvreugd and the presence of white chalcedony at Gifvlei, the ethnographic information that the Flat Bushmen used metal arrowheads and the Grass Bushmen used white stone is confirmed. The fact that the /Xam used different materials to emphasise their individuality shows that emblemic style was not confined to the size and shape of artefacts. Small pieces of beaten iron and numerous anvils that may have been used in the manufacture of metal-tipped arrows at Arbeidsvreugd indicate that this site was occupied within the last thousand or more years when metal was traded from the Tswana or from Europeans. A single gunflint found at

Arbeidsvreugd may have been used in a musket or secondarily as a strike-a-light, but also confirms that the /Xam who lived on this site were familiar with firearms.

Further confirmation of statements made by //Kabbo and /Han≠kass'o was found in the clusters of large quartzite flakes at Arbiedsvreugd as /Han≠kass'o said that they made and used them for cutting up meat. The consistent presence of grindstones, some with well used surfaces, confirms accounts that grass seeds were harvested and ground; the fact that gambro occurs in the vicinity today makes it likely that this too provided a portion of the vegetable diet. There is no indication of digging sticks or bored stones, but these were seen in use in the vicinity in the 1870s. The numerous fragments of ostrich eggshell flask openings are clear evidence for this method of water storage.

There is no indication of the ubiquitous Later Stone Age scraper on the site, but this is not to say that skins were not worked there for there were other stone substitutes (Webley 1990) and the ethnographic evidence makes it clear that skins were cured. The absence of ostrich eggshell bead-making debris, on the other hand, is a neat confirmation of /Han≠kass'o's statement that the Flat Bushmen did not make their own but traded them from the Berg Bushmen.

From the ethnographer's point of view, the results of the archaeological investigation of nineteenth-century /Xam living sites can be likened to ethnographic 'snap' and offer only fragments of information to confirm social practices. The conclusions draw attention to particularistic detail that may be intrinsically interesting, but does not add much to the understanding of /Xam social relations. From the archaeologist's point of view, however, the ethnographic information adds a dimension that is seldom available. Something as apparently mundane as the choice of raw material for arrowheads or the absence of ostrich eggshell bead-making debris, for example, had a deeper significance that would not have been perceived without the ethnography. By contrast, decoration on potsherds was not mentioned by the informants and the archaeological findings suggest that it was not used for emblemic style as it apparently was in the Zeekoei Valley in the Karoo (Sampson *et al.* 1989).

The study has also given information on the layout of a Flat Bushman camp that was otherwise hidden in the ethnographic record, and finally it has shown that despite the presence of herders in the vicinity for a millennium or more, people who occupied the site at Arbeidsvreugd may have eaten mutton and may have intermarried and exchanged goods with Korana herders, but they were not fully integrated into the herder life-style.

## *ACKNOWLEDGEMENTS*

I am grateful to Harriet Deacon, Darryl Seeman and Hannali van der Merwe who assisted with archival research and fieldwork during this project. Facilities offered by the Department of Archaeology at the University of Stellenbosch were much appreciated.

The financial assistance of the Centre for Science Development (formerly the Institute for Research Development) of the Human Sciences Research Council towards this research is hereby acknowledged. Opinions expressed in this publication and conclusions arrived at are those of the author and do not necessarily represent the views of the Centre for Science Development or the Human Sciences Research Council.

I should also like to acknowledge with thanks financial assistance from the Wenner Gren Foundation for Anthropological Research, New York, logistic support from the Department of Archaeology at the University of Stellenbosch, and the numerous farmers and students who helped make this project a pleasure.

# The Bleek and Lloyd Records of Death and Burial

## The Problems that these Present for Archaeologists

Lyn Wadley

More than five hundred Later Stone Age burials are recorded in South Africa (Wadley 1990) and a preliminary survey of some burials is published (Inskeep 1986). Notwithstanding this wealth of Stone Age data, archaeologists have seldom tried to interpret burial practices although hypothetically this should be possible by means of analogy, using ethnographic records of the San. Archaeologists are reluctant to interpret burial practices; this may be attributed to many factors, of which two seem particularly relevant. Firstly, ethnographic data are not readily available because there are so few published accounts of San burial practices. Secondly, there are theoretical difficulties associated with the use of analogy (Wylie 1985) and these have prompted many archaeologists to reject analogical explanations. One of the dangers involves making the assumption that Stone Age people are fossilised San. It would be wrong, for example, to expect modern San religion to be a carbon copy of the religion of Stone Age people; cultures are not static. None the less, the interpretation of burial practices is likely to be better using San concepts than by imposing ideas from a Western cosmology. For this reason, therefore, I examine the Bleek and Lloyd records of San beliefs about death, and of their burial practices. Then I turn to Stone Age burials in South Africa and compare these with the ethnographic record.

Most of the ethnography dealing with beliefs about death is contained in unpublished manuscripts written by Lucy Lloyd, Wilhelm Bleek's sister-in-law. Wilhelm Bleek's remarkable linguistic and ethnographic study of /Xam,

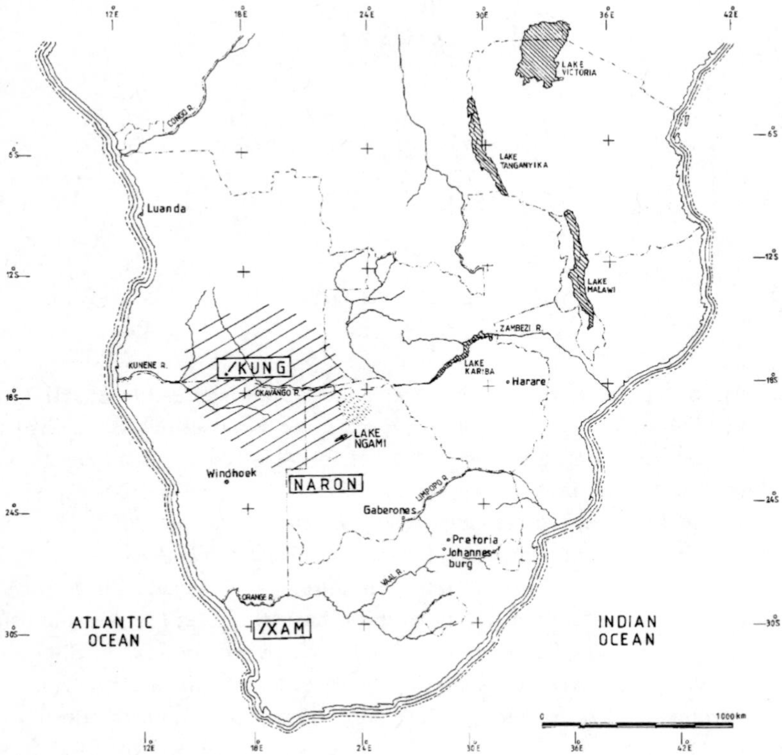


**Figure 1:** *The approximate distribution of /Xam, Naron and !Kung populations*

who originated from the north-western Cape (Figure 1), was undertaken during the space of only five years from 1870 to 1875, the year of his death. During this time Lucy Lloyd worked with Bleek to learn the difficult language and to devise a means of recording it. Lloyd's early participation in the project was fortunate because after Bleek's death she was able to continue the work. Within a few years she expanded the group of narrators to include San other than the /Xam. Bleek had been anxious to record dialects that were different from those of the Southern San and to do this Lloyd hosted two !Kung lads from the Lake Ngami district (Figure 1) from 1879 to 1882. They were !Nanni and Tamme, and they were responsible for many of the unpublished stories of death mentioned here. Two even younger !Kung boys, /Uma and Da, were brought to Lucy Lloyd in 1880 (Bleek and Lloyd 1911).

Lucy Lloyd continued recording San interviews until 1884, and she devoted the remainder of her life to translating and preparing the material for publication. After her death in 1914 the task of translation and of working on a dictionary was taken over by Dorothea Bleek, Wilhelm's daughter. Dorothea's work included the editing of a series of papers on /Xam customs and beliefs (Bleek 1931, 1932b & c, 1933a & b, 1935a, 1936a), and she was also responsible for conducting primary ethnographic research. In 1910 and 1911 she visited Bushmanland and photographed the surviving /Xam (Bleek 1936a). She also studied San of central Angola (Bleek 1928a) and the Naron of Botswana (Bleek 1928b) (Figure 1).

Ironically, Wilhelm Bleek's untimely death seemed to stimulate many of the stories about death that are mentioned here. Perhaps Lucy Lloyd was drawn to the subject through her own grief, but perhaps it was Dia!kwain, a /Xam man clearly devoted to the Bleek family after his two-year sojourn in their household, who sought to offer comfort through his narrations. The discussions of /Xam beliefs about death may have started after an incident that frightened one of the Bleek children. One night, shortly after Wilhelm Bleek's death, one of his children was startled from sleep by an owl making a sound like breathing outside the window. When Dia!kwain heard this he was delighted and told Lucy Lloyd that Wilhelm had returned to see how his little children were getting on (Bleek and Lloyd 1911:xv). This anecdote does not simply point to the origin of the death-related stories, it also illustrates the adaptability of the San belief system which can incorporate new experiences into traditional beliefs.

## SAN BELIEFS ABOUT DEATH

### *Transformation of the Dead into Birds, Small Creatures, Spirits, Rain, Clouds, Stars and Wind*

Although Dia!kwain believed that Wilhelm Bleek's death had transformed Bleek into an owl, there are no other records of this particular transformation among the /Xam. In the same month that Wilhelm died Dia!kwain told Lucy Lloyd that humans who die possess wind and make clouds: 'The hair of our heads will resemble clouds, when we die ...' (Bleek and Lloyd 1911:397-99). This was the beginning of a series of narratives about death, burial, spirits and premonitions that Dia!kwain told Lloyd in the six months before he left Cape Town for the last time. Among the stories he told was one about the angry rain that kills feisty girls, changes their appearance and turns them into stars (Bleek and Lloyd 1911:393). Dia!kwain also said that the heart of a /Xam 'sorcerer' (shaman) becomes a star when he dies: 'his magic makes a star, in order to let his body in which he lived walk about' (Bleek 1935a:24). Dia!kwain's sister, !Kweiten ta //ken added that girls who break food taboos are carried away by a whirlwind and are transformed into frogs (Bleek and Lloyd 1911:203).

One of Dia!kwain's last stories was about his wife's death: after the funeral, on the way home, he and his companions saw an apparition which looked like a small child sitting cross-legged in the salt pan. He explained that when sorcerers are about to take dead people away from their families the dead person takes a form that is different from his or her living appearance and comes to visit the family to say farewell (Bleek and Lloyd 1911:365-69).

All /Xam expected to become spirit people when they died (L.V111.-26.8310) but the Naron of Botswana told Dorothea Bleek of a slightly different belief. They said that only men who had been cut between the eyebrows (probably initiated men) became *//gauwa* (spirit people) or could see *//gauwa*; women only heard them (Bleek 1928b:26). The spirits were said to walk at night and people were afraid of them. Strong winds that howled were called *//gauwa* and it was also believed that the dead were sometimes transformed into birds (Bleek 1928b:46).

Angolan San also mentioned //Gaua who could only be seen by medicine men. Thunder and lightning were caused by //Gaua and those killed by lightning were thought to be //Gaua's victims who thereafter sat in the sky as stars (Bleek 1928a:123).

Among the !Kung *//gauwa* meant 'dream' and 'spirit' as well as 'ghost' (Bleek 1928b:26). This interpretation helps to explain the !Kung boy Tamme's narration:

> (When) a person is ill, (another) person doctors the person. A dream puts a thing into a Bushman ... the dream wears a little apron like the Bushman, a little thing, he wears a little apron. It wears a backdress of mouse's skin ... The dream's body is little, it resembles a Bushman ... a Bushman (who?) dies becomes a dream ... Its heart aches, it kills another Bushman ... (LX1 and X11.4.9260).

Tamme's young companion in the Bleek household, !Nanni, said that his grandfather told him that the dead can be changed into snakes, lizards and even small antelope (Bleek and Lloyd 1911:431). The !Kung would not kill any of these creatures near a grave because they were said to be a dead person's spirit (Bleek and Lloyd 1911:429,431). The form taken by a dead person's spirit was, it seems, determined by the person's cause of death. !Nanni said for example:

> (When) our 'other one', (who) is a man, dies, he becomes a snake; and his snake is a spirit. A snake bites him, he dies, he is a snake. When a woman just dies, the woman has no snake. If a snake bites a woman, (and) the woman dies, the woman is a snake. If a woman merely dies, her spirit is a mere spirit. (Bleek and Lloyd 1911:430).

## *Cause of Death*

San appear to have believed that illness and death were always brought about by spiritual intervention or by unnatural causes such as murder. /Han≠kass'o said that 'sorcerers' resembling lions looked at a person and caused him to die (Bleek 1935a:7). These sorcerers also 'shot' their victims. It is not clear whether the malevolent sorcerers were alive or whether they were spirits of the dead. The reader is confronted with this type of ambiguity in many San stories and, while it is an issue that is of Eurocentric concern, the ambiguity seems not to have been important to the San narrators. San shamans studied by Marshall (1969) and Katz (1982) believed that, through trance, they could transcend the world of the living and enter the spirit world. Thus the distinction between living and dead shamans is rather blurred. A shaman in trance was even said to die (Katz 1982:116), so that ideas about trance and death were strongly connected.

Although the spiritual intervention causing death was thought to have been activated by a person's defiance of social norms, this need not always be the case. /Xam said that a person dies because he is called by the spirits of those who are already dead (Bleek and Lloyd 1911:369; Bleek 1935a:7,29). Shamans in trance saw spirits trying to take someone away and they tried to protect their kinfolk by driving the evil spirits away and by watching over people at night when attack was most likely (Bleek 1935a:27). When in trance, the good shaman might even try to kill his evil counterpart with a stone:

> He kills the other who has bewitched us. He strikes him dead with a stone; as he strikes him, he says, 'This man has been going about killing people, I will kill him knocking him down. (Bleek 1935a:33)

Occasionally shamans would protect people by painting them with nasal blood that fell involuntarily during trance (Bleek 1935a:34). Thus shamans mediated the world of the living and the world of the dead; they fought the spirits who sought victims but sometimes they were unsuccessful and people died despite their efforts.

I have already mentioned that disrespectful behaviour and breaking of taboos could also cause death. The rain would be angered and seek revenge if, for example, a girl was disrespectful to the rain or if she broke the food taboos and ate creatures such as tortoise (Bleek 1933a:303; Bleek and Lloyd 1911: 393). /Han≠kass'o told Lloyd (L.V111.26.8310) that a dead person can be dangerous to his living relatives if he is not properly respected. /Han≠kass'o's grandfather had told him:

> Ye have uttered for us the old people's names, as if the old people were not dead people and they come to harm us, on account of it; because they do not possess their thinking strings. Therefore they are wont to come to harm us if we utter their name, by night (they come as a fighting party, in order that they may kill a person. Therefore the person becomes ill on account of it).

## *The Role of the Dead*

Although spirits could bring ill fortune they could also intercede for their living relations and bring them luck in the hunt or good weather, particularly rain (Bleek 1933b:382). I discuss first the role of the dead in the fortunes of the hunt, and secondly the connection between the dead and rain-making.

Southern San and !Kung believed that dead game medicine men influenced game. Old women whose husbands were having ill fortune in the hunt would therefore try to elicit the cause of this ill fortune by beating the ground with a round grindstone or bored stone (used for weighting a digging stick) while calling out to the dead to look favourably on the band (Bleek 1935a:35-36, 41-43). Dia!kwain told Bleek that his mother did not see the spirits when she beat on the ground, but she talked to them because she felt sure that they would hear her. The !Kung boy, !Nanni, also claimed that women, and never men, beat the stone on the ground (Bleek and Lloyd 1911:429). Used in this context, the bored stone and the grindstone were not merely artefacts with a secular, economic role, they took on a religious meaning in rites to incorporate the dead into the affairs of the living.

Records of the connection between the dead and rain are more common than those for the dead and game. /Han≠kass'o's next description suggests that dead people were thought to be synonymous with the rain. He said that a dead person is:

> A person who rains, the rain falls, taking away his footsteps, so that his footsteps may no longer be there. The rain presently falling takes away his footsteps when we have just put him in (to his grave). (L.V111.-28.8465)

/Han≠kass'o also claimed that spirits of the dead were custodians of the rain:

> Dead people who come out of the ground are those of whom my parents used to say, that they rode the rain ... they bound the rain. Thus they rode the rain, because they owned it. (Bleek 1933a:305)

Because the dead owned the rain their relatives would on occasion plead with them to bring rain (Bleek 1933b:384). Dia!kwain relates how his father called on his great-grandfather to bring rain:

> 'You used to say to me, that when the time came that you were dead, if I called upon you, you would hear me, you would let rain fall for me.' And when father spoke thus, the rain clouds came gliding up, ....rain clouds covered the sky. (Bleek 1933b:384)

Sometimes the spirits were sympathetic and sent rain when it was needed but if the dead withheld rain a shaman would intervene to fetch it. /Xam rainmakers travelled into the spirit world to lead out the rain bull from the sky or a waterpit (Bleek 1933b:376, 1935a:32, 1936a:134). When it was the shaman's turn to die his heart fell from the sky into a waterpit, the same waterpit from which the rainmaking shamans would fetch the rainbull (Bleek 1935a:29,32).

Through their powers over game and rain the dead retained some control over the means of production and reproduction of their living relatives, thus they were not entirely isolated from their families. In turn, the living relatives needed to remember their dead kin and to give them both attention and respect.

I have been able to find only one recent reference to a connection between the dead, rain and game. After the burial of a !Xo man the men who had buried him lit a ritual fire and prayed for rain and fat animals (Heinz 1986). No such practices are recorded among the !Kung, but !Kung ideas about rain and weather patterns were found by Lorna Marshall to be connected to a critical supernatural element, a 'life-force', called *n!ow* (Marshall 1957). *N!ow* was said to exist in all humans and a few important antelope. A child received *n!ow* as an involuntary influence in the womb and was born with it when the mother's uterine fluid flowed into the ground. It was either a 'good' (rain-bringing) *n!ow* or a 'bad' (cold-bringing) *n!ow* and would be recognised as such by the type of weather that followed a child's birth (Marshall 1957). *N!ow* can thus be seen to link control of the weather to reproduction (Biesele 1978:928).

The *n!ow* influence operated in an involuntary way at death as well as at birth: a !Kung mother whose son had a rain-bringing *n!ow* feared her son dead whenever rain fell at an unusual time or was exceptionally heavy because at death a person's particular weather pattern was said to be activated.

Bleek and Lloyd did not specifically refer to *n!ow* among the /Xam but from the narratives it does seem that a similar concept must have been present. Dia!kwain spoke evocatively of the wind:

> When we die, our [own] wind blows; for we, who are human beings, we possess wind; we make clouds when we die ... the wind makes dust,

> because it intends to blow, taking away our footprints, with which we had walked about while we still had nothing the matter with us. (Bleek and Lloyd 1911:397)

When Dia!kwain's father died, Dia!kwain was forewarned by the sudden change in the weather:

> the clouds were acting as they used to do when father said that it was going to rain' ... It was really father's wind ... You know that whenever father used to shoot game, his wind blew like that. (Bleek 1932c:328-29)

Dia!kwain spoke also of an old woman, who was distinguished not only for having a head like that of an ostrich, but also for her ability to invoke the wind. Hunters need to creep against the wind when approaching their prey; after her death, therefore, people would call her name when they wanted the wind to blow (Bleek 1932c:335).

The San narratives about death recorded by Bleek and Lloyd illustrate the depth and complexity of the San belief system. They show how the powers of the living and the dead can either conflict with or complement the interests of each. I turn now to the San burial practices that were recorded by Lloyd and the Bleeks. My intention is to seek material evidence of the complex belief system that surrounds death.

## *SAN BURIAL PRACTICES*

The Naron of the central Kalahari buried their dead in a foetal position. They were fully clothed and most of their possessions were placed with them (Bleek 1928b:35). This excluded ostrich eggshell beads, which were not buried with a woman but were kept by the living. Old women would usually hand their beads down to their daughters before their death (Bleek 1928b:10). Bushes or stones covered the grave, and buchu, an aromatic herb, was burnt at the grave-side. After the funeral the entire Naron group moved to another locality. According to Lloyd's informant, Tamme, moving 'to another country' was also the practice among !Kung (L.X1-X11.4.9236).

The youth !Nanni told Lloyd (L.X1-X11.7.9559) that, among the !Kung, a dead man's possessions were not given away. A man was buried with his head on his bag and he wore his back apron made of the skin of a male jackal. He also wore a girdle and, on his right arm bracelets of jackal ears. Around his neck were two jackal feet and a horn, and on his head was a jackal's tail. Tamme added to !Nanni's description of !Kung burials, saying that a man's bow and his stick were put into the ground with him but that another man took the arrows (L.X1-X11.4.9236). The /Xam said, however, that the brothers of a dying man would take his arrows and bow: 'For he does not see them, he cannot take them, because he is dead and gone' (L.11.13.1295-6). There is no mention of any /Xam grave goods.

In *Specimens of Bushman Folklore* (Bleek & Lloyd 1911:373) there is a drawing by !Nanni (Figure 2) showing the dead man curled into the foetal position with his head on a bag. The drawing shows a side chamber in the main grave.

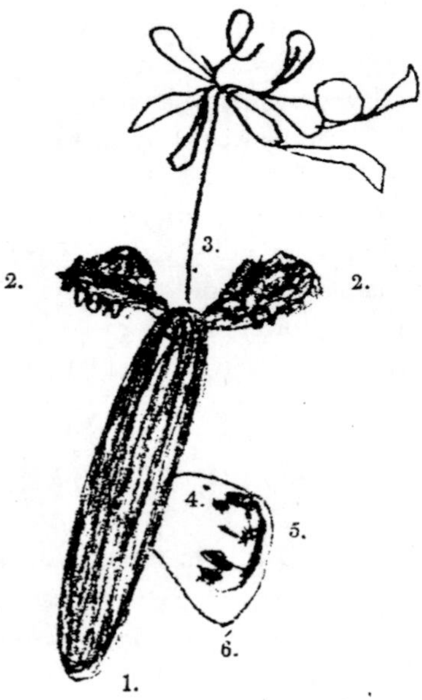


1 { **!kórro** grave. 2 { **ɣá.** earth. 3 { **!kań.** tree. **zãu-ŭ** (the name of the tree, the berries and gum of which are eaten).

4 { **!nųé.** bag (the dead man's bag which is placed underneath his head). 5 { **||ke.** the dead person.

6 { **||gábbe.** the little chamber or hole at the side of the grave, where the body is placed. **!nanni. *July 30th*, 1880**

**Figure 2:** *!Nanni's illustration of a !Kung burial*

!Nanni's observation is vindicated by reports of two recent !Kung burials (Wiessner 1983:2) and a recent !Xõ burial (Heinz 1986). A side chamber of about 200 millimetres width was dug into the wall at the bottom of each grave and the corpse's back was tucked into this.

Tamme's sad description of his younger brother's death and burial mentions only that the grave was filled with earth and sealed with tree trunks; no grave goods were cited (L.X1-X11.3.9215). The !Xõ burial observed by Heinz (1986) was also covered over with branches, and grave goods were absent, save for a pillow, which was placed under the dead man's head to prevent sand getting into his ears. With sand in his ears the dead man would not be able to hear his living relatives.

After her 1910/1911 visit to Bushmanland, Dorothea Bleek reported that /Xam buried their dead far from home and dug graves with the shell of a water tortoise. They dug the graves deep and then smoothed them, making a bed for the dead person with grass or bush. The body was then laid in lengthways, wrapped in skins, and the grave was filled with earth and covered over with bushes (Bleek 1936c:201-202). /Han≠kass'o's account supports Bleek's observation but he adds that /Xam graves were sealed with stones as well as bushes (L.V111.28.8467). There is also an independent record of a dying man asking to be put in his old kaross (L.11.12.1239).

Unfortunately none of the Bleek and Lloyd manuscripts describe the way in which women were buried, and I mention, therefore, the relatively recent !Kung burial of an old woman who had been ill for a long time (Wiessner 1983). The dead woman was sewn into her blanket by the women in her camp, who left her body clothed in a traditional front and back apron and ornamented with bracelets and anklets. The body was laid in the grave with legs slightly flexed, facing east. Then one of the men who had worked himself into a trance sprinkled scented powder from a tortoiseshell compact into the grave. The grave was filled and a large stone placed on the head. Powder was then rubbed and sprinkled on to the participants. Although the grave was half a kilometre from the camp, the group moved the following week. The lack of !Kung grave goods, apart from personal clothing and jewellery, is explained by Wiessner's comment that when a person dies unexpectedly, their possessions are given to *hxaro* partners with a request to continue the relationship with the family. This would not happen when death is anticipated; the elderly pass their *hxaro* partnerships, and presumably their possessions, on to their descendants while they are still alive (Wiessner 1983:4).

This summary of the burial practices recorded by the Bleeks, Lloyd, Heinz and Wiessner suggests that there are some common elements even in such widely separated regions as northern Namibia and the northern Cape. The elements are: burying the dead person fully clothed and wrapped in a kaross, placing the body in a foetal position, and covering the grave with branches and stones. In other details of burial practices there is marked regional variation. Grave goods seem to have been excluded from /Xam burials and from those of !Kung children and some !Kung adults. In contrast, other !Kung adults are reported to have been buried with bags, bows, sticks, bracelets and anklets, and Naron with most of their possessions. Arrows were specifically excluded from !Kung and /Xam graves.

Some form of inheritance rule seems to have applied to all the San groups mentioned here: !Kung possessions were passed on to *hxaro* partners, Naron women inherited their mothers' eggshell beads, and /Xam men inherited their brothers' arrows.

The simplicity of the burial practices recorded here belies the complexity of the San beliefs about the dead. It is difficult to imagine how the archaeologist could deduce beliefs, for example, of the interdependence of the dead and the living or the power of the dead over rain, from the available descriptions of /Xam burials. Nor would it be easy to reconstruct relationships such as those between living shamans and dead people, although a few clues are present such as the sprinkling of buchu or other powders on the dead person, and the use in burials of jackal skins, ears and tail which are also worn by shamans.

I now turn to Stone Age burials in South Africa to investigate continuities between these and the recent San burials.

## *SOUTH AFRICAN LATER STONE AGE BURIALS*

Most Stone Age burial sites in South Africa were found in the coastal regions of the Cape. Here, caves and rock shelters served both as homes for hunter-gatherers and as tombs for their dead. Some of the shelters were repeatedly used as burial grounds: over a hundred skeletons were exhumed from Matjes River Cave alone (Dreyer 1933; Hoffman 1958; Louw 1960). By no means all the Cape burials were in caves or rock shelters: coastal dune and other open site burials were found at Bok Baai, Cape St Francis, Estcourt Midden, Milnerton, Groot Hagelkraal, Knysna, Port Elizabeth and Zuurberg. In the Orange Free State and northern Cape no cave burials have been excavated, all the graves were found at open sites. The open-air graves were often solitary, but there were somewhat larger cemeteries at St Clair (12 graves) and Koffiefontein (about 57 graves). Few Stone Age burial sites were found in the Transvaal, KwaZulu and Natal.

Not only were more Stone Age graves found in the southern Cape coastal area but these often contained a wider variety, and higher frequencies, of grave goods than burial sites elsewhere in the country. The western, eastern and northern Cape burials were less 'elaborate' than the ones in the southern Cape, while those in the Transvaal and Natal were the most austere.

A few skeletons with grave goods have been directly dated using bone collagen, and other burials have been relatively dated through their stratigraphic position or through dating of their grave goods. The only direct date for an early Holocene burial is that of 8260+/−720 BP from Wilton Large Rock Shelter (Deacon 1972). This adult was buried under red painted stones but had no other grave goods. An infant buried without grave goods, in Melkhoutboom, is thought to date to approximately 7300 BP (Deacon 1976:35). The layer D burials from Matjes River and the oldest ones from Oakhurst Cave, assumed to be of early Holocene age, have gravestones, some of which are ochre stained, but few other grave goods (Dreyer 1931; Goodwin 1938; Louw 1960). The infant in Bushman Rock Shelter, possibly dating to the early Holocene, was buried with 145 ostrich eggshell beads around its neck (Plug 1982:61). All the burials thought to date to the early Holocene have a small range and low frequency of grave goods.

Marked temporal differences are evident in Matjes River Cave and Oakhurst Cave, where changes in burial custom are stratigraphically observable. At both caves several of the burials within levels containing Wilton Industry tools, probably dating to the mid-Holocene, contain a wealth of grave goods including ostrich eggshell water bottles, eggshell bead jewellery, shell ornaments, wooden beads and bored stones (Dreyer 1933; Goodwin 1938). In each cave, however, there are also burials that contain no grave goods at all. Other mid-Holocene burials include the Cape St Francis man, buried with a seashell necklace, Middle Stone Age flakes and a grindstone (Thackeray and Feast 1974), and the Welgeluk burial complex with grindstones, shells and ostrich eggshell beads (Hall and Binneman 1987). The Nelson Bay Cave burial 5, thought to be about 5 800 years old, is richly endowed with quartz crystals, more than 800 ostrich eggshell beads, half a beadstone, a tortoise shell bowl, a milled edge hammerstone and several seashells (Inskeep 1987).

Further changes in burial practices occur after about 3500 BP; at this time in the southern Cape there seem to be fewer grave goods than previously in the mid-Holocene. No grave goods were found in the layer B burials of Matjes

River and four Nelson Bay Cave burials (1,2,3 and 4) contain eggshell beads and seashell ornaments, but little else apart from a lower grindstone placed on the body of a nine- to ten-year-old child, directly dated to 2660+/−150 BP (Inskeep 1986, 1987). The Robberg Cave burials (SAM 1145, SAM 1879 and SAM 1871) dated to between 3400 and 3200 BP have no grave goods reported with them (Hausman 1980). The Robberg Cave D burial with a painted stone and seashells does, however, date to 1925+/−33 BP (Rudner 1971) and the Snuifklip open site burial, dated directly to 2300 BP, contained a grindstone, seashells, animal bones and Middle Stone Age tools (Morris *et al.* 1987).

In the south-eastern Cape elaborately ornamented infant burials were found at Klasies River Mouth Cave 5 (Hall and Binneman 1987), and at Melkhoutboom a child was buried with earthen beads, seashells and grindstones (Deacon 1976:36). In the western Cape, the Clanwilliam skeleton (SAM-AP 1449), directly dated to 2230+/−100 BP was found under a rush mat with microliths, seashells and eggshell beads (Sealy and Van der Merwe 1985). Although some graves in the western Orange Free State and the northern Cape contain no grave goods whatsoever, burials dating between about 3000 BP and 100 BP have a wide range of grave goods: bored stones, grindstones, ostrich eggshell water bottles, beads and seashells (Humphreys 1970, 1974, 1982; Humphreys and Maggs 1970; Morris 1984).

In summary, it appears that ochre, seashells and ostrich eggshell beads have the longest tradition as grave goods. They occur in the earliest burials of the late Pleistocene as well as in twentieth-century burials. Notably, the early grave goods are personal ornaments, not tools. New grave goods appear in the mid-Holocene: upper and lower grindstones, bored stones, stone rings, ostrich eggshell water bottles, tortoiseshell bowls, ornaments of seashell, quartz crystals and Middle Stone Age or other stone tools, bonework and even animal or fish bones.

## COMPARISON OF THE ARCHAEOLOGICAL AND ETHNOGRAPHIC DATA

The entire range of grave goods introduced in the mid-Holocene is present in geographically widespread graves that date to the last few hundred years. The chronological differences evident in the use of grave goods provide compelling evidence that hunter-gatherer behaviour was not fossilised. Furthermore, it is clear that the use of grave goods is idiosyncratic. While some burials are richly adorned with grave goods, others contain none. This variability occurs both in graves that are geographically and temporally separate, and in graves of similar ages at single sites.

Not only does the range of Stone Age grave goods change from the early to the mid-Holocene but the range used during the Stone Age is far wider than that used among modern San. The Stone Age southern Cape sites are especially elaborate. It is tempting to suggest that Stone Age beliefs about death in the southern Cape were more complex than those of San interviewed just over a hundred years ago. In favour of this suggestion is the fact that by the 1870s the San had already undergone centuries of contact with pastoralists and farmers, and this contact may have influenced the hunter-gatherer way of life in many ways (Solway and Lee 1990). The hunter-gatherer populations were considerably reduced in those regions most suited to keeping stock and it is possible that by the 1870s the San way of life and material expression of their cosmology had undergone considerable impoverishment.

I have, however, already suggested that the Bleek and Lloyd ethnographies illustrate the danger of making such judgements. While grave goods almost certainly embody symbolism and carry information about belief systems, a lack of grave goods does not automatically imply a belief system less complex than that of people with elaborate burial practices. Bleek and Lloyd's ethnographies show, for example, that the /Xam, who appear to have buried their dead without grave goods, had as rich a belief system as the !Kung who used a variety of grave goods. The absence of grave goods in some burials may be the result of rules of inheritance rather than the result of impoverished symbolism. Arrows are, for example, absent from both ancient and recent graves, and the ethnography referred to earlier suggests that this may be an example of applying the rules of inheritance. /Xam men inherit arrows from their dead brothers, but other social rules, even those which seem to have no bearing on the ritual surrounding death, may also limit the material elaboration of graves. The !Kung practice of giving dead people's possessions to their *hxaro* partners is a prime example. It is important for the archaeologist to know that, among modern hunter-gatherers, there are sometimes obligations to pass certain of the deceased's belongings to living relatives. Without this knowledge it is easy to be misled into asserting a purely symbolic interpretation of grave goods and burial practices. Furthermore, the presence of quartz crystals, for example, in the Stone Age burials is suggestive of shamanistic associations, but at present such an interpretation would be purely speculative.

Although the Bleeks and Lloyd left an invaluable ethnographic heritage, it is clear that it is not possible, using the ethnographic and archaeological data presented here, to explain Stone Age burial practices satisfactorily. There are many attendant problems but the most important of these is the theoretical one. While there is no doubt that social interpretations of archaeological data are possible, we shall not get more than a shadowy impression of Stone Age belief systems from excavated material culture until we can harness a more sophisticated theory.

## ACKNOWLEDGEMENTS

I am grateful to the staff of the Jagger Library, University of Cape Town, for allowing me access to the unpublished Bleek and Lloyd notebooks. I also thank Janette Deacon, David Lewis-Williams and Thomas Dowson for helpful comments on the first draft of this paper. Brigid Ward drew Figure 1.

# Consolidated Bibliography


Aarne, A. & Thompson, S. 1964. *The Types of the Folktale*. Helsinki: FF Communications 184. (Quoted as AaTh)

Alexander, J.E. 1838. *An Expedition of Discovery into the Interior of Africa*. 2 vols. London: Colburn.

Almeida, M.E. De 1957. Duas Lendas Bosquimanas. *Garcia de Orta* 5: 553-58.

Antal, F. 1949. Remarks on the method of art history. *Burlington Magazine* 551,v.XCI, February.

Arbousset, T. & Daumas, F. 1846. *Narrative of an Exploratory Tour to the North-east of the Colony of the Cape of Good Hope*. Translated from the French of the Revd T. Arbousset, by John Croumbie Brown. Cape Town: Robertson.

Barnard, A. 1979. Nharo Bushman Medicine and Medicine Men. *Africa* 49:68-80.

-------- 1992. *Hunters and Herders of Southern Africa*. Cambridge: Cambridge University Press.

Battiss, W.W. 1948. *The Artists of the Rocks*. Pretoria: Red Fawn Press.

Bauman, R. 1975. Verbal art as performance. *American Anthropologist* 77:290-311.

Bauman, R. & Sherzer, J. 1975. The ethnography of speaking. *Annual Review of Anthropology* 4:95-120.

-------- (eds). 1974. *Explorations in the Ethnography of Speaking*. London: Cambridge University Press.

Beaumont, P.B., Morris, D. & Vogel, J.C. 1985. The Chronology and Context of Petroglyphs in South Africa. Unpublished paper presented at the Southern African Association of Archaeologists Biennial Meeting, Grahamstown, September 1985.

Beaumont, P.B. & Vogel, J.C. 1989. Patterns in the age and context of rock art in the northern Cape. *South African Archaeological Bulletin* 44:73-81.

Ben-Amos, D. 1971. Towards a definition of folklore in context. *Journal of American Folklore* 84:5-15.

Berglund, A.I. 1976. *Zulu Thought-Patterns and Symbolism*. Studia Missionalia Upsaliensia 23. London: C. Hurst.

Beyers, C.J. (ed.). 1981. *Dictionary of South African Biography* Vol. IV. Pretoria: Human Sciences Research Council.

Biesele, M. 1975. Folklore and Ritual of !Kung Hunter-Gatherers. Doctoral thesis, Harvard University, Cambridge, Mass.

-------- 1978. Sapience and scarce resources: Communication systems of the !Kung and other foragers. *Social Science Information* 17: 921-47.

--------- 1980. 'Old K"xau'. In Halifax, J. (ed.), *Shamanic Voices: A Survey of Visionary Narratives*. Harmondsworth: Penguin, pp.54-62.

--------- 1986. 'Anyone with Sense Would Know': Tradition and Creativity in !Kung Narrative and Song. In Vossen, R. and Keuthmann, K. (eds), *Contemporary Studies on Khoisan*. In Honour of Oswin Köhler on the Occasion of his 75th Birthday. 2 vols. Quellen zur Khoisan-Forschung 5.1.-5.2. Hamburg: Helmut Buske Verlag, pp.83-106.

--------- 1993. *Women Like Meat: The Folklore and Foraging Ideology of the Kalahari Ju/'hoan*. Johannesburg, Witwatersrand University Press.

Bleek, D.F. 1924. *The Mantis and his Friends*. Cape Town: Maskew Miller.

--------- 1928-29. Bushman Grammar. *Zeitschrift fur Eingebovenen-Sprachen*, 19, 81-98 and 20, 161-74.

--------- 1928a. Bushmen of central Angola. *Bantu Studies* 3:105-25.

--------- 1928b. *The Naron, a Bushman Tribe of the Central Kalahari*. Cambridge: Cambridge University Press.

--------- 1929. Bushman folklore. *Africa* 2:302-13.

--------- 1931. Customs and beliefs of the/Xam Bushmen. Part I: Baboons. *Bantu Studies* 5:167-79.

--------- 1932a. Customs and beliefs of the /Xam Bushmen. Part II: The lion. *Bantu Studies* 6:47-63.

--------- 1932b. Customs and beliefs of the /Xam Bushmen. Part III: Game animals. *Bantu Studies* 6:233-49.

--------- 1932c. Customs and beliefs of the /Xam Bushmen. Part IV: Omens, wind-making, clouds. *Bantu Studies* 6:323-342.

--------- 1933a. Beliefs and customs of the /Xam Bushmen. Part V: The rain. *Bantu Studies* 7:297-312

--------- 1933b Beliefs and customs of the /Xam Bushmen. Part VI: Rain-making. *Bantu Studies* 7:375-92.

--------- 1935a. Beliefs and customs of the /Xam Bushmen. Part VII: Sorcerers. *Bantu Studies* 9:1-47.

--------- 1935b. !Ku~ mythology. *Zeitschrift für Eingeborenensprachen* 25(4):261-83.

--------- 1936a. Beliefs and customs of the /Xam Bushmen. Part VIII: More about sorcerers and charms. *Bantu Studies* 10:131-62.

--------- 1936b. Special speech of animals and moon used by the /Xam Bushmen. *Bantu Studies* 10:163-99.

--------- 1936c. Notes on the Bushman photographs. *Bantu Studies* 10:200-204.

--------- 1956. A *Bushman Dictionary*. New Haven: American Oriental Series Vol. 41. New Haven: American Oriental Society.

Bleek, E. & Bleek, D. 1909. Notes on the Bushmen. In Tongue, M.H., *Bushman Paintings*. London: Clarendon Press, pp.36-44.

Bleek, W.H.I. 1851. *De nominum generibus linguarum Africae Australis, Copticae, Semiticarum aliarumque sexualium*. Bonn: A. Marcus.

-------- 1864. *Reynard the Fox in South Africa: Hottentot Fables and Tales*. London: Trubner.

-------- 1873. Report of Dr Bleek concerning his Researches into the Bushman Language and Customs. Presented to the Honourable the House of Assembly by command of His Excellency the Governor. Cape Town: House of Assembly.

-------- 1875. *Brief Account of Bushman Folklore and Other Texts*. Second Report concerning Bushman Researches, presented to both Houses of the Parliament of the Cape of Good Hope, by command of His Excellency the Governor. Cape Town: Government Printer.

Bleek, W.H.I. & Lloyd, L.C. 1911. *Specimens of Bushman Folklore*. London: George Allen.

Burchell, W.J. 1967. *Travels in the Interior of Southern Africa*. Facsimile reprint. Cape Town: Struik.

Burger, W.A. n.d. Geskiedenis van Kenhardt. Kenhardt Nederlandse Gereformeerde Kerk: Unpublished roneoed typescript.

Burne, C.S. 1915. Obituary: In Memoriam – Lucy Catherine Lloyd. *Folk-Lore* 26: 99-100.

Caraveli, A. 1982. The song beyond the song: Aesthetics and social interaction in Greek folksong. *Journal of American Folklore* 95:129-58.

Chip, H. 1969. *Theories of Modern Art: A Source Book by Artists and Critics*. Berkeley: University of California Press.

Clark, J.D. 1977. Interpretations of prehistoric technology from Ancient Egyptians and other sources. Part II: Prehistoric arrow forms in Africa as shown by surviving examples of the traditional arrows of San Bushmen. *Paleorient* 3:127-50.

Coetzee, A. 1960. *Die Afrikaanse Volkskultuur*. Amsterdam/Cape Town: Balkema.

Collingwood, R.G. 1946. *The Idea of History*. Oxford: Clarendon Press.

Dammann, E. 1961. Die 'Urzeit' in afrikanischen Verschlingemythen. *Fabula* 4:130-37.

-------- 1987. *Was Herero erzahlten und sangen*. Texte, Ubersetzung, Kommentar. Afrika und Ubersee, Beiheft 32. Berlin: Reimer.

Danto, A.C. 1988. Artifact and art. In *Art/Artifact: African art in Anthropology Collections*. New York: The Center for African Art.

Darnell, R. 1974. Correlates of Cree Narrative Performance. In Bauman, R. & Sherzer, J. (eds), *Explorations in the Ethnography of Speaking*. London: Cambridge University Press, pp.315-36.

Deacon, H.J. 1976. *Where Hunters Gathered*. South African Archaelogical Society. Monograph Series 1:1-231.

-------- 1989. The origins of modern people, *Homo sapiens sapiens*. Final Report to Human Sciences Research Council.

Deacon, J. 1972. Wilton: An assessment after fifty years. *South African Archaeological Bulletin* 27:10-48.

-------- 1986. 'My place is the Bitterpits': The home territory of Bleek and Lloyd's /Xam San informants. *African Studies* 45:135-55.

--------- 1988. The power of a place in understanding southern San rock engravings. *World Archaeology* 20:129-40.

--------- 1992. *Arrows as Agents of Belief amongst the /Xam Bushmen.* Margaret Shaw Lecture 3. Cape Town: South African Museum.

Degh, L. & Vazsonyi, A. 1976. Legend and Belief. In Ben-Amos, D. (ed.), *Folklore Genres.* Austin: University of Texas Press, pp.93-123.

De Kock, W.J. (ed.). 1976. *Dictionary of South African Biography* Vol. 1. Pretoria: Human Sciences Research Council.

Dornan, S.S. 1909. Notes on the Bushmen of Basutoland. *Transactions of the South African Philosophical Society* 18:437-50.

--------- 1925. *Pygmies and Bushmen of the Kalahari.* London: Seeley, Service and Co. Repr. 1975, Cape Town: Struik.

Dowson, T.A. In prep. Bushman Rock Art and Changing Perceptions of Southern Africa's Past. Doctoral thesis, University of the Witwatersrand.

Dreyer, T.F. 1931. Report on the Skulls of a Pre-Bushman Race from the Knysna. In Dreyer, T. F. and Lyle, A. (eds), *New Fossil Mammals and Man from South Africa.* Bloemfontein: Nationale Pers, pp.41-60.

--------- 1933. The archaeology of the Matjes River Rock Shelter. *Transactions of the Royal Society of South Africa* 21:187-209.

Dundes, A. 1980. Texture, Text and Context. In Dundes, A. (ed.), *Interpreting Folklore.* Bloomington: Indiana University Press, pp.20-32.

Dunn, E.J. 1872/73. Through Bushmanland. *Cape Monthly Magazine* 30:374-84; 31:31-42. Reprinted in Lewin, A.M. (ed.), *Selected Articles from the Cape Monthly Magazine (New Series 1870-76).* Cape Town: Van Riebeeck Society, 1978.

--------- 1931. *The Bushman.* London: Griffin.

Eliade, M. 1972. *Shamanism: Archaic Techniques of Ecstasy.* New York: Routledge and Kegan Paul.

Engelbrecht, J. A. 1935. The Tribes of Wikar's Journal. In Mossop, E.E. (ed.), *The Journals of Wikar, Coetse and Van Reenen.* Cape Town: Van Riebeeck Society, pp.221-38.

--------- 1936. *The Korana.* Cape Town: Maskew Miller.

--------- 1956. Introduction. In Bleek, D.F., A *Bushman Dictionary.* American Oriental Series, Vol. 41. New Haven: American Oriental Society.

--------- n.d. Introduction to A *Bushman Dictionary* by D.F.Bleek. Typescript. (BC 151)

Findlay, D.A. 1977. The San of the Cape Thirstland and L. Anthing's 'Special Mission'. Honours essay, University of Cape Town.

Freilich, M. 1975. Myths, method and madness. *Current Anthropology* 16:207-26.

Georges, R. A. 1969. Toward an understanding of storytelling events. *Journal of American Folklore* 82:313-28.

Giliomee, H. 1981. Processes in Development of the Southern African Frontier. In Lamar, H. & Thompson, L. (eds), *The Frontier in History.* New Haven: Yale University Press.

Goodwin, A.J.H. 1938. Archaeology of the Oakhurst Shelter, George. *Transactions of the Royal Society of South Africa* 25:229-324.

-------- 1945. Some historical Bushman arrows. *South African Journal of Science* 41:429-43.

Gordon, R.J. 1992. *The Bushman Myth: The Making of a Namibian Underclass*. Boulder, San Francisco, Oxford: Westview Press.

Grobbelaar, P.W., Hudson, C.W. & Van der Merwe, H. 1977. *Boerewysheid.* Cape Town: Tafelberg.

Guenther, M. 1975. The trance dancer as an agent of social change among the Farm Bushmen of the Ghanzi District. *Botswana Notes and Records* 7:161-66.

-------- 1975/76. The San trance dance: Ritual and revitalization among the Farm Bushmen of the Ghanzi District, Republic of Botswana. *Journal of the South West African Scientific Society* 30:45-53.

-------- 1976. From Hunters to Squatters: Social and Cultural Change among the Ghanzi Farm Bushmen. In Lee, R.B. & DeVore, I. (eds), *Kalahari Hunter-Gatherers*. Cambridge, Mass.: Harvard University Press, pp.120-33.

-------- 1983/84. Bushwoman: The position of women in Bushman society and ideology. *Journal of Comparative Sociology and Religion* 10/11:12-31.

-------- 1986. *The Nharo Bushmen of Botswana: Tradition and Change.* Hamburg: Helmut Buske Verlag.

-------- 1988. Animals in Bushman Thought, Myth and Lore. In Ingold, T., Riches, D. & Woodburn, J. (eds), *Property, Power and Ideology in Hunting and Gathering Societies*. Oxford: Berg, pp.192-202.

-------- 1989. *Bushman Folktales: Oral Traditions of the Nharo of Botswana and the /Xam of the Cape*. Stuttgart: Franz Steiner Verlag.

-------- 1990. Convergent and Divergent Themes in Bushman Myth and Art. In Kohl, K., Muszinski, H. & Strecker, I. (eds), *Die Vielfalt der Kultur*. Berlin: Dietrich Reimer Verlag, pp. 237-54.

Gutmann, B. 1909. *Dichten und Denken der Dschagganeger*. Beitrage zur östafrikanischen Volkskunde. Leipzig: Evangelisch-Lutherische Mission.

Hall, S. and Binneman, J. 1987. Later Stone Age burial variability in the Cape: A social interpretation. *South African Archaeological Bulletin* 42:140-52.

Hammond-Tooke, W.D. 1977. Lévi-Strauss in a garden of millet: The structural analysis of a Zulu folktale. *Man* 12:76-86.

-------- 1988. The 'mythic' content of Zulu folktales. *African Studies* 47:89-100.

Haring, L. 1972. Performing for the interviewer: A study of the structure of context. *Southern Folklore Quarterly* 36:383-98.

Hausman, A.J. 1980. Holocene Human Evolution in Southern Africa: The Biocultural Development of the Khoisan. Doctoral thesis, State University of New York, Binghamton.

Heikkinen, T. 1985. Hei//om and !Xu stories from North Namibia. Unpublished MS.

-------- 1986. Phonology of the !Xũ dialect spoken in Ovamboland and western Kavango. *Southern African Journal of African Languages* 6(1):18-28.

-------- 1987. An outline of the grammar of the !Xũ language. *Southern African Journal of African Languages* 7 (Supplement 1).

Heinz, H-J. 1966. The Social Organization of the !Ko Bushmen. Master's dissertation, University of South Africa, Pretoria.

-------- 1975. Elements of !Ko Bushmen religious beliefs. *Anthropos* 70:17-41.

-------- 1986. A !Ko Bushman Burial. In Vossen, R. and Keuthmann, K. (eds), *Contemporary Studies on Khoisan.* In Honour of Oswin Köhler on the Occasion of his 75th Birthday. 2 vols. Quellen zur Khoisan-Forschung 5.1.-5.2. Hamburg: Helmut Buske Verlag, pp.23-36.

Hewitt, R.L. 1986a. *Structure, Meaning and Ritual in the Narratives of the Southern San.* Hamburg: Helmut Buske Verlag, Quellen zur Khoisan-Forschung 2.

-------- 1986b. The Anteater's Laws: Animal Classification and the Social Order. In R. Vossen and K. Keuthmann (eds), *Contemporary Studies on Khoisan 2.* In Honour of Oswin Köhler on the Occasion of his 75th Birthday. 2 vols. Quellen zur Khoisan-Forschung 5.1.-5.2. Hamburg. Helmut Buske Verlag, pp.37-49.

Hodder, I. 1986. *Reading the Past: Current Approaches to the Interpretation in Archaeology.* Cambridge: Cambridge University Press.

Hoffman, A. C. 1958. New excavations in the Matjes River Rock Shelter. *South African Museums Association Bulletin* 6: 342-48.

How, M.W. 1970. *The Mountain Bushmen of Basutoland.* Pretoria: Van Schaik.

Humphreys, A.J.B. 1970. The remains from Koffiefontein burials excavated by W. Fowler and preserved in the McGregor Museum, Kimberley. *South African Archaeological Bulletin* 25:104-15.

-------- 1974. Note on a date for a burial from the Riet River. *South African Journal of Science* 70:271.

-------- 1982. Cultural material from burials on the farm St Clair, Douglas area, Northern Cape. *South African Archaeological Bulletin* 37:68-70.

Humphreys, A.J.B. and Maggs, T.M.O'C. 1970. Further graves and cultural material from the banks of the Riet River. *South African Archaeological Bulletin* 25:116-26.

Humphreys, A.J.B. & Thackeray, A.I. 1983. *Ghaap and Gariep: Later Stone Age Studies in the Northern Cape.* Cape Town: South African Archaeological Society Monograph 2.

Hymes, D. 1967. Models of the Interaction of Language and Social Setting. In Macnamara, J. (ed.), Problems of Bilingualism. *Journal of Social Issues* 23:8-28.

-------- 1972. Models of the Interaction of Language and Social Life. In Gumperz, J.J. & Hymes, D. (eds), *Directions in Sociolinguistics.* New York: Holt, Rinehart & Winston, pp.35-71.

Inskeep, R.R. 1986. A Preliminary Survey of Burial Practices in the Later Stone Age, from the Orange River to the Cape Coast. In Singer, R. and Lundy, J.K. (eds),

*Variation, Culture and Evolution in African Populations*. Johannesburg: Witwatersrand University Press, pp.221-39.

--------- 1987. *Nelson Bay Cave*. Oxford: British Archaeological Reports International Series 357 (i and ii).

Jacobson, L. 1987. The size variability of ostrich eggshell beads from central Namibia and its relevance as a stylistic and temporal marker. *South African Archaeological Bulletin* 42:55-58.

Jantunen, T. 1967. *Pahkinansydan*. Helsinki: Suomen Lahetysseuran Kustannusliike.

Junod, H.A. 1912. *The Life of a South African Tribe*. Vol. 1: The Social Life. Neuchatel: Attinger.

--------- 1913. *The Life of a South African Tribe*. Vol. 2: The Psychic Life. Neuchatel: Attinger/London: Macmillan.

KH – see Schmidt 1989.

Kallaway, P. 1982. Danster and the Xhosa of the Gariep: Towards a political economy of the Cape frontier 1790-1820. *African Studies* 41:143-60.

Katz, R. 1982. *Boiling Engergy: Community Healing among the Kalahari !Kung*. Cambridge, Mass.: Harvard University Press.

Kirby, P.R. 1936. A study of Bushman music. *Bantu Studies* 10: 205-52.

Kirshenblatt-Gimblett, B. 1975. A Parable in Context: A Social-Interactional Analysis of Storytelling Performance. In Ben-Amos, D. & Goldstein, K. (eds), *Folklore: Performance and Communication*. The Hague: Mouton, pp.105-30.

Köhler, O. 1975. Geschichte und Probleme der Gliederung der Sprachen Afrikas. In Baumann, H., *Die Volker afrikas und ihre traditionellen Kulturen* I. Wiesbaden: Steiner, pp.141-373.

--------- 1981. *Les Langues Khoisan*. Paris: Centre de la Recherche Scientifique.

Krüger, D.W. & Beyers, C.J. (eds). 1977. *Dictionary of South African Biography*. Vol. III. Pretoria: Human Sciences Research Council.

Kuper, A. 1986. *South Africa and the Anthropologist*. London/New York: Routledge and Kegan Paul.

Lebzelter, V. 1934. *Eingeborenenkulturen in Südwest-und Südafrika*. Leipzig: Hiersemann.

Lévi-Strauss, C. 1970. *The Raw and the Cooked*. London: Jonathan Cape.

Lewis-Williams, J.D. 1979. 'Led by the nose': Observations on the supposed use of southern San rock art in rain-making rituals. *African Studies* 36:155-59.

--------- 1980. Ethnography and iconography: Aspects of southern San thought and art. *Man* 15:467-82.

--------- 1981. *Believing and Seeing: Symbolic Meanings in Southern San Rock Paintings*. London: Academic Press.

--------- 1983. *The Rock Art of Southern Africa*. Cambridge: Cambridge University Press.

--------- 1986. Paintings of Power: Ethnography and Rock Art in Southern Africa. In Biesele, M. (ed.), *The Past and Future of !Kung Ethnography: Critical Reflections and*

*Symbolic Perspectives, Essays in Honour of Lorna Marshall.* Quellen zur Khoisan-Forshung. Hamburg: Helmut Buske Verlag.

——— 1987a. Beyond Style and Portrait: A Comparison of Tanzanian and Southern African Rock Art. In Vossen, R. and Keuthmann, K. (eds), *Contemporary Studies on Khoisan 2*. Quellen zur Khoisan-Forshung. Hamburg: Helmut Buske Verlag.

——— 1987b. A dream of eland: An unexplored component of San shamanism and rock art. *World Archaeology* 19:165-77.

——— 1988. 'People of the eland': An Archaeo-linguistic Crux. In Ingold, T., Riches, D. & Woodburn, J. (eds), *Hunters and Gatherers 2: Property, Power and Ideology*. Oxford: Berg, pp.203-11.

——— 1990a. *Discovering Southern African Rock Art*. Cape Town, David Philip.

——— 1990b. Keynote address: The first art historians' rock art symposium. *Current Perspectives in South African Art and Architecture*. Proceedings of the Sixth Annual Conference of the South African Association of Art Historians.

——— 1991. Upper Palaeolithic art in the 1990s: A southern African perspective. *South African Journal of Science* 87:422-29.

Lewis-Williams, J.D. and Biesele, M. 1978. Eland hunting rituals among Northern and Southern San groups: Striking similarities. *Africa* 48:117-34.

Lewis-Williams, J.D. and Dowson, T.A. 1988. The signs of all times: Entoptic phenomena in Upper Palaeolithic art. *Current Anthropology* 29:201-45.

——— 1989. *Images of Power: Understanding Bushman Rock Art*. Johannesburg: Southern Books.

——— 1990. Through the veil: San rock paintings and the rock face. *South African Archaeological Bulletin* 45:5-16.

Lewis-Williams, J.D., Dowson, T.A. & Deacon, J. 1993. Rock art and changing perceptions of southern Africa's past: Ezeljagdspoort reviewed. *Antiquity* 67: 273-91.

Lewis-Williams, J.D. & Loubser, J.H.N. 1986. Deceptive Appearances: A Critique of Southern African Rock Art Studies. In Wendorf, F. and Close, A.E. (eds), *Advances in World Archaeology* Vol. 5. New York: Academic Press, pp.253-89.

Lichtenstein, H. 1930. *Travels in Southern Africa, in the years 1803, 1804, 1805 and 1806*. Vol. II. Cape Town: Van Riebeeck Society.

Limon, J. E. & Young, M. J. 1986. Frontiers, settlements, and development in folklore studies, 1972-1985. *Annual Review of Anthropology* 15:437-60.

Lloyd, L.C. 1889. *A Short Account of Further Bushman Material Collected.* Third Report concerning Bushman Researches, presented to both Houses of Parliament of the Cape of Good Hope, by Command of His Excellency the Governor. London: David Nutt.

Long, U. (ed.). 1956. *The Journals of Elizabeth Lees Price written in Bechuanaland, Southern Africa 1854-1883*. London: Edward Arnold.

Louw, J.A. 1976. Bleek, Wilhelm Heinrich Immanuel. *Dictionary of South African Biography* 1:82-85.

Louw, J.T. 1960. Prehistory of the Matjes River Rock Shelter. *Memoirs of the National Museum, Bloemfontein* 1.

Lüthi, M. 1961. *Volksmarchen und Volkssage*. Zwei Grundformen erzahlender Dichtung. Bern/Munchen: Francke.

--------- 1962. *Es war einmal ... Vom Wesen des Volkmarchens*. Gottingen: Vandenhoeck and Ruprecht.

Maggs, T.M.O'C. 1967. Microdistribution of some Typologically Linked Rock Paintings from the Western Cape. In Hugot, H.J. (ed.), *Proceedings Sixième Congrès Panafricain de Préhistoire*, Dakar, pp. 218-20.

Maingard, L.F. 1937. *The Weapons of the /Auni and the ≠Khomani of the southern Kalahari*. Johannesburg: Witwatersrand University Press, pp. 277-83.

--------- 1962. *Korana Folktales*. Grammar and Texts. Johannesburg: University of the Witwatersrand Press.

Malinowski, B. 1926. *Myth in Primitive Psychology*. New York: W.W. Norton & Co.

Malinowski, M. 1965 [1935]. *Coral Gardens and their Magic*. Bloomington: Indiana University Press.

Manhire, A.H. 1981. Rock Art of the Sandveld. Honours essay, University of Cape Town.

Manhire, A.H., Parkington, J.E. & Yates, R.J. 1985. Nets and fully recurved bows: Rock paintings and hunting methods in the Western Cape, South Africa. *World Archaeology* 17(2):161-74.

Maquette, J. 1986. *The Aesthetic Experience: An Anthropologist Looks at the Visual Arts*. New Haven: Yale University Press

Marais, J.S. 1962. *The Cape Coloured People, 1652-1937*. Johannesburg: Witwatersrand University Press.

Marshall, L. 1957. N!ow. *Africa* 27(3):232-40.

--------- 1959. Marriage among !Kung Bushmen. *Africa* 29:335-65.

--------- 1960. !Kung Bushman bands. *Africa* 30:325-55.

--------- 1961. Sharing, talking and giving: Relief of social tensions among !Kung Bushmen. *Africa* 31(3):231-49.

--------- 1962. !Kung Bushman religious beliefs. *Africa* 32: 221-51.

--------- 1969. The medicine dance of the !Kung Bushmen. *Africa* 39:347-81.

--------- 1976. *The !Kung of Nyae Nyae*. Cambridge, Mass.: Harvard University Press.

Maxwell-Mahon, W.D. 1981. Lloyd, Lucy Catherine. *Dictionary of South African Biography* 4:315-16.

Mazel, A.D. 1987. The Archaeological Past from the Changing Present: Towards a Critical Assessment of the South African Later Stone Age Studies from the early 1960s and the early 1980s. In Parkington, J. & Hall, M. (eds), *Papers in the*

*Prehistory of the Western Cape*. Oxford: British Archaeological Reports International Series 332(ii), pp.504-29.

McCall, D.F. 1970. Wolf courts girl: The equivalence of hunting and mating in Bushman thought. *Ohio University Papers in International Studies*. Africa Series 7.

McCall, D. and Bay, E. (eds). 1975. *African Images: Essays in African Iconology*. New York: Africana Publishing.

Mitias, M. 1980. Hegel on the Art Object. In Steinkraus, W. and Schmits, K. (eds), *Art and Logic in Hegel's Philosophy*. New Jersey: Humanities Press.

Morris, A.G. 1984. An Osteological Analysis of the Protohistoric Populations of the Northern Cape and Western Orange Free State, South Africa. Doctoral thesis, University of the Witwatersrand, Johannesburg.

Morris, A.G., Thackeray, A.I. and Thackeray, J.F. 1987. Late Holocene human skeletal remains from Snuifklip, near Vleesbaai, southern Cape. *South African Archaeological Bulletin* 42:153-60.

Morris, D. 1988. Engraved in place and time: A review of variability in the rock art of the northern Cape and Karoo. *South African Archaeological Bulletin* 43:109-20.

Murphy, W.P. 1978. Oral literature. *Annual Review of Anthropology* 7:113-36.

Orpen, J.M. 1874. A glimpse into the mythology of the Maluti Bushmen. *Cape Monthly Magazine* 9(49):1-13. Repr. 1919. *Folklore* 30:139-56.

Panofsky, E. 1955. *Meaning in the Visual Arts*. New York: Doubleday Anchor Books.

Paredes, A. & Bauman, R. (eds). 1972. *Toward New Perspectives in Folklore*. Austin: University of Texas Press.

Parkington, J. 1989. Interpreting paintings without a commentary: Meaning and motive, content and composition in the rock art of the Western Cape, South Africa. *Antiquity* 63:13-26.

Paulme, D. 1976. *La mère dévorante. Essai sur la morphologie des contes africains*. Paris: Gallimard.

Penn, N.G. 1986. Pastoralists and pastoralism in the northern Cape frontier zone during the eighteenth century. *South African Archaeological Society Goodwin Series* 5:62-68.

Plug, I. 1982. Bone tools and shell, bone and ostrich eggshell beads from Bushman Rock Shelter (BRS), eastern Transvaal. *South African Archaeological Bulletin* 37:57-62.

Potgieter, E.F. 1955. *The Disappearing Bushmen of Lake Chrissie*. Pretoria: Van Schaik.

Raper, P.E. & Boucher, M. 1988. *Robert Jacob Gordon: Cape Travels, 1777 to 1786*. Vol. 2. Johannesburg: Brenthurst Press.

Rosenthal, E. & Goodwin, A.J.H. 1953. *Cave Artists of South Africa*. Cape Town: A.A. Balkema.

Ross, R. 1975. The !Kora wars on the Orange River, 1830-1880. *Journal of African History* 16:561-76.

Rudner, I. 1970. Nineteenth-century Bushman drawings. *South African Archaeological Bulletin* 25:147-54.

Rudner, J. 1971. Painted Burial Stones from the Cape. In Schoonraad, M. (ed.), *Rock Paintings of Southern Africa. South African Journal of Science* Special issue 2:54-61. Johannesburg: South African Association for the Advancement of Science.

Sampson, C.G., Hart, T.J.G., Wallsmith, D.L. & Blagg, J.D. 1989. The ceramic sequence in the Upper Seacow Valley: Problems and implications. *South African Archaeological Bulletin* 44:3-16.

Schapera, I. 1930. *The Khoisan Peoples of South Africa.* London: George Routledge & Sons.

Scheub, H. 1975. *The Xhosa Ntsomi.* Oxford: Clarendon Press.

Schmelen, J.H. [1815]. Diary. In Schmidt, S., Auszuge aus dem Tagebuch 1815/16 des Missionars Heinrich Schmelen in Bethanien. *Namibiana* 1.3(1979):53-68.

Schmidt, S. 1973. Die Mantis religiosa in den Glaubensvorstellungen der Khoesan-Volker. *Zeitschrift fur Ethnologie* 98(1):102-27.

——— 1977. Das Kind unter den Pavianen. *Mitteilungen der SWA Wissenschaftlichen Gesellschaft* 18/2:3-7.

——— 1979a. Auszuge aus dem Tagebuch 1815/16 des Missionars Heinrich Schmelen in Bethanien. *Namibiana* 1.3:53-68.

——— 1979b. The rain bull of the South African Bushmen. *African Studies* 38: 201-24.

——— 1980. *Märchen aus Namibia.* Volkserzahlungen der Nama und Dama. Märchen der Weltliteratur. Dusseldorf/Cologne: Diederichs.

——— 1982a. Khoisan Folktales: Original Sources and Republications. *African Studies* 41:203-12.

——— 1982b. Theophilus Hahn, zum 140. Geburtstag, am 24.12.1842. *Mitteilungen der SWA Wissenscbaftlichen Gesellschaft* 23/8-9:2-7.

——— 1984. Lucy Catherine Lloyd (1834-1914). *Mitteilungen der SWA Wissenschaftlichen Gesellschaft* 25/5-6:1-5.

——— 1986a. Heiseb-Trickster und Gott der Nama und Dama in Südwestafrika/Namibia. In Vossen, R. and Keuthmann, K. (eds), *Contemporary Studies on Khoisan* 2. In Honour of Oswin Köhler on the Occasion of his 75th Birthday. 2 vols. Quellen zur Khoisan-Forschung 5.1.-5.2. Hamburg: Helmut BuskeVerlag, pp.205-56.

——— 1986b. Tales and Beliefs about Eyes-on-His-Feet. In Biesele, M. *et al.* (eds), *The Past and Future of !Kung Ethnography: Critical Reflections and Symbolic Perspectives. Essays in Honour of Lorna Marshall.* Quellen zur Khoisan-Forschung 4. Hamburg: Helmut BuskeVerlag, pp. 169-94.

——— 1988. Die Vorstellungen von der mythischen Urzeit und der Jetztzeit bei den Khoisan-Volkern. In Vossen, R. (ed.), *New Perspectives on the Study of Khoisan.* Quellen zur Khoisan-Forschung 7. Hamburg: Helmut Buske Verlag, pp. 29-45.

——— 1989. *Katalog der Khoisan-Volkserzahlungen des sudlichen Afrikas / Catalogue of the Khoisan Folktales of Southern Africa.* 2 vols. Quellen zur Khoisan-Forschung 6.1-6.2. Hamburg: Helmut Buske Verlag.

Schultze, L. 1907. *Aus Namaland und Kalahari*. Jena: Fischer.

Sealy, J. C. and Van der Merwe, N. J. 1985. The first accelerator radiocarbon dates in South African archaeology. *South African Archaeological Bulletin* 81:350-51.

Sellers, J.M. 1977. Lloyd, William Henry Cynric. *Dictionary of South African Biography* 3:530.

Shaw, E.M. 1976. Bleek, Dorothea Frances. *Dictionary of South African Biography* 1:80-82.

Sherzer, J. & Darnell, R. 1972. Outline Guide for the Ethnographic Study of Speech Use. In Gumperz, J.J. & Hymes, D. (eds), *Directions in Sociolinguistics*. New York: Holt, Rinehart & Winston, pp.548-54.

Silberbauer, G.B. 1965. *Bushman Survey*. Gaberones: Bechuanaland Press.

——— 1981. *Hunter and Habitat in the Central Kalahari Desert*. Cambridge: Cambridge University Press.

Skotnes, P. 1990. Rock art: Is there life after trance? *De Arte* 44:16-24.

Snyman, J. W. 1980. The Relationship between Angolan !Xũ and Zu/'hõasi. In Snyman, J.W. (ed.), *Bushmen and Hottentot Linguistic Studies*. Pretoria: University of South Africa, pp.1-58.

Solomon, A. 1988. Division of the Earth: Gender, Symbolism and the Archaeology of the Southern San. Master's dissertation, Department of Archaeology, University of Cape Town.

——— 1992. Gender, representation and power in San ethnography and rock art. *Journal of Anthropological Archaeology* 11:291-329.

Solway, J. S. and Lee, R. B. 1990. Foragers, genuine or spurious? *Current Anthropology* 31:109-46.

Spohr, O.H. 1962. *Wilhelm Heinrich Immanuel Bleek. A Biobibliographical Sketch*. Varia Series 6. Cape Town: University of Cape Town Libraries.

——— 1965. *The Natal Diaries of Dr W.H.I. Bleek, 1855-1856*. Translated from the German with some additional material and notes by O.H. Spohr. Cape Town, Balkema.

Stow, G. W. 1905. *The Native Races of South Africa*. London: Swan, Sonnenschein.

Stow, G.W. & Bleek, D.F. 1930. *Rock Paintings in South Africa: From Parts of the Eastern Province and Orange Free State; Copied by George William Stow; With an Introduction and Descriptive Notes by D.F. Bleek*. London: Methuen.

Strauss, T. 1979. *War Along the Orange: The Korana and the Northern Border Wars of 1868-9 and 1878-79*. University of Cape Town: Centre for African Studies Communication 1.

Tedlock, D. 1972. *Finding the Centre*. New York: Dial.

Thackeray, F. and Feast, E. C. 1974. A midden burial from Cape St Francis, eastern Cape Province. *South African Archaeological Bulletin* 29:92.

Theal, G.M. 1910. *The Yellow and Dark-Skinned People of Africa South of the Zambesi*. London: Swan Sonnenschein. Repr. 1969, New York: Negro University Press.

-------- 1911. Introduction. In Bleek, W.H.I. & Lloyd, L.C., *Specimens of Bushman Folklore*. London: George Allen, pp.xxv-xl.

Thomas, E.M. 1988. *The Harmless People*. Cape Town: David Philip.

Thomas, E.W. 1950. *Bushman Stories*. Cape Town: Oxford University Press.

Thompson, G. 1968. *Travels and Adventures in Southern Africa*. Vol. II. Reprint edition. Cape Town: Van Riebeeck Society.

Toelken, B. 1979. *The Dynamics of Folklore*. Boston: Houghton Mifflin.

Tongue, Helen M. 1909. *Bushman Paintings*. Oxford: Clarendon Press.

Trumpelmann, G.P.J. 1976. Hahn, Johannes Theophilus. *Dictionary of South African Biography* 1:344-46.

Turner, M. 1988. *Shipwrecks and Salvage in South Africa, 1505 to the Present*. Cape Town: Struik.

University of the Cape of Good Hope. 1912. Honorary Degrees Commission, University Council Minutes, 16/17 Sept.

Van der Merwe, H. 1987. Water: Lewegewer vir die Boesmanland. *Tydskrif vir Volkskunde en Volkstaal* 43/2:22-32.

Vialls, C.C. 1908. A Bushman tradition. *African Monthly* (Grahamstown) 4:303-04.

Vinnicombe, P. 1976. *People of the Eland*. Pietermaritzburg: University of Natal Press.

Von Wielligh, G.R. 1917-1921. *Boesman Stories*. 4 vols. Cape Town: Nasionale Pers.

Vorbichler, A. and Brandl, R.N. 1979. *Die Oralliteratur der Balese-Efe im Ituri-Wald (Nordost-Zaire)*. Studia Instituti Anthropos 34, St. Augustin.

Wadley, L. 1987. *Later Stone Age Hunters and Gatherers of the Southern Transvaal*. Oxford: British Archaeological Reports International Series 380.

-------- 1990. Symbolic Grave Goods in the Stone Age of South Africa. Proceedings of the Conference on Hunting and Gathering Societies, May 1990, University of Alaska, Fairbanks, pp.277-92.

Webley, L. 1984. Archaeology and Ethnoarchaeology in the Leliefontein Reserve and Surrounds, Namaqualand. MA dissertation, University of Stellenbosch.

-------- 1986. Pastoralist ethnoarchaeology in Namaqualand. *South African Archaeological Society Goodwin Series* 5:57-61.

-------- 1990. The use of stone 'scrapers' by semi-sedentary pastoralist groups in Namaqualand, South Africa. *South African Archaeological Bulletin* 45:28-32.

Werner, A. 1968. *Myths and Legends of the Bantu*. London: Cass.

Westphal, E.O.J. 1971. The Click Languages of South and East Africa. In Berry, J. and Greenberg, J.H. (eds), *Linguistics in Subsaharan Africa*. Vol. 7 of Sebeok, T. (ed.), *Current Trends in Linguistics*. The Hague: Mouton, pp.367-420.

Wiessner, P. 1983. Social and ceremonial aspects of death among the !Kung San. *Botswana Notes and Records* 15:1-5.

Winter, J.C. 1988. Der 'Hottentottische Mythos vom Ursprung des Todes': Ein Lehrstuck um Aufrichtigkeit und Luge. In Möhlig, W.J.G., Jungraithmayr, H. &

Thiel, J.F. (eds), *Die Oralliteratur in Afrika als Quelle zur Erforschung der traditionellen Kulturen / La litterature orale en Afrique comme source pour la decouverte des cultures traditionnelles*. Collectanea Instituti Anthropos 36. Berlin: Reimer.

Wylie, A. 1985. The reaction against analogy. *Advances in Archaeological Method and Theory* 8:63-111.

Yates, R.J., Golson, J. & Hall, M.J. 1985. Trance performance: The rock art of Boontjieskloof and Sevilla. *South African Archaeological Bulletin* 40:70-80.

Yates, R.J. & Manhire, A.H. 1991. Shamanism and rock paintings: Aspects of the use of rock art in the south-western Cape, South Africa. *South African Archaeological Bulletin* 46:3-11.

Yellen, J.E. 1977. *Archaeological Approaches to the Past*. New York: Academic Press.

-------- 1990. The transformation of the Kalahari !Kung. *Scientific American* April:72-79.

## *Works of Reference*

*Dictionary of South African Biography* (*DSAB*). 1968. Cape Town: Nasionale Boekhandel.

*Standard Encyclopaedia of Southern Africa* (*SESA*). 1973. Cape Town: NASOU.